DATE DUE

~~OC 1 '96~~			
~~DE 13 '96~~			
~~NO 13 '97~~			
~~AP 21 '99~~			
~~OC 25 '99~~			
~~MR 31 '00~~			
~~JE 6 '02~~			
~~MY 9 '02~~			
MR 18 '03			
~~MY 28 '03~~			
~~JE 11 '03~~			
DE 12 '05			

DEMCO 38-296

The Mexican Dream

J. M. G. Le Clézio

THE
MEXICAN
DREAM

*Or, The Interrupted Thought
of Amerindian Civilizations*

Translated by Teresa Lavender Fagan

THE UNIVERSITY OF CHICAGO PRESS   *Chicago and London*

J.M.G. LE CLÉZIO was born in Nice in 1940. In 1963 he received the Renaudot Prize for his first novel, *Le procès-verbal*. He has studied the Indian civilizations of pre-Columbian Mexico since 1971 and has published translations of Mayan sacred texts and an evocation of three sacred villages in the land of the Maya, *Trois villes saintes* (1980). Two of his novels are soon to be available in English from David Godine.

Map on pages vi–vii by Philip Schwartzberg

The University of Chicago Press, Chicago 60637
The University of Chicago Press, Ltd., London
©1993 by The University of Chicago
All rights reserved. Published 1993
Printed in the United States of America
02 01 00 99 98 97 96 95 94 93   1 2 3 4 5

ISBN: 0-226-11002-8 (cloth)
Originally published in French as *Le rêve mexicain ou la pensée interrompue;*
©1988 Editions Gallimard.

Library of Congress Cataloging-in-Publication Data
Le Clézio, J.-M. G. (Jean-Marie Gustave), 1940–
    [Rêve mexicain, ou, La pensée interrompue. English]
    The Mexican dream or, The interrupted thought of Amerindian
civilizations / J.-M. G. Le Clézio : translated by Teresa Lavender
Fagan.
        p.   cm.
    Includes bibliographical references.
    1. Indians of Mexico—Philosophy. 2. Indians of Mexico—First
contact with Europeans. 3. Mexico—History—Conquest, 1519–1540.
4. Mexico—Civilization—Indian influences. I. Title. II. Title:
Interrupted thought of Amerindian civilizations.
F1230.L3413   1993
972'.018—dc20   93-17029
                                                              CIP

∞The paper used in this publication meets the minimum requirements of the
American National Standard for Information Sciences—Permanence of Paper for
Printed Library Materials, ANSI Z39.48-1984.

Contents

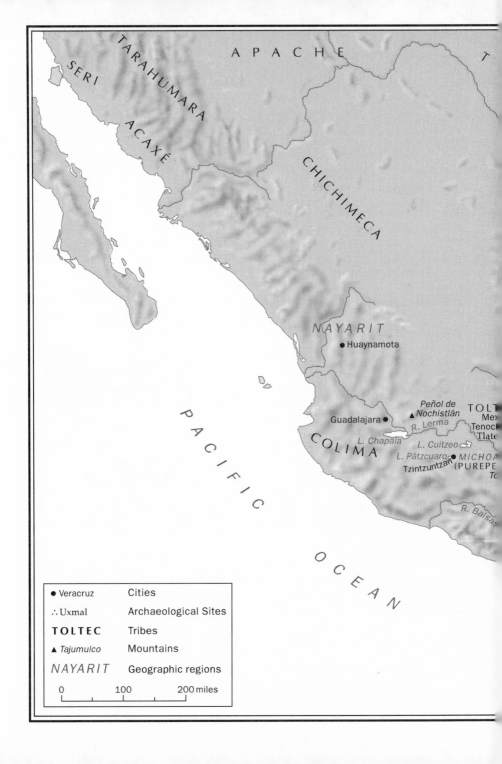

SERI

TARAHUMARA

ACAXÉ

APACHE   T

CHICHIMECA

NAYARIT

● Huaynamota

Peñol de   TOL
▲ Nochistlán   Me
Guadalajara ●   R. Lerma   Tenoc
                                              Tlate
L. Chapala   L. Cuitzeo
COLIMA   L. Pátzcuaro ● MICHOA
Tzintzuntzan (PUREPE
                                     Tc

R. Balsas

PACIFIC

OCEAN

● Veracruz	Cities
∴ Uxmal	Archaeological Sites
TOLTEC	Tribes
▲ *Tajumulco*	Mountains
NAYARIT	Geographic regions

0   100   200 miles

A
S

Pánuco

HUAXTEC

OTONAC

Tajín∴

∴Teotihuacán
●Texcoco
nalco ∴Tlaxcala
▲●Malinche ●Veracruz
cíhuatl *Citlaltépetl*
▲Cholula *(Orizaba)*
cíhuatl
HUATL *Popocatépetl*
luding ●Cempoala ●Villahermosa
TEC) OLMEC ●La Venta

MIXTEC
Monte Albán∴●Oaxaca
●Mitla
ZAPOTEC
Tehuantepec●

G U L F

O F

M E X I C O

●Mérida ∴Chichen Itzá
●Mani ∴Cozumel
Uxmal∴ ∴Tulúm
Campeche● YUCATÁN
PENINSULA
Chan●
Santa Cruz
MAYA

R. Usumacinta
R. Candelaria

Palenque∴ Uaxactún∴
TZOTZIL ∴Piedras Negras ∴Tikal BELIZE
DZENDAL ∴Yaxchilán
San Cristóbal
de las Casas

Coatzacoalcos

R. Grijalva

Tacaná∴ R. Motagua
Tajumulco▲ Kaminaljuyú R. Ulúa
∴Copán
●Guatemala HONDURAS
Atitlán▲ City
▲Acatenango

●San Salvador

Translator's Note

Translating *Le rêve mexicain (The Mexican Dream)* has been a moving and enlightening task. For this is a special book, one which forces the reader to rethink—and to re-feel—the history of the Conquest of Mexico and the fate of the Amerindian peoples. Beyond describing the extraordinarily rich and complex cultures of those peoples, M. Le Clézio makes the American adventure and the effect it had on the lives and civilizations of Indian populations—and consequently on our own—an immediate, disturbing issue.

One of the ways in which the author achieves this is through his use of many original texts, written in Spanish or in Nahuatl by those who experienced first-hand the events he describes. Wherever possible I have used the standard English-language translations of those texts, and have cited the appropriate references. When published translations could not be obtained, I translated directly from Le Clézio's French versions.

For the use of the following English-language texts I would like to gratefully acknowledge their publishers:

Doubleday, for the use of selected sentences from *The Bernal Diaz Chronicles*. Translation copyright © 1956 by Albert Idell. Used by permission of Doubleday, a division of Bantam Doubleday Dell Publishing Group, Inc.

The University of Oklahoma Press, for the use of selected sentences from *The Chronicles of Michoacan*, edited and translated by Eugene R. Craine and Reginald C. Reindorp, copyright © 1970 by the University of Oklahoma Press; and for the use of two sentences from *The Mescalero Apaches*, by C. L. Sonnichsen, copyright © 1958 by the University of Oklahoma Press;

Fisk University Library, for the Fisk University Press (no longer in existence), for the use of selected sentences from *A History of Ancient Mexico*, by Bernardino de Sahagun. Translated by Fanny Bandelier. Copyright © 1932, Fisk University Press.

Paulist Press, for the use of selected lines of poetry from *Native Mesoamerican Spirituality*, edited by Miguel Leon-Portilla, copyright © 1980 by the Missionary Society of St. Paul the Apostle of the State of New York;

University of New Mexico Press, for the use of two sentences from *Federal Control of the Western Apache*, by Ralph Hedrick Ogle, copyright © 1970 by the University of New Mexico Press;

Farrar, Straus & Giroux, for the use of excerpts from *The Peyote Dance* by Antonin Artaud. Translation copyright © 1976 by Farrar, Straus & Giroux, Inc. Reprinted by permission of Farrar, Straus & Giroux, Inc.

1   The Dream of the Conquerors

T HE DREAM BEGAN ON FEBRUARY 8, 1517, when, from the deck of his ship, Bernal Díaz first saw the great white city of the Maya, the city the Spanish would later name "Great Cairo." The dream continued the following March 4, when Díaz saw approaching his ship "ten large canoes, called piraguas, . . . filled with Indians. They were hollowed from single logs so large that many of them could hold forty Indians" (Idell: p. 19).[1]

This was the soldier Bernal Díaz's first encounter with the Mexican world. The dream could begin, still free of any fear or hatred.

The Indians came with no fear, and "more than thirty came on board and we gave to each a string of glass beads [and] they . . . examined the ships for a good while" (Idell: p. 19).

There was thus wonderment on both sides. Bernal Díaz and his companions were amazed at the size of the cities, the beauty of the temples, and the ugliness of the Mayan idols, those "bas-reliefs of snakes and other reptiles, as well as pictures of evil-figured idols, and something like an altar covered with drops of blood. There were other idols that carried the sign of the cross, all painted so that we admired them as something never before seen or heard about" (Idell: p. 21).

As for the Indians, they wondered at the appearance of the strangers. They asked them if they had come "from where the sun rises," and then for the first time they told the legend which later Captain Cortés and his men would use to their great advantage, the legend "that [their] ancestors had foretold that men with beards would come from the east and rule over them" (Idell: p. 31).

In the beginning the dream was like any genesis: the strangers gave names to the land, to the bays, to the islands, to the mouths of rivers: *boca de Términos, río Grijalva, montaña San Martín, isla de Sacrificios.*

And they asked for gold. Gold was already the "currency" of the dream. And the Indians, who sensed the dangers associated with possessing that metal, diverted the strangers, saying only "Colua, Colua" and "Mexico, Mexico." As later the Carib Indians would speak of Peru.

There was also the Spaniards' first meeting with the ambassadors of Montezuma, king of Mexico. Here, too, one can sense the beginning of the dream of the conquest and the destruction of the Aztec empire; one senses the destiny of the Mexican people. On the banks of the great river shaded by trees, Montezuma's ambassadors are seated on their mats. They wait. Behind them warriors stand armed with their bows and hatchets made of obsidian, and carrying large white banners. When the Spanish arrive, the Aztec priests greet them as they would their gods, burning incense in their presence. The ambassadors then give them the gifts Montezuma sent for the strangers. In memory of the white banners, the river is henceforth called *río de Banderas*, the river of the Flags.

Thus began the *True Story*, with that meeting of two dreams. There was the Spanish dream of gold, a devouring, pitiless dream, which sometimes reached the heights of cruelty; it was an absolute dream, as if there were something at stake entirely different from the acquisition of wealth and power; a regeneration in violence and blood to live the myth of Eldorado, when everything would be eternally new.

On the other side was the ancient dream of the Mexicans, a long-awaited dream, when from the east, from the other side of the ocean, those bearded men guided by the Feathered Serpent Quetzalcóatl would come to rule over them once again. Thus, when the two dreams and the two peoples met, the one demanded gold and riches, whereas the other wanted only a helmet to show to the high priests and the king of Mexico, since, as the Indians said, it resembled those once worn by their ancestors, before they disappeared. Cortés gave them the helmet, but demanded that it be brought back to him filled with gold. When Montezuma saw the helmet, Bernal Díaz tells us, "he was more than ever convinced that we were the people spoken of by his ancestors as coming to rule his land" (Idell: p. 58).

From that imbalance rose the tragic results of the coming together of two worlds. It was the extermination of an ancient dream by the frenzy of a modern one, the destruction of myths by a desire for power. It was gold, modern weapons, and rational thought pitted against magic and gods: the outcome could not have been otherwise.

Bernal Díaz knew this, but despite the passing of time, he sometimes could not help expressing his bitterness or his horror at what had been destroyed. The *True Story* sometimes has the tone of an epic poem, but more often Bernal Díaz describes the Conquest as it truly was: the slow, difficult, and unavoidable progress of a destruction, the plundering of the Mexican empire, the end of a world. It is not surprising that *The True Story of the Conquest of Mexico* was for a long time cursed and judged injurious to the glory of the Conqueror Hernán Cortés.

For Bernal Díaz del Castillo wrote his book with two purposes in mind: on the one hand, to tell the truth about the wars of the Conquest, without hiding the smallest detail, without attempting the slightest flattery. That goal was a settling of accounts by Bernal Díaz,

the uneducated soldier—"illiterate idiots like me" (Díaz: p. 614)—
with the court historians such as Gomarra who had heaped lavish
praise on Hernán Cortés.

On the other hand, in writing his *True Story* Díaz sought to relive
his oldest dream. Of these two motives, there is no doubt that the
second was most important to Díaz. Granted, he was irritated by
the errors of the historians/chroniclers of the Conquest, by their
complacency and their affectation, as well as by the bias of Bartolomé
de Las Casas, the bishop of Chiapas and the author of the pamphlet
which revealed the "black legend" of the Conquest and which was
read throughout all of Europe: *The Devastation of the Indies: A Brief Account.* Bernal Díaz's simplicity, indeed his taste for simplification,
made him detest excess. His own bias was in fact one of the simplest. When Cortés undertook the conquest of the Mexican territories, he was not acting on his own behalf, but in the name of the
Spanish crown. It was therefore not Díaz's place, as a simple soldier,
to judge the actions of his captain, except sometimes to protest irritably when people wanted to see Cortés as a disinterested hero,
or when Cortés himself seemed to forget his former comrades in
arms. For example, when Cortés embellished his blazon with the arrogant motto addressed to the king: "Me, to serve you, without
equal," Bernal Díaz made a correction: He [Díaz] and his comrades
had helped their captain to "earn that glory, that honor, and that
status" (Díaz: p. 616).

But that taste for truth and an irritated reaction to the court historians would not have been enough to turn a soldier into a writer.
There was something more. When he began to write his chronicle,
Bernal Díaz was nearing the end of his days. Most of those involved
in the epic were dead, some during the battles with the Indians,
others from illness or old age. Hernán Cortés himself, the Marqués
del Valle, after experiencing political setbacks and disgrace, died
alone, the victim of an apoplectic seizure following an insulting
shock—the breaking of his daughter's engagement. She was abandoned by a young Castilian nobleman. Cortés died on December 2,

1547, in Spain, far from the Mexican land. His ashes alone were sent to New Spain, to be buried in Coyoacán.

The other Conquerors were also dead: Pedro de Alvarado, whom the Indians had named *Tonatiu*, the Sun, owing to his great beauty; Cristobal de Olid, the Conqueror of Michoacán, whom Bernal Díaz compares to Hector; Sandoval; Francisco de Montejo, the Conqueror of Yucatán; Luis Marin; Cristobal de Olea, the "very valorous soldier" who saved Cortés's life at the cost of his own. Dead also was the world they had conquered; it had disappeared, reduced to nothingness. Dead also were the last kings of Anáhuac: Montezuma, Cacamatzin, Cuitlahuatzin, and Cuauhtemoc, taking with them the secret of greatness, and the beauty of the legend. Dead also the Indian world with its cities more beautiful than Salamanca or Venice, its tall temples, its stone palaces covered with gold and paintings, its holy books and fabulous gardens. Dead, like the water of the large, beautiful lake in which the high temple towers and the palace courtyards were reflected, and upon which the piraguas bringing fruit and wealth to the great marketplace in Tenochtitlán [Aztec capital, located where Mexico City now stands] once glided. At the time when Bernal Díaz wrote his account nothing remained of that splendor, and the lake was nothing more than a dried-out basin in which a few stalks of corn were growing.

Thus when Díaz took up his pen, "like a good pilot who heaves the lead to discover the shallows of the sea before him when he senses they are there" (Díaz: p. 53), it was an attempt to rediscover the old dream, the one he had lived through during those two intense and tragic years alongside Cortés and his Conquerors. He didn't write to attain the glory of a historian (he quickly found out that his book was too true to be read by his contemporaries), but with the single hope that he would be recognized by generations to come: "Because," he says, "I am an old man of eighty-four and have lost my sight and my hearing. It is my fortune to have no other wealth to leave my sons and descendants except this, my true story, and they will see what a wonderful one it is" (Idell: p. 9).

The True Story of the Conquest of Mexico is not a book meant for others. For the old soldier it was above all the enjoyment of reliving, while writing about it, the excitement of that fabulous adventure. Along with him we relive that strange and cruel dream, a dream of gold and new lands, a dream of power, that sort of absolute adventure, when the new world discovered by Columbus still appeared for a brief moment as fragile and ephemeral as a mirage, before it disappeared forever. For he who watches in this tragedy is also he who destroys.

Thus began the dream, through the eyes of Bernal Díaz. We know of no other event like it in the history of the world, except perhaps the first confrontation in Europe between the neolithic peoples who came from the East and the primitive hunters. But no witness ever wrote of that great drama.

What is most striking in Díaz's account is the apparent combination of two abilities among the crew of adventurers who, united around Cortés, left to conquer the American continent: the expertise of sailors and that of horsemen.

They were sailors by necessity, those men who gathered on the island of Cuba, the springboard of all expeditions. They knew the ruses of the sea, and how to count only on themselves.

But they were also horsemen. Like the Huns and the Mongols before them, they had the advantages of the hunter: speed and endurance. It is no exaggeration to compare the conquistadors with the hordes that migrated from central Asia. Before departing, Cortés chose his men and horses with great care. He did not learn this from his easy conquest of the Antilles; his intuition made him aware of the determining role horses and their riders would play in the war against the Indians. It is difficult to imagine the Mexicans' terror when they first saw armored horsemen galloping toward them, brandishing long, threatening spears. This first apparition must have been as terrifying as the elephants of Alexander's army. For a long time, as Bernal Díaz recounts, the Indians believed "that the horse and its rider was all one animal." And, like a good commander, Cortés happily used a trick to increase the Indians' fear of horses. After making a stallion smell the scent of a mare in heat, he had it led not far from a place where the chiefs of Tabasco were assembled. The horse, Díaz writes, "began to paw the ground and neigh with excitement, looking toward the Indians, from which direction came the scent of the mare. The chiefs thought his wild cries were at them and stood like ghosts. Cortés had orderlies lead the stallion away and explained that he had given orders to the horse not to be angry, as we were all friendly and wished only for peace" (Idell: p. 50).

Horses were more important than men: to dress the wounds the horses sustained in battle, the Spaniards thought nothing of using human fat taken from the cadavers of their enemies.

Later, during the terrible battles with the México, captured horses, like men, would be sacrificed on the altar of the gods and their heads placed on display. Horses were such an integral part of the Conquest that they were long reserved only for the Spaniards; Indians were not allowed to ride, nor to bear arms.

Thus when Cortés set out from the island of Cuba with his army on February 10, 1519, Díaz conscientiously gave an exact accounting of his crew: 508 soldiers, 100 sailors, and 10 horses. It was this minimal crew that left to conquer a continent.

In retrospect Bernal Díaz considered the folly of such an undertaking to be obvious. He certainly saw it as one of those reckless, thoughtless acts which belong to the realm of dreams.

At the center of that particular dream was a man upon whose shoulders the entire expedition weighed: Hernán Cortés. This man, whose portrait Díaz gradually unveils for us, was truly the beginning and the end of that dream. Without him there might very well have been no Conquest, in the primitive and violent sense he gave to the term. Like most of the men with Cortés, Díaz admired him, but he feared and hated him at the same time. This man as clever as Ulysses, as cruel and ambitious as Attila, and as self-assured as Caesar was the one who created the dream of gold and new power which intoxicated all those who followed him. Who in fact was he? At the end of his account Díaz gives an unemotional portrait of Cortés, one which does not, however, conceal a certain antipathy—it certainly does not convey the warm friendship Díaz expresses for the dethroned King Montezuma, or the admiration he felt for the young hero Cuauhtemoc. Díaz describes Hernán Cortés:

He was of a good stature and strong build, of a rather pale complexion, and serious countenance. His features were, if faulty, rather too small; his eyes mild and grave. His beard was black, thin, and scanty; his hair in the same manner. His breast and shoulders were broad, and his body very thin. He was very well limbed, and his legs rather bowed; an excellent horseman, and dexterous in the use of arms. He also possessed the heart and mind, which is the principal part of the business. I have heard that when he was a lad in Hispaniola, he was very wild about women, and that he had several duels with able swordsmen, in which he always came off with victory. He had the scar of a sword wound near his under lip, which appeared through his beard if closely examined, and which he received in one of those affairs. (Keatinge: pp. 479–80)

Díaz's admiration was probably also due to Cortés's reputation as a cultivated man: "He was congenial with his men, something of a poet, and wrote well. He knew Latin, and I have been told that he was a bachelor at Law" (Idell: p. 391).

But what Díaz admired most about him was his coolness and daring—which verged on recklessness—in all aspects of war. It was to that recklessness that Cortés owed his most daring victories.

In short, through the episodes of the *True Story*, Bernal Díaz paints the portrait of an awesome predator: a leader, a strategist, a horseman, but also a man determined to win before all others, a man who wanted to bend the world to his will. He was an ambitious individualist intent on obtaining great wealth, and to do so he readily stole from those around him, both friends and enemies.

A child of the Middle Ages, an adventurer, this military leader benefited from the moral support of the greatest king of the European Renaissance, Emperor Charles V, in whose name Cortés conquered both land and men. It was a strange set of circumstances that, to the ruin of the Mexican empire, linked the pillaging of the adventurer from Extremadura to the name of the most powerful emperor of Europe, the heir to the realm of the Caesars.

One can see how Hernán Cortés prefigured the hero of the romantic era: he was clever, swift, unscrupulous, and he handled intrigue as well as he did his sword; he was well suited to conquer a world. He knew he was not just at the head of five hundred soldiers, but also on the tip of the Western and Christian world, like the longest tongue of the hydra that was to devour the world. And when his conquest was achieved and he was ennobled under the name of Marqués del Valle, was it by chance that he chose the phoenix to decorate his coat of arms, a bird which already suggested the Napoleonic eagle? With his brooding and hungry air, the extraordinary daring of his campaigns, his cold cruelty but also the tears he sometimes shed over the bodies of those he had sacrificed, Hernán Cortés prematurely evoked the legendary figure of another military leader who would conquer the world.

When he finally landed, first on Cozumel, then on the Punta de las Mujeres (Cape of Women), as his ships advanced along the Yucatán coast and he encountered the last of the *calacheoni* (or *halach unic* ["True Man," the religious and political leader of the village. *Calacheoni* is the Spanish misspelling]) of the Mayan world; then later when he met with Montezuma's emissaries on the banks of the Río de Banderas, and with the Totonac Indians at Cempoala: who were those men who greeted him? They were probably not the gentle "lambs" Bartolomé de Las Casas speaks of in his indictment; but they were completely foreign to the Spanish world, as different from Cortés and his men as they would have been if they had lived a thousand years apart.

The Maya, the Totonacs, and the México were profoundly religious tribes, completely subservient to the order of the gods and to the rule of their priest-kings. They practiced ritual war, waged using magic as much as strategy, and in their eyes the outcome of a battle, determined in advance according to mysterious agreements between celestial powers, was not to obtain land or wealth, but to render the triumph of the gods, who were fed on the hearts and blood of the defeated. Naively led by the myth of the return of their ancestors and of the divine Feathered Serpent, Quetzalcóatl/Kukulcán, the Indians were blinded; they were incapable of seeing the true motives of those whom they had already named *teules*, or gods. And by the time they finally understood that the return of those bearded men who had come from "where the sun rises" marked an unprecedented slaughter out of which no one would escape unscathed, it was too late. The Spaniards had taken advantage of the Indians' hesitation to penetrate into the very heart of their empire, to sow discord and to seize land and slaves.

It is that fatality which gives the conquistadors' adventure its tragic grandeur: in the unfolding of Bernal Díaz's account of the battles, the interviews, the surrendering of villages, we perceive the growing shadow which ultimately covered the Mexican land. Paralyzed, terrorized, incapable of reacting, of speaking, the Indians endured a true nightmare which held them prisoners of their own magic and led them to their deaths.

How could they have saved themselves, those Indians who formed but a whole, a single and same soul controlled by their gods, subject to the will of their kings and priests, when there appeared before them the individualistic, skeptical man of the modern world? Granted, faith accompanied Cortés's soldiers and came to Bernal Díaz's aid in the most crucial moments of the Conquest. But for Cortés wasn't that faith above all the symbol of Spanish power which was henceforth to reign over those new lands? As an able military leader Cortés knew this well when he attacked the Indians he intended to subdue in what was most precious and vital to them: he had their idols thrown to the foot of their temples, and he replaced them with symbols of the Christian faith. Abandoned by their ancestral gods, the Indians experienced the greatest anguish; they knew in advance they would ultimately be defeated.

Such were the worlds which collided during those two terrible years: the individualistic and possessive world of Hernán Cortés, the world of the hunter, the gold pillager who killed men and seized women and land; and the collective and magical world of the Indians, growers of corn and beans, peasants subjected to a clergy and a militia, adoring a sun-king who was the representative of their gods on earth. It is this story of hopeless confrontation which Bernal Díaz relates, and it was out of that confrontation that the dream was born, for it is also the tale of the end of one of the last magical civilizations.

Although Cortés the pillager took no notice of this, Díaz at least sensed something, a disturbance, a regret, which occasionally took hold of him while he was contemplating the beauty which was soon to disappear in another outbreak of fighting. Because of Díaz's doubts the *True Story* was a book cursed by his contemporaries, for it showed very well where the real glory and grandeur lay. Without that magical world, without the ritual languor of the Indian nations, without the splendor of that condemned civilization, Hernán Cortés would have been only a bandit at the head of a gang of adventurers. The grandeur was not born out of Cortés or his daring actions; it came from the Mexican world that he so eagerly sought to destroy.

Devastation—despite its exaggerations, Bartolomé de Las Casas's pamphlet indeed told of things that needed to be told. *The True Story of the Conquest of Mexico* is also that of *The Devastation of the Indies*.

Cortés's design was brutal, unequivocal. He had prepared everything with great care, and from his first encounters on Mexican land, his attitude left no doubt. Following the bloody battle at Rio de Grijalva, a victorious Cortés took possession of the land in the name of the king of Spain, as Bernal Díaz relates, "by drawing his sword and making three cuts in a huge tree, called a ceiba, that stood in the court, proclaiming that if anyone should object, he would defend his action with his sword and shield" (Idell: p. 45). Cortés's gesture was symbolic, for the ceiba was the sacred tree of the Maya, who believed it was the pillar supporting the vault of heaven.

Later the Indians attempted to free themselves from that sign of enslavement, and there occurred the first great battle waged by Cortés against the Indian world. It was also the first massacre, for in only a few hours the harquebuses, the crossbows, the iron swords, and the long spears of the horsemen—and undoubtedly also an inexpressible agony which paralyzed the Indians—caused more than eight hundred deaths within the ranks of the Mayan warriors.

Cortés's victory over the armies of the town of Tabasco was to have two important, mainly symbolic, consequences for the Conquest. The first was that the Spaniards earned the reputation of being invincible warriors, "gods," which ultimately led to the defeat of Montezuma. The second was that among the gifts offered as signs of peace to the Spanish captain the defeated *halach uinic* included the woman who was to be the essential instrument of the Indians' destruction: a young, very beautiful captured Indian girl whom the Spaniards baptized that very day under the name of Doña Marina and who became Cortés's companion and interpreter during his conquest of her land.

Thanks to Malintzin, the "Malinche"—whom Bernal Díaz calls "our tongue"—during his advance toward Anáhuac Cortés was able to use his most formidable, most efficacious weapon: speech. [Malintzin was the name originally given to Cortés by the Indians; later it came to be associated with Doña Marina.]

The gifts Cortés presented to the chiefs of Yucatán and to Montezuma's ambassadors also had symbolic value. Was it by chance that he chose to give them those *cuentas verdes,* that is, green-tinted glass beads? One can imagine Cortés before he set sail having his ships loaded with cases of those precious trinkets. For he had heard explorers of the West Indies who had gone before him tell of the magical power which the Indians attributed to the color of jade, the most precious of stones, the symbol of the color of the center of the earth.

The Maya called those "green stones" *kan*, symbols of prayer and destiny, and the Aztecs called them *chalchiuis*, the ornaments of the gods. Was this a coincidence or rather a cunning trick by the conqueror? When they were given those stones [as the Indians referred to the glass beads, which they associated with the *kan* stones] the Indians saw Cortés and his men as representatives of the gods who had come to distribute the mysterious and distressing message of their final destiny.

In exchange for their glass beads what did the visitors receive? They received what they had been seeking ever since they landed on American soil: gold. And we see again how the conquistadors' demands assumed a symbolic value: for the Indians, gold was the metal of the gods par excellence—the Maya called it *takin*, the excrement of the sun. The Indians didn't use it as money because it was reserved for the temples, for the "idols," sometimes to make amulets or sacred jewelry. It decorated the robes of princes and the insignia of captains, for it was a sign of divine power.

By constantly demanding gold everywhere they went, the Spanish adventurers succeeded in plunging their Indian enemies into great agony. Was gold not the primary tribute for the gods? These strangers who had come from "where the sun rises" brought that curse, that insatiable madness with them. At first they were satisfied with the gifts the chiefs and the Mexican emissaries presented to them. But soon their thirst for gold could no longer be quenched. In their quest for gold they killed, they destroyed, they tortured anyone who got in their way.

This recalls the story told by Bartolomé de Las Casas in his *Devastation of the Indies*: when the Spaniards undertook the conquest of Cuba, an Indian chief named Hatuey assembled his followers and spoke of the foreigners in these terms: "They are by nature wicked and cruel . . . because they have a God they greatly worship and they want us to worship that God, and that is why they struggle with us and subject us and kill us." In his house he had a basket full of gold and jewels, and, pointing at it, he said: "You see their God here, the

God of the Christians." Thus to escape the Spanish curse, the Indians threw all the gold they had into the river. And when the Spanish arrived they did not spare Hatuey. Las Casas adds that a Spanish monk, wanting to comfort the king while he was waiting to be burned at the stake, was asked by Hatuey: "Do the Spanish go to the Heaven you told me about?" When he received an affirmative reply the Indian said, "Then I prefer to go to Hell."[2]

Gold had symbolic value for the Indians; since it belonged directly to the gods, it was their treasure. By demanding it the Spanish thus proved that they were *teules*, gods. But it was also the symbol of the history which was unfolding. Without knowing it, by giving the Spaniards gold—the lavish gifts of Montezuma which were meant to mollify those awesome messengers from beyond—the Mexicans gave their conquerors a terrestrial power they could never have anticipated. For the golden wheels, the jewels of Montezuma's father, Axayacatzin, the precious treasures of the gods, melted down, turned into bars, then sent back to Spain, were used as collateral to finance more expeditions to the New World. Gold was a pact with destiny, for it was the Indians themselves who provided their conquerors with the financial means to exterminate them. How could they have known this? Could the Indians of the rural, religious, and feudal world of the Aztec empire ever have imagined the moral upheaval which was shaking Europe in the Renaissance, and which ultimately led to colonial expansion, when the warrior, the head of troops, became the ally and the supplier of a power in search of new frontiers? Gold was the very soul of the Conquest, its true God, as Las Casas said. Gold was also its dream money, and the insatiable rapine of the conquistadors was only the beginning of the modern frenzy.

Indeed, it is in this meeting of two dreams—one of magic, the other of gold—that one can see where the truth (and where falsehood) actually lay. The Mayan and Totonac chiefs, then Cacamatzin, king of Texcoco, and Montezuma, king of Mexico, gave the Spanish what was most precious, most sacred to the Indians: gold, jade, and turquoise. They also gave them cloth, food, and slaves. They even gave them the most beautiful, the most noble of their women—they gave their own daughters. What did they receive in return? "Green stones," glass beads, *margaritas* stones (twisted glass). When Cortés met Montezuma for the first time at the gates of the city of Mexico he placed one of those famous *margaritas* necklaces around the king's neck; Montezuma in turn placed a string of gold beads carved in the shape of shrimp around Cortés's neck, a piece of "marvelous workmanship," says Bernal Díaz. One cannot help thinking that Cortés and his men must have laughed up their sleeves at such a good deal: glass beads for gold ones. The colonial era was off to a good start.

Contrary to this were the dreams and magic which inhabited the Indian world when the Spaniards arrived. Even before meeting them, before being slaughtered by their weapons, the Indians knew that the strangers had come to rule over them. The Maya, the Tarascans, and the Aztecs had listened to their prophets and their diviners. They had been troubled by omens and dreams: eclipses, comets, falling meteorites, and recurrent nightmares announced the coming of terrible events. In the lands of Michoacán a slave woman of the lord of Ucareo, named Uiquixo, gave a strange account of the apparition of the goddess Cuerauaperi, mother of the gods, at her house. The slave told that she had been led to a place where all the gods of the universe were gathered, their faces covered with black paint, and the gods said: "Leave off the sacrifice of men and bring no more offerings with you because from now on it is not to be that way. No more kettle drums are to be sounded, split them all asunder. There will be no more temples or fireplaces, nor will any more smoke rise, everything shall become a desert because other men are coming to the earth."[3] In Mexico City, as Father Beaumont recounts in his *Crónica de Michoacán*, one heard "in the air, in various places, ominous voices telling of the end of that Indian monarchy," and there was brought before King Montezuma and his diviners a huge bird with a mirror on its head, and in the mirror "the sun was reflected with a sort of baneful and melancholy light."[4]

The Spaniards, however, were completely sure of themselves, and rarely doubted the positive outcome of their bold undertaking. Was this an unawareness of or a blindness to the reality of things? I believe rather that they truly represented the soldiers of the modern era; they were fundamentally materialistic and relied above all on their technology and weaponry.

As they advanced, who could beat them, who could hold them back? The beauty of the gifts Montezuma sent them, far from frightening them, was incentive to continue their marching onward. Magic was of little concern to them: when Montezuma, in the depths of his despair, sent a delegation to Cortés to halt his progress, he chose as his ambassador a prince by the name of Quintalbor, because, as Díaz says, he "looked like Cortés both in face and in body" (Idell: p. 58). This idea of presenting Cortés with his double was rooted in magic, which indeed shows the level upon which history was unfolding for the Aztecs. It was also a sign of the extreme attention the king of Mexico was paying to events. Each day he was told of yet another vassal being defeated: first the Totonacs, then the Tlaxcaltecas, the Cholultecas, and the people of Texcoco. Irrepressibly, despite gifts, despite sacrifices to the god of war, Huitzilopochtli, despite magic and ambushes, the band of Conquerors tightened its grip on the Mexican capital, while the ranks of mortal enemies of the México continued to expand.

In addition to European weaponry and strategy, Hernan Cortés used his most fearsome instrument of domination: speech.

As a man practiced in the art of court intrigue, he knew that his only chance of winning was in using trickery. For, after all, the Spaniards were only a handful of men, with few supplies, isolated on a continent they hardly knew, marching toward danger. And there were thousands, indeed, millions of Indians; they were masters of the land and water, sure of their strength. Under normal circumstances, the disproportion of forces was such that the Conquerors should not have survived more than a few hours on that new land.

Here we see the great value of Captain Cortés. If he was worthy of going down in history, it was not due to his courage or to his faith, and even less to the greatness of his adventure. It was due to his cunning trickery.

His initial setbacks might be attributed to the fact that the Maya had not left him time to speak. His later defeats—particularly the one known as the Sorrowful Night, when Cortés and his men were driven from Mexico and had to abandon most of their gold and many soldiers into the hands of the Aztecs—were due to the Indians having understood (a bit too late) that they should not listen to Cortés's words.

For Cortés owed the essence of the Conquest less to his sword than to his words—and to her who was named Doña Marina.

Cortés knew that to conquer he had to divide. As a contemporary of Machiavelli, Hernán Cortés quickly recognized the weak point of his enemy, the Mexican giant: In Montezuma's desire to rule too much, the empire had become weak. Each nation was the enemy of its neighbor, but especially of Mexico/Tenochtitlán. Cortés had no difficulty in inciting nations one after the other to rise up against the tyrant Montezuma, by promising them assistance and a share of the final spoils. He did the same with his own men.

Upon arriving at Cempoalla, the large Totonac city, Cortés began by imprisoning Montezuma's emissaries, who had come to collect a tribute of gold and captives. Then he secretly freed two of them so Montezuma would think he was his ally. He then publicly reprimanded the Totonacs for having allowed the two prisoners to escape, and held the three others hostage on his boat. He threatened the Totonacs with his departure, and the Indians, fearing the wrath of Montezuma, begged Cortés to stay, and declared themselves ready to submit to the authority of the king of Spain. Cortés, a man who knew the law, had them perform an act of allegiance before a public scribe named Diego de Godoy. Finally, when Montezuma sent further emissaries, Cortés returned the three hostages to them, saying he had saved them from the Totonacs. He found his friendship rewarded, as always, with sumptuous gifts. The art of political intrigue could hardly be raised to greater heights.

At the mercy of the Spanish, the Totonacs not only had to submit, but they had to witness, impotently, the destruction of their gods. Before the terrified eyes of the high priests and the chiefs, Cortés had his men crush the images of their gods in the temple of Cingapacingo. Fifty Spanish soldiers, having climbed to the top of the pyramid, pushed the statues, which then rolled to the bottom of the stairs. Bernal Díaz writes: "Some were like horrible dragons as large as calves, others were half men and half dog, of evil appearance. When they saw them this way, in pieces, the chiefs and priests wept and closed their eyes and begged for pardon, wailing that it wasn't their fault that we had broken them" (Idell: p. 83).

The massacre of the gods was a harbinger of the massacre of men, and of the fall of the gods from atop the great temple of Huitzilopochtli which was the end of that world.

Then began the slow climb toward the city of Mexico/Tenochtitlán. Aided by Totonac warriors, the Spaniards waged their first great battle against the Tlaxcaltecas, allies of Montezuma. Fifty thousand Indians rallied around the Tlaxcalteca war chief, Xicotenga the Younger. On their banners there figured a "large white bird with open wings" which Bernal Díaz describes as a sort of ostrich. The battle was fierce and deadly. The Spaniards had to bury their dead in secret in order not to belie their legend of immortality. Negotiations with the chiefs of Tlaxcala enabled Cortés to obtain the surrender of the Tlaxcalteca nation, but the Spanish soldiers were so demoralized that they spoke of retreating. It took all of Cortés's verbal artistry to convince them: "It was better to die, as is told in the tales of chivalry, than to live with dishonor."

Xicotenga the Younger, as he was about to surrender, made a gesture which shows well the state of mind of the Indians: He sent Cortés food, incense and feathers, and women. And here is his message to Cortés: "If you are [evil] *teules* (lords), as the Cempoallans say, and wish to sacrifice, you can take these four women and eat their hearts and flesh, but as we do not know your manner of sacrificing, we have not done it here before you. If you are men, eat the chickens, bread, and fruit. If you are tame *teules*, we have brought copal for incense and parrot feathers; make your sacrifice with them" (Idell: p. 110).

Cortés and his men could then enter as conquerors and allies into the great city of Tlaxcala, received as friends and brothers by Xicotenga the Elder, Massecasi, and other chiefs, all of whom gave them their own daughters as companions.

From then on the progress toward Mexico met no obstacles. Supported, fed, and guided by the mass of the Indian population, which was living both in fear of the *teules* and in hatred of the Mexica, the Conquerors were no longer the band of starving and worried adventurers they were in the beginning. They now had strength and numbers on their side.

Strangely, and in spite of himself, the image Bernal Díaz gives of Cortés's army is of some legendary and horrifying animal. There can be no doubt that the Indians, terrified by those men on horseback with helmets of iron carrying long spears (an image which survives even today in the name given the Spanish—*gachupines*, those who have spears), in seeing that marching army were reminded of their myths of fabulous and monstrous creatures. We think in particular of the myth of the Minotaur. That creature ruled first over the Indian civilizations: Huitzilopochtli, the god of war, Tezcatlipoca, the god of the sky, and Tlaloc, the god of rain, demanded heavy tributes in blood from the peoples living around Mexico City.

But when Cortés and his men arrived, an even heavier tribute was required. Food, gold, riches, and slaves had endlessly to be sent to the Spaniards and their allies. Díaz speaks of this tribute as an inexhaustible source of abundance, but did he know that the richness of those lands was only apparent? As the Spanish army continued its advance, and as its ranks increased with Indian mercenaries, there was ruin along its path. The meager harvests of the Indian peasants were pillaged, their reserves and treasures depleted. Why would the Conquerors have been concerned about that when all those riches—corn, poultry, fruit, cloth, jewelry—came to them so easily? The Indian peoples were giving to a new Minotaur in order to rid themselves of the old one. They gave the Spanish everything—gold, precious stones, slaves, women—undoubtedly with the illusion that those foreign *teules*, once their mission was completed and Mexico destroyed, would return to where they had come from, on the other side of the sea.

But the tribute the Indians had to pay the Minotaur only became greater, in Cholula, Texcoco, and Tenochtitlán. They continuously had to give the Conquerors new treasures, women, captives, whom they branded using a red-hot iron with the sign which alienated them forever: the ⚓ of war.

And later, after the Conquest, although the Mexican land was bloodless, starving, depopulated by flu and smallpox epidemics, the Minotaur continued to demand its share of food, women, slaves, and gold.

The *oidor* (adviser) Ceynos visited New Spain in 1530, and what he saw horrified him: "During the seven years of its government (Cortés's administration), the natives have suffered many deaths, and they have been treated very badly, they have been robbed and violated, men have taken advantage of their bodies and their goods without any thought of order or consequences, or measure."[5]

Reduced to slavery after the Conquest, the Indians had to pay an ever-increasing tribute to the new Minotaur and devote most of their time to working in its service, on plantations, in cities, and in silver and gold mines. They sometimes worked more than eleven hours a day, with no salary. They paid more taxes than they did to their former masters: there was the *moneda forera* (the king's share), the *aljama* (the fifth), the *fonsadera* (a war tax), the *alcabala* (sales and purchasing duties), the *almojarifazgo* (transport duties), the *chapín* (the queen's share), the tithe, not counting the direct levies by the owners of the haciendas. The *encomiendas*, properties bestowed by the crown upon Spanish nobles, enabled the complete exercise of such predatory behavior. In an accounting of the tributes paid by the Indians of the province of Cuernavaca to their master, Hernán Cortés, Bishop Zumarraga denounced the abuses: Each day, in addition to the various taxes destined for the crown, every adviser of Cortés's *encomienda* received seven young turkeys, several portions of game, partridges, corn, chocolate, spices, and seventy eggs. Later the Councils of State Diego Ramirez and Lorenzo Lebron de Quiñones denounced these abuses and attempted to temper the monstrous appetite of the Minotaur. But during the Conquest and in the years that followed, the Conquerors devoured almost all of the inhabitants and the wealth of New Spain.

That, too, was part of the "dream" of the Conquest. While those mysterious and destructive *teules* were advancing toward his city, King Montezuma sought in vain to divert their progress, to change the course of destiny. He increased his ambushes, his magical traps, his embassies, and gifts. Following the fall of Cholula, he hoped that Cortés would choose the easiest route to Mexico, and he prepared a final ambush. Cortés, being a seasoned soldier, thwarted the trap; he descended upon Mexico through the sierra route between the high volcanoes guarding the city. The first of the Conquerors, the Spaniard Diego de Ordaz, climbed the Popocatépetl volcano, and from atop its crater, 5,450 meters high, he discovered the extraordinary landscape of the valley of Mexico, its huge lake, its floating gardens, its white cities connected by causeways.

Cortés and his men had been dreaming of Mexico for such a long time! We can imagine Diego de Ordaz's description of it when he returned to the bivouac. There is something legendary in that first sighting of the forbidden capital by Western man, for that sighting bore the sign of the coming destruction. Montezuma had tried to persuade Cortés to retreat, for he knew that when the *teules* arrived, there would no longer be any hope: their destiny would have been fulfilled.

The story of the Conquest of New Spain, as it is written by Bernal Díaz del Castillo, is one of two opposing wills to speak which intersected, sought each other out, attempted to convince before confronting each other: The wily and threatening words of the Spaniard and the anguished and magical speech of the Mexican king. These two wills could not have met except, occasionally, with the help of the brilliant diplomacy of Doña Marina, the companion of Cortés. For those two tongues were completely foreign to each other: whereas the one inhabited a world of rituals and myths, the other expressed the pragmatic and dominating thought of Renaissance Europe.

Bernal Díaz admired the gift and art of speech of Hernán Cortés, who with only a few words could turn the most difficult situations to his advantage, when, for example, his men wanted to abandon their struggle and return to Cuba. In the portrait Díaz paints of Cortés, there is a note which explains well the true nature of the man: "Cortés was very fond of play, both at cards and dice, and while playing he was very affable and good humoured. He used frequently at such times those cant expressions which persons who game are accustomed to do" (Keatinge: p. 481).

It was certainly that cynical and unscrupulous language that Cortés spoke while he was advancing toward the interior Mexican territory. Thus when he wanted to frighten Montezuma's emissaries at Cempoalla, he presented to them, at the head of a battalion of Totonac warriors, a soldier named Old Heredia, a Basque who had, says Bernal Díaz, "a bad twitch in his face," which was half-covered with scars, he was blind in one eye, had a huge beard, and was lame in one leg. The soldier, Cortés thought, would make a very good scarecrow, and the captain told him: "because you are so ugly they will think that you are an idol" (Idell: p. 79).

It was that language, sometimes mocking, sometimes threatening, which Cortés used to inspire his men; and it was the language of a dice player which he used to trick, frighten, or divert the strength of his Indian adversaries. We can understand how the Indians had been fascinated by that "big-talker" who could play on all levels of emotion, from love to anger. He loved them, he said, and he came on behalf of a great king who lived beyond the seas, and who wanted to deliver them from the yoke of the Mexica. But beneath those "loving" words, Díaz says, were lurking domination, plundering, and slavery.

Montezuma procrastinated; he sent delegation after delegation; he debated, revealed his weakness, his anguish, to his adversary. If only the Indian had used the strength of silence! In that cruel and fatal game, to speak was to recognize the other, to allow him to enter into your heart. It was to show to one's vassals, one's allies, that the proud reign of Tenochtitlán was on the verge of ending, just as all the legends had proclaimed.

Then came the great Cacamatzin, king of Texcoco, to welcome Cortés. He arrived on a palanquin carried by eight princes, while servants swept the dust from the path in front of him. This was the meeting of a king who was equal to a god with the man who was feared as a god. This encounter opened the way to Mexico.

Here, perhaps, is one of the most striking moments of Bernal Díaz del Castillo's *True Story*: the march of the Spanish soldiers, cavalry at the head, along the causeway over the lake toward the great city of Mexico/Tenochtitlán. In Díaz's memory, the image is as pure and dazzling as a dream—for at that moment everyone had the feeling of living in a dream, comparable to the "enchantments" told about in the book of *Amadis*: "Some of our soldiers asked if what we saw was not a dream. It is not to be wondered at that I write it down here in this way, for there is much to ponder over that I do not know how to describe, since we were seeing things that had never before been heard of, or seen, or even dreamed about" (Idell: p. 139). All around them, endlessly before them, on the sky-blue lake, there spread out white cities, stone palaces, floating gardens, courtyards filled with trees, overshadowed by the tall outlines of the pyramids. The Spanish Conquerors advanced slowly on the long causeway that crossed the lake, from the city of Ixtapalapa to Tenochtitlán, in the twilight that must have blurred the shapes of the volcanoes and revealed, as if through a fog, the magical and distant shadows of the tall temples of Tlatelolco and the palaces of Montezuma. And as they silently advanced, their eyes filled with those marvels, they were greeted by the great princes of Anáhuac and by crowds of warriors and Mexican people. At that moment they must surely have felt a shiver from the greatness, to be living that moment of history and legend; those soldiers, the messengers of destruction, bearers of death, whose destiny depended entirely on that encounter with the power of Mexico/Tenochtitlán.

And while writing about it, Bernal Díaz could not help voicing his admiration, his wonderment mixed with sadness: "I stood looking, thinking that never in the world would lands like these be discovered again, for at that time we had no knowledge of Peru. Today all that was there then is in the ground, lost, with nothing left at all" (Idell: p. 140).

Upon the large causeway that went across the lake the great king in person, Montezuma, like a legendary god, finally came to meet Cortés: He was carried beneath a canopy made of feathers and gold, wearing his robes set with precious stones, and sandals with golden soles. No one could look at his face, and when he walked, mats were placed before him on the ground. It was this king, this living god, who then made his way toward Hernán Cortés, who greeted him at the doors of Mexico/Tenochtitlán. For more than a year they had been seeking each other out through words, and Montezuma's anguish had been growing every day. That moment was otherworldly, tragic. It was the supreme moment of the meeting of two worlds, two civilizations—the one, divine power; the other, the power of gold and weapons. There is something vertiginous in that meeting, for the future of the Western world clearly hinged on its outcome. By admitting the strangers into his universe, by seeking to come to terms with them, Montezuma, without knowing it, sealed the defeat of his world, for the white man never shares. Cortés meant to exclude the Indian world, and once he reduced it to slavery, he set the stage for the conquest of the entire American continent, from Canada to the Tierra del Fuego. Without gold, without the raw materials, above all without the work of slaves, what might the fate of Europe and its "industrial revolution" have been?

But the world of dreams and myths was condemned with the arrival of that handful of adventurers. They were lodged by Montezuma in the palace of his father, King Axayacatzin, and in the neighboring temples—were they not in fact gods? Fed, served, guarded by those they had come to destroy, they could secretly prepare their plans for attack, break open the funerary vault filled with sacred treasures, and dream at the sight of the piles of gold which shone upon the walls of the temples.

Who was Montezuma, that legendary king, who seemed to abandon himself to his fate? From Bernal Díaz del Castillo's account he sometimes resembled a Renaissance prince, refined and taken with luxury. But he was also a legendary king, a half-god. There is something almost incongruous in the portrait Díaz presents of him; for those Spaniards, those adventurers who became heroes in spite of themselves, could not be the equals of those kings and princes of divine essence. If there was an abyss which separated the Conquerors' and the Indians' ways of thinking, there was also one regarding their customs. It was the abyss which separated the spiritual chief of the most civilized people of Central America from the European barbarians, Cortés and his soldiers. In Montezuma's court there was the baroque refinement of an Oriental prince—the Mikado of Japan, for example—coupled with the natural nobility of a man born and raised to rule. This was a subject of wonderment for a man of as modest origins as Bernal Díaz, who knew nothing of European nobility. But above all there was something which neither he nor Cortés, nor any of the other Conquerors could understand: Montezuma was not just a man, not just an army chief; he was the representative of the gods on earth, an "idol." This is why no one could look at his face or approach him directly. He lived surrounded by rituals like a god, and when he ate he was hidden behind a screen. It was that supernatural monarch whom the Spanish, through an act of audacity which barbarians alone could have dreamt up, later seized and held hostage in his own father's palace.

One might question the reason for Montezuma's submissiveness. How could such a powerful king, he who made all of Mexico tremble, who commanded the largest and best-organized army in the New World, in the shelter of his palace, surrounded by his guards and his high priests, in the center of a city which at that time must have had more than a million inhabitants, how could he have so easily accepted that humiliation, that destruction of his power? Was he irresolute? A coward? Perhaps as soon as the Spaniards had entered his city he understood through an illuminating, inevitable intuition that his people were alone, hated, divided, and that he would never be victorious through force in the face of such a coalition. So he accepted the situation, he sought to buy time, he consulted the oracles.

The reason for this tragedy, I believe, is found entirely in the realm of magic. Dreams, the predictions of magi, legends, signs from heaven—everything told Montezuma of the end of his reign, of the arrival of the *teules*. Knowing he was condemned in advance by the gods, persuaded that nothing could change the course of destiny, he wanted to take upon himself the largest part of the tragedy which was about to unfold.

If it is true that Montezuma appeared weak, irresolute, gripped by that inner turmoil which was to destroy most of the great Indian kingdoms, it is also true that in the face of the irreversible, he proved to be a true leader who sought first to spare his people and his city.

Montezuma was above all the representative on earth of the god Huitzilopochtli. He wore the symbols of that god, the "seal and that insignia of [Huitzilopochtli]" which he tore from his wrist when Cortés and his men took hold of him, something—Bernal Díaz says—"he did only when he gave an important order that, once given, was to be complied with" (Idell: p. 170). Deeply religious, Montezuma must have been torn until his dying day between the desire to avenge the affronts the foreigners committed against his gods and his total submission to a destiny he believed was inescapable.

In this confrontation between America and Western Europe, between gods and gold, we can clearly see who were the civilized and who were the barbarians. In spite of their bloody sacrifices, despite ritual anthropophagy, despite the tyrannical structure of that theocracy, there can be little doubt that it was the Aztecs—like the Maya, or the Tarascans—who could be called civilized. Bernal Díaz del Castillo, like all those who participated in colonization, wanted to believe that the destruction of the Indian world was justifiable because it was a world devoted to demons. Thus, like the chronicler Motolinia, he justified the massacre of Cholula because it brought about the conversion of the Indians; and for that same reason he justified the massacre of Tlatelolco and the bloody destruction of the city of Mexico/Tenochtitlán. And yet it is in the actions and the words of the vanquished that we find the lost splendor of that civilization. When Cortés and his men climbed to the top of the main temple and Cortés asked Montezuma to renounce his gods, the Mexican king could not contain his anger: "Señor Malinche, if I had thought that you would so insult my gods, I would not have shown them to you" (Idell: p. 160).

When the foreigners had set up camp in his father's palace and after they had broken into his tomb to assess its treasures, Montezuma first sought to expiate the sin committed against the gods; he fasted, he prayed, he offered up sacrifices.

The Mexican gods, like those of the Maya, were uncompromising and terrible. The arrival of the Spanish must have been seen by the Indians as an exemplary punishment. Until the final moment the Mexica warriors believed that at the conclusion of their trials their gods would ultimately bring them victory. While the Spanish advanced, found allies, prepared their assault on the capital, the Indians concerned themselves with their gods. They increased their offerings and sacrifices, and what Bernal Díaz readily saw as a sign of demoniacal cruelty was fundamentally only a consequence of the Conquest: wherever the Spanish went the pyramids and sacred altars flowed with the blood of expiatory and propitiatory victims. Indeed, day and night, night and day, during the three months of the siege of Mexico/Tenochtitlán, one heard without interruption the beating of the drums that accompanied human sacrifices on the altar of Huitzilopochtli.

The Mexican gods were part of that tragic dream; they were the principal actors in it. When for the first time Bernal Díaz saw the gods of the Aztecs on the temple of Huitzilopochtli in Tlatelolco, he was struck by their frightening appearance. In his imagination those statues representing creatures who were half-men, half-beasts were exactly like those of the infernal European Middle Ages: for, of course, the canons of the art of the Renaissance could not admit the symbolics of Indian art: Huitzilopochtli, writes Díaz, "had a very broad face with monstruous, horrible eyes . . . [and his body] was circled with great snakes made of gold and precious stones, and in one hand he held a bow and in the other some arrows. A small idol standing by him they said was his page; he held a short lance and a shield rich with gold and precious stones. Around the neck of [Huitzilopochtli] were silver Indian faces and things that we took to be the hearts of these Indians, made of gold and decorated with many precious blue stones" (Idell: p. 159). As for the god Tezcatlipoca, he had "the face of a bear and glittering eyes, made of their mirrors, which they call *tezcal*. It was decorated with precious stones the same as [Huitzilopochtli], for they said that the two were brothers. This Tezcatlipoca was the god of hell and had charge of the souls of the Mexicans. His body was girded with figures like little devils, with snakelike tails" (ibid.). At the highest part of the temple in a sort of recess, there was another figure that was "half man and half lizard, covered with precious stones and with a mantle over half of it. They said that its body was filled with all the seeds there are in all the world. It was the god of sowing and ripening." (Idell: p. 160).

These were the Aztec gods which Cortés and his men, with a mixture of curiosity, greed, and horror, discovered at the highest point of the great temple of Mexico. A few months later the Spaniards would throw those statues down the steps of the pyramid, after stripping them of the riches that covered them.

The dream of the Conquest seemed gradually to lose its marvelous quality, while Cortés and his soldiers remained in the city. For Montezuma that dream became a nightmare when he was taken from his own palace and held hostage in his father's palace, which the foreigners had transformed into a fortress. Montezuma then felt the weight of an incomprehensible error upon him—it was perhaps a punishment being inflicted on him by those gods whom Cortés had insulted during his first visit to the temple. For Bernal Díaz the imprisonment of Montezuma, one of those mad acts of audacity which made up the history of the West, was an act dictated by God. For the Indians it was a sacrilegious act, since the king was as untouchable as the gods themselves. It would ultimately cause them great anguish. The inevitability they, like Montezuma, felt at that time was linked to a mysterious will, beyond all human understanding. At the beginning of the Conquest, when the Indians believed that the foreigners were gods, their anguish was very great; and it became even greater when they discovered those foreigners were men. From then on nothing could appease their will to fight back.

Chained up, powerless, uttering "great cries," says Díaz, Montezuma witnessed the torturing of his army chiefs, burned alive by the Spaniards for having attacked the Spanish at Veracruz and for having collected tributes in their place. Like gold, the chain was one of the symbols of the Conquest, one of those nightmarish signs which the Spanish brought to the New World. As soon as Cortés had secured the imprisoned Montezuma, he sent messengers to the coastal town of Veracruz to get a long chain of wrought iron which he had brought along in his ships for a purpose. The chain was intended to make the great chiefs of the Mexican army his prisoners.

In my opinion there is something nightmarish in the image of that long chain from beyond the sea, which slowly climbed the slopes of the mountains, from village to village, carried by Indian slaves, going through forests and cornfields, to the foot of the Popocatépetl volcano, and finally arriving at Mexico/Tenochtitlán, going across the lake along the causeway, to the palace where the Spanish had imprisoned the last Mexican king. In any event it was the symbol which Cortés, having become Marqués del Valle after the Conquest, would choose to illustrate his blazon: the heads of the last seven kings of Anáhuac all chained together.

The Conquerors' chain was indeed the symbol of that fatality. Each time a new humiliation was heaped upon Montezuma, he seemed paralyzed by pain. When Cortés, during one of those judicial ceremonies he used to make his will official, demanded that Montezuma submit to the king of Spain, "Montezuma and his chiefs, showing much emotion, gave fealty to His Majesty. Montezuma could not keep back his tears, and he was so dear to us and we were so much affected at seeing him cry that our own eyes were saddened," writes Bernal Díaz (Idell: p. 184).

The other symbol of the fall of Mexico/Tenochtitlán was, again, the gold that brought it about. In his father's palace, where he was being held hostage, Montezuma continued to rule; he rendered justice, he organized, he commanded his vassals. But behind him it was Cortés who collected the tributes.

The conquered had to pay a very heavy duty, and it came from the treasure of Axayacatzin, Montezuma's father, which was pillaged. The Spaniards extracted everything from the funerary vault that was made of gold; they had it melted down, and thus transformed the sacred jewelry of the former king of Tenochtitlán into bars three inches thick, worth, as Díaz specifies, 600,000 pesos. This fabulous fortune was to be divided up, a process during which Cortés proved no less rapacious than the Pizarro brothers were a few years later in Peru. Cortés kept the same share the king received—a fifth—for himself, while most of the soldiers received scarcely more than 100 pesos each. Revolt was rumbling momentarily among Cortés's men, but the dice player knew how to wield the phrases he needed to make promises, to appease.

These are the true symbols of the Conquest: the chain and gold ingots. At the time of the insurrection, when the gods Huitzilopochtli and Tezcatlipoca responded to Cortés's offers of peace through the mouths of the oracles, they said in effect that they could not remain in a place where they were so ill-treated by the *teules*, and where sacred gold was transformed into "bricks." And Montezuma, when Cortés asked him to place a cross at the top of the temple, cried out in shock: "Oh, Malinche, how can you wish to cause the loss of this whole city?" (Idell: p. 194).

The most maleficent act in the history of the Conquest was the massacre at the great temple of Mexico. Cortés was away from the capital to fight his enemy and rival, Navarez, and had left the garrison and his royal hostage in the hands of his lieutenant, Pedro de Alvarado, whom the Indians had named "the Sun." Alvarado and his soldiers watched the high priests and the war chiefs prepare the feast of the god Huitzilopochtli in the temple courtyard. Here is a description of the massacre as related by a Mexican of Tlatelolco who in 1528 gave his anonymous account in the Nahuatl language:

At that time they asked *Montezuma* how they should celebrate the feast of their god. He told them:
Put all his ornaments on him. Do that.
At that time it was when the Sun (Alvarado) gave his orders: they are already chained up, *Montezuma*, and the *Tlacochcalcatl* of *Tlatelolco Itzcohuatzin*.
It was when they hung a prince of Acolhuacan by the name of *Netzalhualquentzin*, near the stone ramparts.

Then the king of *Nauhtla*, named *Cohualpopocatzin*, died. They pierced him with arrows, and then, still alive, they burned him.

For that reason the *Tenochcas* of the Gate of the Eagle stood guard. On one side were the rooms of the *Tenochcas*; on the other, the rooms of the *Tlatelolcas*.

Then they were told that *Huitzilopochtli* had put on his ornaments. Then they put his finery on *Huitzilopochtli*, his paper clothing, all his accoutrements. They put all that on.

Then the Mexicans began to sing. They did that the first day.

But they could not do it the second day: they began to sing, and it was then that the *Tenochcas* and the *Tlatelolcas* were killed.

Those who were singing and dancing were completely unarmed. They wore only the decorated mantle, turquoise stones, jewels on their lips, necklaces, tufts of heron feathers, amulets made with the feet of a deer. And those who played the drums, the old men, wore their calabashes filled with powdered tobacco to snuff, and their bells.

It was those men whom they began to strike down first; they knocked them over, they struck their hands, they slapped their faces, and then they killed them all, without exception. And those who were singing and looking around them were also killed.

They knocked us down, they mistreated us for three hours. It was in the Sacred Courtyard that they killed everyone.

Then they entered into the chambers of the temple to kill everyone: those who carried water, those who were feeding the horses, those who were grinding grain, those who were sweeping, those who were standing guard.

But King *Montezuma*, accompanied by the *Tlacochcalcatl* of *Tlatelolco*, *Itzcohuatzin*, who supplied the Spaniards with food, said:

"Oh lords—Enough! What are you doing there? Oh, the poor, poor people! . . . Do they have shields? Do they have clubs? But they are completely unarmed!"

And when the captain (Cortés) returned, the Sun (Alvarado) had already killed us all.[6]

According to Bernal Díaz the massacre at the temple of Mexico/ Tenochtitlán was a counterattack by Alvarado, who was threatened by an Aztec plot. And in the bloody disorder following the massacre, he even speaks of the miraculous intervention of the Virgin and of the "lord Santiago" [Saint James, patron of the Conquerors]: during the battles there appeared a great *tecleciguata*, a great lady, who threw dirt into the Indians' eyes and blinded them, while a blond *teule* rode on his white horse striking them down (Díaz: p. 265).

The massacre at Tlatelolco was the moment of rupture between the two worlds. For a few months, terror, despair, and also that sort of fascination the Indians experienced for the foreigners who came to bring them new things enabled their cohabitation. The massacre at Tlatelolco was the signal for a war without mercy which the Indians waged to expulse the Spanish in an attempt to regain their equilibrium, their power, and their gods.

As always, Cortés, having hastily returned from the coast of Cempoalla, decided to strike at the jugular. Using his sword and his harquebus, with the help of a few soldiers he cleared a path to the temple. With his men he climbed to the top of the pyramid and set the idols on fire.

There could henceforth be no mercy on either side. Besieged in the palace, without food or water, the Spaniards were condemned. There then occurred one of the culminating incidents of the tragedy, the death of King Montezuma, "in year 2 silex," according to the anonymous chronicler. The man who was too submissive to destiny, enchained by the Conqueror, was led to the battlements. He was forced to speak to his subjects, to the war chiefs. But it was too late. The Mexicans replied: "Oh, Lord, our great lord, how greatly we are afflicted by your misfortune, and that of your sons and relations! We have to let you know that we have already raised one of your kinsmen to be our lord" (Idell: p. 248).

Montezuma, rejected by his people, ceased to exist. When Cortés wanted to use him one last time (not without previously having called him a "dog"), Montezuma spoke these single words, which are surely the saddest of this *True Story*. He said to Cortés: "What more does Malinche want from me? I do not want to live." (Idell: p. 247).

These were in fact his final words, for, dragged by force onto the battlements, he was struck by a stone thrown by a warrior of his own people, and he allowed himself to die from the wound. Cortés had the body of the immolated ruler given to his enemies, less out of magnanimity than as a ruse, for he knew that the sight of the murdered king would plunge the Indians into the greatest sorrow, and that he would then have a few days of peace in which to prepare his escape.

During the night of July 10, 1520—less than a month after their astonishing entrance into the Aztec capital—in a cold rain, the Spaniards fled without glory, losing a large number of their men, horses, and their gold spoils in the battle. It was this defeat for Cortés, later known as the Sorrowful Night, that Bartolomé de Las Casas called a "very just and holy war."

Henceforth the Mexica no longer gave in. But it was too late. Despite that victory, the ultimate extermination of the Indian world could no longer be prevented.

The reconquest of Mexico/Tenochtitlán was achieved thanks to Cortés's chief weapon—his ability to speak—which enabled the Spaniards to assemble all the enemies of the Aztecs for the final attack. But it also came about with the help of the most fearsome ally of the Europeans: smallpox. In only a few hours the disease decimated the population of the capital, striking down the most courageous of men, such as Cuitlahuac, the new king of Mexico. Later it was again smallpox, known as *cocoliztli* (infernal sickness), that accomplished the colonists' work of destruction, especially during the year 1545 when, according to historians' estimates, it must have caused close to 800,000 deaths. That disease was a decisive weapon in the conquest of Yucatán and Central America, for it was often spread intentionally by Spanish soldiers using contaminated rags.

Following the ephemeral victory of the Sorrowful Night, while the Mexica were making sacrifices to their gods and praying for their dead, Cortés and his men began the long march to encircle and isolate the capital, and recruited one after another all the Aztecs' vassal nations. Xicotenga (baptized Don Lorenzo de Vargas) and Netzahualpinzintli, king of Texcoco (baptized Don Hernán Cortés in honor of the Conqueror), provided food and the support of their warriors.

The great army, composed essentially of Indians hostile to the Mexica, followed the Conquerors, says Díaz, like "the birds of prey that followed our army in Italy in order to feed on the dead bodies that were left on the field after a battle" (Idell: p. 315).

The devouring monster, the Minotaur, surrounded the city of Mexico spreading blood and terror. Wherever there was resistance the Spaniards indulged in plundering. The horse was one of their greatest assets in those open-air wars which took place on the plains. Cortés, obsessed with order and justice, in front of witnesses drafted an act which justified the seizing of slaves. All prisoners of war, men and women alike, were branded on the face with the sign of war, the $\mathcal{F}$. They were then distributed among the Conquerors. Their repression was sometimes extremely brutal, as in Tepoztlán, where all the houses were burned down, "to strike fear in the other towns," writes Díaz. He adds that everywhere the Spaniards took "a great deal of spoils, both of cloth and of good-looking girls" (Idell: p. 321).

Famine, the consequence of war and epidemics, was an even more sinister shadow of that Minotaur which was depopulating the surroundings of Mexico. Living through that, witnessing it all, there can be little doubt, the Indians believed they had been abandoned by their gods, and that the end of their race was at hand.

To the devouring extermination by the Spanish there responded the cruel magic of the Indians. The soldiers captured during the Sorrowful Night were sacrificed on the altar of Huitzilopochtli and the skin of their faces sent to the principal vassals of Mexico. Everywhere, without interruption, the echo of war cries, the whistling of the Indians, and the obsessive noise of their drums were heard.

Xicotenga the Younger arrived from Tlaxcala to join the attack against Mexico/Tenochtitlán, along with his warriors carrying banners decorated with the fabulous "white bird," and they paraded in front of the Spaniards crying "Castilla! Castilla" [Castile, from which most of the Conquerors came] and "Tlaxcala! Tlaxcala!"

The attack began on May 13, 1521. Cortés managed to add around twenty-five thousand Indian allies to his troops. It was then no longer a matter of magic or daring; it was sheer numbers that would conquer the Mexicans.

Isolated, its fresh-water supply cut off, without food, Mexico/Tenochtitlán nevertheless managed to resist for three long months, each day heroically repelling the assault of the Spaniards on their causeways and on the lake. During those battles, it sometimes seemed that destiny was vacillating, as in Xochimilco, when Cortés fell from his horse "Romo" and was taken prisoner by the Mexica warriors. But Cristobal de Olea succeeded in saving his life.

As told in Bernal Díaz's *True Story*, this final act of the Mexican tragedy reveals a legendary hero: the young Cuauhtemoc, the new king of Mexico/Tenochtitlán, who was later to become one of the symbols of the Independence of Mexico. Cortés, who saw him as a worthy enemy, tried to seduce him with promises of peace and pardon. But Cuauhtemoc didn't respond. He knew that silence was his greatest strength.

Bernal Díaz del Castillo was surely the first to assert the legend of the young warrior king: "He was a young man around twenty-five years old, and kindly for an Indian" (Idell: p. 378); and Díaz adds that at the time of his capture "he had the appearance of a man of quality, both in features and in body. His face was somewhat large and cheerful, with eyes more grave than gay . . . His complexion was somewhat lighter than that usual to Indians. They said that he was a nephew of Montezuma, son of one of his sisters, and was married to a daughter of the same Montezuma, a very beautiful woman, and young" (Idell: p. 384).

Cuauhtemoc was the pure hero of that dreamed legend. Brave to the point of recklessness, he understood—as his uncle Montezuma had undoubtedly suspected—before everyone else that the outcome would be inevitable. When Cortés, discouraged by the fierce resistance of the Mexicans, made them offers of peace, the young king finally replied: "It would be better for us all to die here fighting than to become their slaves." (Idell: p. 378).

In those words, and in the silence he subsequently offered in response to Cortés's seductive words, is found the ultimate grandeur of his dying world.

Magic was thus the final intoxication of those condemned men. An intoxication made bloody by the sacrifices of the Spanish soldiers captured during the battle of Tlatelolco, as if the gods could be reborn for a moment from the disaster, when all around them men were dying of hunger, illness, exhaustion. The final days of the Mexican capital seem linked to that nightmare, to that mortal intoxication.

The Spaniards, beaten down, listened in the very depths of their souls to the rhythmic beating of the drums announcing the deaths of their companions.

"As we retreated," writes Bernal Díaz, "we heard peals of sound from the great *cu* [temple] where the idols of [Huitzilopochtli] and [Tezcatlipoca] were. They were beating a drum that had a most sorrowful sound, like an instrument of demons, and could be heard two leagues away. With it were tambourines, conch shells, horns, and whistles" (Idell: p. 364). The music of the sacrifices resounded terribly for the Spaniards, who knew their companions were dying, and while writing about it, Díaz again shivered at the horror of those moments: "The mournful drum of [Huitzilopochtli] sounded again, accompanied by conch shells, horns, and something like a trumpet. All of them together made a terrifying sound, and as we looked at the high *cu* from which it came, we could see our companions who had been captured in the defeat of Cortés being forced up the steps to be sacrificed. When they had them up on the open space before their cursed idols, we saw them put plumes on the heads of many of the prisoners, and with some things like pitchforks they made them dance before [Huitzilopochtli]. After the prisoners had danced, the Mexicans bent them backward over some stones, somewhat narrow, that they used for sacrificing, and with stone knives they sawed through their chests, took out their beating hearts, and offered them to their idols. Then they kicked the bodies down the steps. There were butchers waiting below to cut off the arms and legs. They flayed the faces, and later cured them with mud so that they were like glove leather, with the beards still on. These they kept for their fiestas, when they got drunk and ate the meat with *chilmole* [sauce made with wild tomatoes, hot pepper, and mint leaves].

"They sacrificed all the others in the same way, eating the legs and arms and offering the hearts and blood to their idols. The torsos they threw to the tigers, lions, and snakes that they kept in [the house of animals]" (Idell: pp. 368–69).

Thus that was the last cannibal feast Mexico/Tenochtitlán celebrated before dying. The intoxication of that feast continued until the very last moment. Each night Bernal Díaz and his companions heard the obsessive and tragic sound of "the accursed drum." For it was, he says, "the most evil and the most mournful sound that it would be possible to invent" (Idell: p. 376). It sounded far over the land, and they played other, even worse instruments, they did diabolical things, lit huge fires, and continued loud shouting and whistling.

But hunger, thirst, and illness ultimately broke down the final resistance of the Mexican people. Under the pressure of Cortés and the men from Tlaxcala, Cuauhtemoc abandoned the center of the city, the palaces, and the temples. The Spaniards burned the idols. While attempting to escape on board a piragua, the young king was captured by one of the Spanish brigantines which had cut off the lake route, piloted by a certain Garcia Holguin. Brought before Cortés, Cuauhtemoc uttered only these heroic words, as reported by Díaz: "Señor Malinche, I have done what I was obliged to do in the defense of my city and my people. I can do no more. I have been brought before you by force as a prisoner. Take that dagger from your belt and kill me with it quickly" (Idell: p. 383).

But Cortés didn't kill him. He held him hostage for a long time, torturing him to find out where the treasure of his uncle Montezuma was hidden, and, not being able to obtain what he wanted, had him shamefully strangled, along with his cousin, the lord of Tacuba, upon his return from an expedition to Honduras.

Before the hero of the Mexican resistance died that unjust death, Díaz reports, he spoke one last time to Cortés:

"Oh, Malinche! I have understood for a long time that you were going to make me die in this way, and I have guessed the falsity of your words, for you are making me die unjustly" (Díaz: p. 490). The murder of Cuauhtemoc marked the end of the Aztec dynasty. Cuauhtemoc's capture, notes Díaz, took place on "the thirteenth of August, at the hour of vespers on the day of San Hipolito in the year 1521" (Idell: p. 384).

Then there was silence. It was that silence which shocked Díaz the most in the days that followed the fall of Mexico/Tenochtitlán. For "now that [Cuauhtemoc] was captured, all of us soldiers were as deaf as though up to now we had been in a bell tower with all the bells ringing. For the ninety-three days of the siege there had been constant cries and whistles day and night, the shouts of Mexican captains giving orders on the causeways, others crying to the canoes, putting in palisades, and making barricades. In addition to all this their accursed drums and horns never stopped sounding from their towers and oratories, so that it was impossible to hear anyone talk. Now that [Cuauhtemoc] was captured, all the noise and voices stopped" (Idell: p. 384).

That silence represented the death of a people. After the ruses and the dirty dealings—the mocking and wily language of the dice player—after the clamor, the imprecations, the "whistling" of the Indians, and the obsessive rhythm of the drums in the temple of Huitzilopochtli, silence closed in over that annihilated world. It reigns forever over it, keeping its secrets, its myths, its dreams, all that the Conquerors, through a privilege they sometimes sensed without really understanding, briefly perceived before they destroyed it.

Years later, distanced by time, Bernal Díaz wrote his *True Story* to rediscover that beauty, that life. But what he discovered above all was an inevitable impression of the disaster at the heart of the legend: everything had been razed, thrown to the ground, put to death: "I swear that all the houses on the lake were full of heads and corpses. I have read of the destruction of Jerusalem, but I cannot believe that the massacre was greater than that of Mexico, although I cannot say for certain. The streets, squares, houses, and courts were filled with bodies so that it was almost impossible to pass" (Idell: p. 385).

That silence, which closed in on one of the greatest civilizations in the world, carrying off its words, its truth, its gods, and its legends, was also in a certain way the beginning of modern history. The fantastic, magical, and cruel world of the Aztecs, the Maya, and the Purepecha [Tarascans] would be succeeded by what is called civilization: slavery, gold, the exploitation of land and men—everything that announced the industrial era.

And yet, by disappearing into silence, as if it turned back toward the very origin of time, the Indian world has left an indelible mark, somewhere, on the surface of our memories. Slowly, irresistibly, legends and dreams have returned, sometimes restoring, in the midst of the ruins and wreckage of time, what the Conquerors could not erase: the faces of the ancient gods, the faces of the heroes, the immortal desires of dances, rhythms, words. Bernal Díaz del Castillo leads us into a dream whose outcome we do not yet know.

2 The Dream of Origins

N THE AFTERMATH OF THE CATASTROPHE that annihilated Mexico/Tenochtitlán, silence covered the last magical civilization, its songs, its rites, its words. It was the silence of death, of barbarism, comparable to the fate of Rome in the fourth century. But it was even more shocking, since the Indian civilization was destroyed just as it was coming into full bloom, at the conclusion of a Conquest that lasted only a few months. It was the silence which follows a destructive cataclysm, when all the forces which united that world were unleashed to destroy each other.

Rivalries, war, illness, and famine annihilated everything. The ancient world was bled dry. The nobility, the warriors, all active members of that society disappeared. Fernando de Alva Ixtlilxóchitl wrote about it: the number of dead in Mexico was "more than two hundred forty thousand men, and among them, almost all the Mexican nobility."[1]

In the heart of that silence the work of Bernardino de Sahagun was born, his *History of Ancient Mexico*[2] upon which the memory of the people of Mexico was established. Over the ruins of one of the most beautiful and innovative cities in the history of mankind there reigned the silence of death, and for that reason it was essential to rediscover the memory of the lost beauty and grandeur.

For the soldier Bernal Díaz del Castillo, who fought alongside Hernán Cortés, writing the story was a way of rediscovering those days of wonderment, as all the witnesses of the epic had already died. It was also a way of telling the truth against the lies of the court historian Gomarra. Bernardino de Sahagun's inspiration was different. His *History* was to be a summa which would be (as would the *Codex Florentinus* upon which it is based) the great book of the Mexican people, its ultimate monument. Like the ancient pyramids, like the myths of the wandering Chichimeca, the *History* offers the world—to those who destroyed it—a sacred remembrance. The mystery, the dream of origins go beyond the creator of this book, for he is but the interpreter of a language whose complete meaning he was unable fully to understand. The holder of a secret he was unable to measure, Sahagun was not a historian in the modern sense of the word. He was like a man who, unawares, while following his nose came upon an immense and inexhaustible treasure.

It was the treasure of the Mexican language, and, as he himself said, "a treasure for knowing many things worthy of being known" ("To the Sincere Reader," book 1), this summa of information, one of the most detailed ever written, is also a book of dreams. A double dream: on the one hand the dream of the Franciscan who came to the New World following the tragedy of the Conquest. For that religious man, the fearsome mystery of the Conquest—which was of divine will—was the annihilation of a world, with all its cruelty and demoniacal cults, but also with its beauty, its harmony, and its grandeur. For Sahagun, to understand all that was to touch upon the mystery of human destiny. In those pages heavy with reality, there is something dreamlike, as if while he was writing Bernardino de Sahagun was drawn ever more deeply into that fabulous past of a destroyed people.

In the dream of origins there is horror, admiration, and compassion all at the same time. While looking for the ancestral roots of others, Sahagun discovered his very own; he was henceforth connected to that world of forgotten legend and splendor.

The other dream belonged to the last survivors of that people, when, gathered before the Franciscan, they spoke for the last time. Before disappearing, those men expressed themselves beyond their own ruin. There is neither illusion nor vanity in their ultimate message. On the contrary, they showed the same mystical force which had animated the Mexican people, and which seemed to be prolonged in a dream of eternity. This is surely the most profound meaning of memory. Through the voice of the Conqueror who destroyed it, that civilization could express for men of all time that which was once its life, its language, its laws, and its gods. All those prayers, those songs, hopes, suffering—could they disappear with the men who had borne and lived them?

It is the coming together of these two dreams that moves us most in this memory: the Spanish chronicler's dream of recreating the world and the dream of eternal life of the last speaking men of the *Codex Florentinus*. They complete each other, and give all their truth to those whom the historian Angel Maria Garibay calls the "half-breeds of culture." Alone, each of those dreams was impossible. Without the passion and the insatiable curiosity of the Franciscan, without his labor and his desire to save that treasure, there can be no doubt that those documents written in the Nahuatl language would never have reached us. But without the informers' will to survive, without their creative power, without the genius of their language, without their poetry, there can also be no doubt that Sahagun's undertaking would have failed, and would have resulted only in a falsified and moralizing inventory. Here, in this major work for the first time—and perhaps for the only time—in the history of the world, two enemy cultures, completely foreign to each other, were able to meet face to face.

They had the same dream. It was to go beyond destiny by saving what could be saved from oblivion. In this book there is more than curiosity—one senses a feeling of urgency and haste. Feverishly, the Indian authors—priests, poets, scholars, doctors—recounted, dictated their memories, sometimes writing them on sheets of agave paper, as the temple scribes used to do. They were quick to tell all they knew, even going beyond the wishes of the Spanish friar, as if they had understood in the tragedy of their defeat that only the future could be offered to them, and that they would henceforth be speaking to other men, those not yet on the earth, in order to bequeath to them the treasure of their lives.

It is this haste, this wish for the future which went beyond the despair and the humiliation of the vanquished, beyond their suffering and deaths, this wish to tell everything, to reinvent everything through words, which makes the book truly Indian. Granted, without the Franciscan's organization, without the use of alphabetic writing, without the unexpected sanctuary the monasteries offered them from the violence of the armed conquerors, this testimony would never have seen the light of day. Bernardino de Sahagun's work is that of a compiler and a moralist, but also that of a protector.

However, what is shocking and touching in the *History* comes entirely from the Indian world. For in it we witness the survival of the Indian people of Mexico, their beauty, their grandeur, their faith, and their philosophy. The dream of origins is above all that of the Mexican people, and it is that dream which drew the Spanish chronicler into his adventure.

A dream of immortality: for Bernardino de Sahagun, writing his book was a way of recognizing the beauty and harmony of that civilization annihilated by the violence of the Conquest. If he saw the conquest of the Indians as a "punishment for the war they had waged against the Christians sent by God on that voyage" (Sahagun: p. 721), he also knew he had to write his summa "to know the quality [he says the *carat*] of that Mexican people, which we have not yet recognized" (Sahagun: Prologue, p. 18).

The sense of a historic catastrophe motivated his entire undertaking, as if, in the ultimate effort of the Indian testimony, Sahagun hoped to save that which divine will had condemned. We already see the West's ambiguity during the age of Conquests. In his "Account by the author which is worthy of note," which he substitutes for chapter 28 of book 10—written entirely in Nahuatl—Sahagun recognizes the role the Spanish played in the moral decadence which followed the Conquest of Mexico. The banning of the *calmecac* (colleges where young men received religious, moral, and artistic instruction), drunkenness, the abandonment of traditions and the dissolution of customs, the loss of values of austerity and modesty were the direct consequences of the Spaniards having seized power. "It is shameful for us," Bernardino de Sahagun courageously writes, "that the native Indians, wise and ancient sages, knew how to provide the remedies for ills that this earth sends to its inhabitants, alleviating natural vices through contrary efforts. And we allow ourselves to follow our bad tendencies. Granted, we are seeing the growth of a race, as much Spanish as Indian, that is impossible to govern and difficult to save: neither fathers nor mothers can do anything to keep their sons and daughters away from the vices and pleasures that this land provides" (Sahagun: p. 580).

Indeed, all the great writers who were witnesses of the Conquest, from Motolinia to Bartolomé de Las Casas, deplored that decadence of morality. The destruction did not occur in only one generation. It was a catastrophe whose consequences are still felt today, even after four hundred years. If we consider that it was the shock of the Conquest which managed to engender four centuries of poverty and social imbalance on the once thriving lands of the Aztec empire, as well as that sort of "defeatist complex" (according to Norman Martin) created by Western colonial powers which today is called "underdevelopment," we can better measure the historical and philosophical importance of Sahagun's Indian summa.

A book at the crossroads, written at the time of the shaking of the ancient world, announcing the modern age of Mexico, this account is not just a scientific document; it is also the voice of a people who wished to survive through their testimony.

Its will is urgent, burning. Already, when the ancient priests of Huitzilopochtli, the ancient scribes of the temples, and the surviving dignitaries from the court of Montezuma were dictating their memories, in Tepeopulco near Texcoco, then in Tlatelolco, while the images of a lost reality were receding into time, myth was replacing experienced truths. The myth of a golden pre-Hispanic age, made up of harmony and happiness, of riches and power. Without understanding it, Bernardino de Sahagun was participating in that myth. And it was that myth which seduced and bewitched him. The origins of the Indian people, their magical and lavish kingdom, with its rituals, its dreams, the abundant beauty of its images and the cruelty of its sacrifices—Sahagun gathered up all of that, infused it with his own culture, to the point of combining the demoniacal figures of the Aztecs with the pagan myths of the Greco-Roman West. We are quite far from a simple accounting; no other traveler of that time was so caught up in, transported, and transformed by the story of another culture.

What fascinated Bernardino de Sahagun above all was the magic, the mystery of that people who lived united with their gods through boundless faith.

At the time Sahagun was writing, the old faith was still alive: "The sins of idolatry, and idolatrous rituals, superstitions, auguries, abuses and ceremonies have not yet completely disappeared" (Sahagun: Prologue, book 2).

As a good evangelist Sahagun evaluated the danger represented by the survival of magic. In his exhortation at the conclusion of book 1, he reproaches the Indians for taking "as their gods governing the universe, fire, or spirits, or wind, or the cycle of the stars, or floods, or the sun and the moon." The Holy Scriptures recognized only one God, and thus the indigenous gods were "all demons." Idolatry was the "principle of fornication," and the "abominable cult of the idols is the beginning and the end of all evil" (Sahagun: p. 54). Sahagun uses the language of the "extirpators," and of the inquisitors, who condemned to eternal darkness all those who remained faithful to the religions of their ancestors. In his opinion Huitzilopochtli, the god of war, was a "sorcerer, the friend of the devil, the enemy of men, horrible, frightful, cruel, sly, an instigator of wars." Tezcatlipoca was Lucifer himself, "the father of all evildoing and all lies" (Sahagun: p. 60). But those qualifiers were in fact only literal translations of the god's second name, Necoc Yaotl, the sower of discord, the enemy. For Bernardino de Sahagun, Quetzalcóatl was not a god, but a "mortal and carnal man, who, despite a virtuous appearance, according to what was told, was only a great necromancer, a friend of devils." He attempted to destroy the idea of Quetzalcóatl's return (that idea the Conquerors used to inspire fear in the Indians): "What your ancestors tell you, that Quetzalcóatl went to Tlapallan and that he is to return, and that you must wait for him, is a lie, for we know that he is dead and his body has returned to the earth. As for his soul, the Lord our God has thrown it to hell where it endures eternal torment" (Sahagun: p. 61).

Bernardino de Sahagun believed it was black magic which caused the destruction of the Indian empires: "All your ancestors endured continual wars, famines, slaughter, and in the end God sent his servants the Christians against them, who destroyed them and all their gods" (Sahagun: p. 59). Yet Sahagun couldn't help feeling sorry for them: "Oh, the most sorrowful, the most unfortunate of nations!"

Without any doubt Sahagun demonstrates the contradiction shared by all men of conscience in that war-torn time. The idolatry, the cruel rituals of the Indians horrified him, and yet their faith and magic touched him as well, captivating him through their element of the superhuman. Sahagun justified his book by claiming the necessity of preventing evil and of converting the pagans. But one cannot help sensing his attraction to the world he claimed to be converting. He must have entirely recognized that magical force. He had a taste for a complete adventure, which led him beyond the limits of propriety into a sort of forbidden realm. By completely preserving the past of that pagan world, Sahagun promised the survival of the Indian soul.

First there were rituals. Rituals established the history of the Indians of New Spain and determined the nature of those peoples. Daily or special rituals were ties that connected men to each other and linked them to the secret power of the gods. For those magical peoples the gods were everything, and the real world was of very little importance. Rituals took the place of laws, art, morality, history, and even language. For Bernardino de Sahagun, a man of the European Renaissance before he was a man of the cloth, such a devotion, such power attributed to magic was more than shocking, it was incomprehensible.

And yet that incomprehension in the face of Indian fanaticism, his repulsion in the face of the bloody cruelty of their religion, gave way to curiosity, as if Sahagun sometimes felt light-headed before the beauty and the strength of Indian magic. Perhaps this was the first seduction by the "primitive" peoples, whose life and beliefs seemed so new, so true, of that already aged Western society. The cruel and bloody rituals of the Aztec people were not just scenery; they were life and death, lavish and iridescent with masks, costumes, regalia of feathers, gold, and turquoise. Abruptly, with the shock of the Conquest, the sober and puritanical man of the Christian Inquisition encountered, through their violent and upsetting nature, peoples who through their rituals were identified with the gods. The shock of the Conquest was thus also felt by the Conquerors: how could they not have felt disturbed, intoxicated by it?

What was striking in an Aztec ritual, as Sahagun describes one, was the extreme precision of every detail, of every article of clothing, of every body painting, of every instrument the dancers carried. Sahagun only retranscribed into Spanish the phrases given orally through the catechism of the *calmecac*, those military and religious colleges. But one indeed senses that he was enthralled by that pagan catechism; he appears dazzled by its splendor, by its intensity. The

dancers, warriors, priests, and even the men who were to be sacrificed were no longer simple mortals: they became gods, for ritual led
them into another world which magnified and changed their existence. It was truly a matter of transfiguration: in the appendix to
book 2, regarding the feast called *ixnextiua,* which means "to search
for good luck," Sahagun notes: "It was their belief that on this festival
all the gods were dancing, and therefore all the natives who danced
were dressed in diverse fancy costumes, some impersonated birds,
others different animals; some represented the bird called "tzinitzcan," others butterflies; some dressed like drones, others like flies,
still others like beetles; some carried on their backs a sleeping man
who, they said, represented sleep" (Bandelier: p. 146).

Those sacred ballets which were prepared with exquisite attention to detail at the time of festivals were the very figuration of the
other world, of its gods; they asserted the preexistence of magic and
myth over all of real life. It was that which troubled and fascinated
Sahagun, and inspired him to assemble his pagan summa. Although
twenty years after the terrible massacre of the Conquest everything
had disappeared, through the enchanting words of the last survivors
there emerged on that deserted land the fantastic figures of dancers,
priests, musicians, and gods who appeared to have descended among
their people to lead them again in their mysterious rituals.

Festivals of the sun, of fire, of war, of water, of women, of merchants: these fundamental rituals led men into another realm where
defeat had had no consequence. In witnessing the resurgence of
those figures, those gestures, the painted faces, feather headdresses,
emerald-studded shields, in hearing once again the obsessive rhythm
of the drums, the trumpets, the incantations, by breathing again
the perfume of the incense and the bitter odor of sacrificial blood, the
Spanish chronicler could not escape the fascination of magic. The
book then ceased to be an inventory; it was an inverse voyage back
to the origins of time, to the sources of mystery. There, in that violent and beautiful world, every moment of the day and night was

devoted to the gods, to the forces of the beyond. Every thing, every being had its place in the sacred dance, and the memory of the Indians, with the help of Bernardino de Sahagun, beckons us in turn into that ritual, full of anxiety and curiosity.

The Sun

When the day dawned over Anáhuac, the offerings began. "Every day of the world," writes Sahagun, "they offered blood and incense to the sun; at sunrise they at once offered blood from their ears, and the blood of quails whose heads they tore off and, snatching them up while their blood still flowed, they raised them toward the sun like offertories, saying as they did so, 'The sun, called tonametl xiuhpitontliquauhtleoamitl, has risen, we do not know how it will end its course this day, nor do we know whether some misfortune will befall the people;' then, addressing the sun directly, they exclaimed, 'Our Lord fulfill your duty (ministry) prosperously (luckily).'" During the day, Sahagun reports, they offered blood to the sun four times, and once more during the night. "When they made the first offering of the night they greeted the night saying, 'The lord of night has come, who is called Ioatltecutli; we do not know how he will perform his ministry or finish his course'" (Bandelier: p. 166).

The sun was at the very center of the Indian religion, among the Toltecs, the Aztecs, and the Maya. It reigned over Cihuatlampa, the House of the Sun, which was the destination of warriors killed in battle. Male children were dedicated to the sun at birth, and when a boy baby was baptized the priest raised him to the sky and spoke to the sun: "Lord Sun, and you, Tlaltecuhtli, who are our mother and father, see this child here who is like a bird with rich feathers, which we call *zacan* or *quecholli*; he is yours, and I want to offer him to you, Lord Sun, who are also called Tonametl, and Xipilli, and Quauhtli, and *Ocelotl*, you who are spotted brown and black like the jaguar, and who are brave in war" (Sahagun: p. 399).

A young man, during the ceremony of the *telpochcalli* (the house of youth), was also dedicated to the sun, for he promised to "feed and quench the thirst of the sun and the earth with the flesh and blood of his enemies" (Sahagun: p. 334). Those who died in battle were "presented to the sun very clean and smooth and resplendent like precious stones" (Sahagun: p. 318). The king himself was promised to the sun, for, said the nobles who elected him, if he died in combat he would go "to the place of men as valiant and courageous as eagles and jaguars, those who rejoice and offer a feast to the Sun, whom we call *tiacauh in quauhtleuanintl*" (Sahagun: p. 328). All sacrifices, the smoke of sacred pyres, blood, or the heart that was torn beating from the victim were all offered first to the sun.

The festival of the sun occurred in the lunar calendar of 260 days, undoubedly predating the solar calendar, in the month *ce ocelotl* (One Jaguar), in the House *nahui olin* (Four Movement). The blood of quails, incense, and human hearts were offered to that unique god. During eclipses albinos were sacrificed, while invoking the pity of that star: "It will never shine again, eternal darkness will reign over us, and demons will descend, coming to devour us!" (Sahagun: p. 431).

However, the supreme god, he who ordered all life on earth, was not at the center of the mythology of the Indians of Central America. In his chapter on "Natural Astrology," Sahagun transcribes "ridiculous fables" invented by Satan: the creation, at Teotihuacán, before the assembly of gods, of the first light; how Tecuciztecatl was chosen to be the sun, and the "poxed" Nanauatzin to be the moon. Taking turns, under the watch of the ancestral gods, they had to enter into the fire and, as the legend had it, "when the sun came out, it was very red, and it seemed to strut around from one place to another; none could look at it, for it blinded the eyes, and shone by throwing its rays all around; and its rays spread in all directions. Then the moon came out, from the same eastern region as did the sun; first the sun appeared, then behind it came the moon. Following the order in which they had entered into the fire, they thus came out, having become the sun and the moon" Sahagun: p. 455). The legend adds that to extinguish the moon, one of the gods present at Teotihuacán threw a rabbit into its face, the mark of which can still be seen on the surface of that satellite.

Fire

The lord of fire was Xiuhtecuhtli (the precious lord, the color of jade and grass), the "ancient god, father of all gods . . . who lived in the reservoir of water surrounded by crenels, encircled by stones similar to roses" (Sahagun: p. 319). This was surely one of the most ancient gods of Mexico, whose cult survived the complicated rituals of the sedentary civilizations. Like the sun-god, he is associated with Tezcatlipoca, the master of the sky, "directing and governing all, invisible and untouchable, the creator and knower of all things and all thoughts." This archaic divinity appeared in a number of ceremonies, venerated in different forms, such as that of the "fire stones," or the sacred pyres which the penitent had to feed before confessing his sins to the priest of Tezcatlipoca. It is undoubtedly he whom one sees in the face of the Kinich Kakmo, the Ara [Macaw] of fire with the face of the sun venerated by the Maya in the temple at Izamal, or in the god of the Tarascans, Curicaueri, the ancient fire, to whom the Indians of Michoacán offered sacred pyres in which they burned incense and cloth. In the way Bernardino de Sahagun describes them, these rituals of fire evoke an ancient fascination, although the chronicler elsewhere refutes such idolatrous beliefs. That god of fire, that creator—"Our father the fire"—whom he compares to Vulcan, and whom the Aztec also called Yxcocauhqui (yellow face), Cuecaltzin (ardent flame), or Huehueteotl (the old god), was adored, says Sahagun, because he burned, enflamed, and consumed and "all these are effects which cause fear" (Bandelier: p. 33); for the Spanish priest, fire was both the symbol of divine power and that of hell. And although Sahagun placed this god among the "minor gods," his mythological importance dominated Indian rituals.

Thus, at the time of the festival of fire, at the end of the month of *izcalli*, the god of fire was represented with the attributes of a lord, wearing lordly clothes and headdress, and seated on his throne. And while the music of the drums and rattles resounded, the parents of children dedicated to the god made offerings of small animals they had captured: snakes, frogs, fish, *axolotl* lizards, and they cooked them in the fire and gave them to their children to eat. The god's image, Sahagun reports, was then painted to represent "a naked man whose chin was dyed black with a resin called *ulli*, and a bib of red stone in the parting of the chin. On the head he had a crown of paper painted in different colors and with diverse designs; on top of the crown were several green feather tufts imitating flames . . . In his left hand he carried a shield with five green stones which are called chalchivites, placed over a gold plate covering almost the entire shield" (Bandelier: p. 35). In his right hand he held a sort of scepter, made from a round gold plate with a hole in the center, with two globes on either end, one larger than the other, with a feather attached to the smallest. They called that scepter *tlachialoni*, which meant "lookout" or "observatory," because he hid his face behind it, looking through the hole in the sheet of gold. In addition, on his back he wore "feathers which represented a dragon's head" (Sahagun: p. 40).

This masked god, crowned with flames and resembling the body of a dragon, was the one to whom the most cruel of all human sacrifices was dedicated, at the time of the feast of the tenth month, *xocotlhuetzi* (the fruit falls, i.e., the month of August). At that time the *xocotl* tree was erected, decorated with paper garlands, by three priests chosen from among the tallest. They also used paper to decorate the statue of a man made out of kernels of corn. They then summoned the masters of the slaves who were to be immolated. "Their entire bodies were dyed yellow, and their faces a bright reddish color. They wore plumes in the shape of butterflies made of red parrot feathers on the head. In the left hand they carried a shield adorned in white plumes with a fringe hanging down from the lower edge. The center field of this shield bore tiger or eagle feet, drawn for that purpose . . . The bodies of the captives were painted white, the belt (sash) which girded their loins was of paper, and they wore also stoles of white paper which reached from the shoulder to the armpit. They also wore hair (a sort of wig) made of small strips of paper. On the head they wore a coif of white plumes; also a lip-ring made of feathers. Their faces were painted a bright reddish-color, and the cheeks black" (Bandelier: pp. 109–10). Masters and slaves danced for half the night. Then the masters cut off the hair on the top of the captives' heads, using a knife they called "the claw of the sparrow-hawk"; the masters kept the cut hair in special chests which they stored under the roof of their houses. At daybreak, the captives were led to the sacred pyre of Tlatacouan, and after all their paper adorn-ments and clothes had been burned, their faces spread with anesthe-tizing powder (*yiauhtli*), "to make them lose consciousness and so [they] would not feel their death so much" (Bandelier: p. 59), they were thrown one after the other into the flames of the fire. But the cruel torture did not end there, for the victim, "while in this (in-fernal) agony, the priests called Quaquacuiltin pulled him (or them) out with gambrels (grappling irons) and placed, one after the other on the block they called techcatl, and at once cut the breast from nipple to nipple or a little below, and tore the heart out and threw it at the feet of the statue of Xiuhtecuhtli, god of the fire" (Bandelier: p. 111).

Slaves were also sacrificed to the god of fire during the festival of merchants, in the presence of the representative of *paynal*, the "page" of Huitzilopochtli, while the high priest danced "inside a paper snake, which he moved as if it were walking all alone; in its mouth they stuck red feathers so that it looked as if fire were emanating from it." The paper snake was called *xiuhcoatl*. Then, seated on a throne covered with a jaguar skin, the lord witnessed the sacrifice of the captives.

The most extraordinary festival of all those celebrated by the Indians of America was surely the *Toxiuh molpilia* (the binding of our years), which took place at the end of every century, at the end of a cycle of fifty-two solar years. This was the festival of the new fire, which seems to have played an important role throughout all of Central America, among the Aztecs, the Toltecs, and also the Maya, where it was called *Tup Kak,* the extinction of fires. It was the most beautiful, the most tragic, and the most meaningful of festivals, since it took place at the time when, according to the Indians' counting of time, all the stars having completed their cycle, the entire cosmos would begin again the revolution which led it from the year One Rabbit to another year One Rabbit.

For the Aztecs, living in complete submission to the divine order, that moment was one of doubt, of anguish. For the fate of the entire world was at stake during the five final days without a name, the *nemontemi,* the "vain days" which marked the entrance into the new century. "That night," writes Bernardino de Sahagun, "they lit the new fire, and before lighting it they extinguished the fires in all the provinces, villages, and houses of New Spain, and all the princes, all the temple ministers went in a great solemn procession. They left from here, from the temple of Mexico City, in the early hours of the night, and they went to the top of the mountain near Iztapalapan, which they call Uixachtecatli, and they arrived at the top of that mountain around midnight, and there they built a solemn temple for this ceremony; having arrived there, they observed the constellation of the Pleiades, whether it was high in the sky, and if not they waited until it arrived; and when they saw that it had passed the middle of the sky, they knew that the movement of the sky would not end, and that it was not the end of the world, but that they would live another fifty-two years with the certainty that the world would not end. At that same hour, on the mountains that bordered the entire province of Mexico, from Texcoco, Xochimilco, and Quauhtitlan, there were great masses of people assembled waiting to see the new fire, for it was the signal that the world would continue" (Sahagun: p. 260).

There was something tragic and dreamlike in that terrifying wait for the end of the world which the Christian Sahagun could not accept, because for him it had the inevitable sense of a damnation: it was, he says, "an invention of the devil so they would renew the pact they had made with him . . . by plunging them into terror of the end of the world and by making them believe that he was prolonging their time and was having mercy on them, by allowing the world to continue" (Sahagun: p. 260). But the emotion of the myth was so intense that it dominated the words of the Spanish conqueror, as if that festival of the end of the world had not been played out; we can imagine the whole valley of Mexico plunged into darkness, the anguish growing, men and women believing they heard the voices of the *tzitzime*, those evil beings, devourers of men, and everyone fearing "it was the end of the line of men and that that night and that darkness would be never ending, and that never again would the sun be born or rise" (Sahagun: p. 439).

The priests then arrived, each one wearing the insignias of his god, and they began to walk slowly, silently, "and they were then called *teonenemi*, which means, they walk like gods" (Sahagun: p. 430).

Then, at a given moment a man was sacrificed, enabling the entire universe to continue on its course. They chose a warrior, captured during combat, chosen from among the most courageous, who had to bear, by the date of his birth, the name of his destiny. Born on the first day of the year, he was called *xiuhtlamin*, he who arrowed the new year. The high priest placed a piece of wood upon his chest and quickly rubbed the tapered stick between his hands, thus producing a spark. When the fire caught "the captive's chest was immediately opened, his heart ripped out and thrown into the fire, which they kept fanning, and then the whole body was consumed in the flames" (Sahagun: p. 439). And all around the people who were waiting in anguish, seeing the fire rise up, "immediately cut their ears with knives, collected their blood and threw it in the direction where the light had appeared" (Sahagun, p. 440); fire was then taken to all parts of the province by runners carrying torches, and, says Sahagun, "it was an admirable sight, that multitude of fire in all the villages, to such a degree that it seemed to be daylight." The last ceremony of the new fire took place in 1507, according to Sahagun; "they did it in complete solemnity, for the Spanish had not yet come to that land" (Sahagun: p. 440).

Water

For the Indian nations of middle America, water was the most precious of goods, the divine element which sustained life on earth. It was water that engendered the sacred liquid—blood—which men offered to the gods in exchange for the fertilization of the land.

The most ancient gods of the Mexican pantheon were perhaps the Tlalocs—the Chac gods among the Maya of the Yucatán. They were gods of fertility and rain, the tutelary divinities of the mountains and the volcanoes which surrounded the valley of Mexico, providers of the water of the sky. "All prominent mountain peaks," writes Sahagun, "especially such around which rain clouds will gather, they imagined to be gods, therefore they made of each an image according to their idea" (Bandelier: p. 45).

Water was central to the myths of the destruction of the world since, according to the Aztecs, water was the cause of the end of the first terrestrial age, "Atonatiuh, which means sun of the water," when the world "was ended by a flood and an inundation, where all men were drowned and all things created perished."[3] According to Father Ramirez's account, the Tarascans believed that after having twice created men, the third time the gods "destroyed them through a flood lasting five days, during which all springs and all rivers opened up, and there fell so much water that it drowned them all along with everything on the earth that had been created, according to what was told, by the goddess of hell."[4]

Water was also central to the myths of genesis: the terrestrial paradise was *tlalocan*, the realm of the Tlalocs, gods "of the greenery and of freshness" (Sahagun: p. 316); it welcomed those whose death was associated with rain or water: those struck by lightning, drowned, with dropsy. The very origin of the gods was water, for the Mexican peoples, the Chichimeca, the Toltecs, the Maya, had come from the sea, like Quetzalcóatl, the hero-god; later other gods would come from the sea, the *teules* wearing beards and armor, who would carry out the conquest of Mexico.

The sea was *ilhuicaatl,* "water joined to the sky, for the ancient inhabitants of this land believed that the sky was joined to the water in the sea, as if it were a house whose walls were the water and the sky was placed on them" (Sahagun: p. 699); the water was also *teoatl,* the water of the gods.

Among the Maya, the water principle was portrayed by the cross, whose center represented the heart of the world. The Chac gods were present at the time the earth was created, and their divine essence was represented by the "humidity of the sky" (the clouds). Water was yet the final symbol, that of death, as were the openings of the Maya's sacred wells, or the River Chiconahuapan, which flowed along the border of hell in Aztec mythology. The very origin of water was one of the fundamental myths, as Bernardino de Sahagun relates:

The ancients of this land believed that all rivers came out of a place they called *tlalocan,* which is like terrestrial paradise, the place where a god named Chalchihuitlicue reigned; and they also said that the mountains built upon it are full of water, and their outer walls are made of earth, as if they were large water vases, or like houses full of water. And when the time will come, the mountains will shatter, and all the water contained in them will flow out, to annihilate the earth. From this comes the custom of naming those mountains where people live *altepetl,* which means mountain of water, or mountain full of water. They also said that rivers came out of the mountains, and it was that god Chalchihuitlicue who sent them . . . The sea enters into the earth along its veins and its canals, and goes under the earth and mountains; and where there is a passage, it springs forth, either through the roots of the mountain, or in the plains of the earth . . . And although the water of the sea is salty, and the water of the rivers fresh, it loses its bitterness, or its salt, by being filtered through the earth, the rocks, the sand. (Sahagun: p. 700)

The myth of the birth of rivers and the flood is associated with the paradise *tlalocan*, where the goddess Chalchiuhtlicue [whom Sahagun incorrectly identified as a god], sister of the Tlaloc gods, lived. That goddess, writes Sahagun, was painted in the shape of a woman with a yellow face, wearing a crown of blue paper, and a sky-blue *huipil* [gown]. In the left hand she was holding a shield adorned with a water-lily petal, and in her right hand "a cup with a cross on it, which was made just like the cross on the tabernacle in which the holy sacrament is carried" (Bandelier: p. 29). This goddess was celebrated in the month of *etzalqualiztli*, which even today corresponds to the festival of the first rains, the celebration of Santa Cruz, at the beginning of June. In earlier times there were pilgrimages in honor of the Tlalocs, in Citlaltepec, on the banks of a lake called Temilco. Captives were sacrificed, and their bodies were thrown into the whirlpool of Lake Texcoco. In the first month of *atlacahualo*, and in the third month of *tozoztontli*, a large number of young children were sacrificed, until the first rains fell.

The festival of water culminated during the sixth month, *etzalqualiztli*, during which there were rituals of purification. After the blood sacrifices, writes Sahagun, "there were four houses near the water's edge where the priests were to bathe, and these houses they called aiauhcalli, which means houses of fog. They faced the four cardinal directions of the world . . . One of them, whom they called Chalchiuhquacuilli, spoke and said: 'coatl icomocaian, amoiotl, icaoacayan; atapalcatlyne-chiccana oaianaztapilquecuetlacaian,' which means: this is a place of snakes, of mosquitoes, of ducks and cyperus! As soon as he had uttered these words, all the others threw themselves into the water and began to paddle in the water with their feet and hands, making much noise, shouting and screaming and imitating the water fowl, some squawking like ducks or geese, others imitating the aquatic bird known to them as *pipitzti*; others the sea-raven and still others the white or the gray heron" (Bandelier: p. 91).

These strange, sometimes violent rituals granted the priests a sacred freedom, with a view to their purification; the festival culminated in bloody sacrifices.

Water again intervened in the ceremonies of shamanic curing, as in the one Sahagun describes regarding the god Ixtlilton, whose name means "the little negro": "They made a tabernacle of painted boards where his image stood. In his oratory or temple were a good many glazed earthenware tubs and water jars with water, all of which were covered with boards or comales; the water they contained was called *tlilalt,* meaning 'black water.' When a child was ill they took it to the temple of god [Ixtlilton] and, uncovering one of these jars, they gave the sick child some of that water to drink, and the water cured it" (Bandelier: p. 38).

The water ritual par excellence was the bath. For the Aztecs, as for most of the Indian nations of middle America, the use of the warm bath (or *temazcal*) was not just for hygienic reasons or for pleasure. It was also a magical act, during which the man or the woman surrendered their body to *xochicaltzin,* the flowered house, that is, to "our mother, the oven of the bath, whom we call Yaolticitl, the doctor of the night, who is the goddess of baths, she who knows all secrets" (Sahagun: p. 374).

Births were carefully prepared in the *temazcal* with the help of an experienced midwife, or *ticitl.* Labor was made easier with hot baths, and through the absorption of a decoction made from the *cihuapactli* root (*Montanoa tomentosa*), which facilitated the birth. We can assume that in some cases the birth actually occurred in the water, following a technique which modern medicine has just recently rediscovered. Right after it was born the baby was washed, dedicated to the goddess Chalchiuhtlicue, during a first baptism which was to purify it of all soiling acquired during its birth.

The midwife spoke to the child, whom she called "the fingernail and the hair of our dead lords, of our vanished lords" (Sahagun: p. 390). After cutting the umbilical cord, she spoke to the water of the first bath, saying: "Very holy lady, you whose name is Chalchiuhtlicue, or Chalchiuhtlatonac, here is your servant, born into this world, sent here by our mother and father who are called Omete-cuhtli and Omecíhuatl, who live in the nine skies, the place where the gods live; we do not know what talents he has received." She then plunged the child into the water, saying: "Enter, my son—or daugh-ter—into this water, which we call *metlalac* or *tuxpalac*; be washed by it, that he who resides everywhere cleans you, and be purified of all the evil that has been with you since the world was created" (Saha-gun, p. 386).

Then the diviner Tonalpouhque consulted the sacred almanac to determine the day of the great baptism, during which the child would receive its name. During that ceremony the midwife, her face turned toward the west, said: "Oh eagle! Oh jaguar! Oh valiant man, my son! . . . You have been born and raised in your home, which is the home of the supreme gods, of the Great Lord and the Great Lady who reign over the nine skies. Our son Quetzalcóatl, who is every-where, has granted you his favor. Now join yourself to your mother, the goddess of water, she whom we call Chalchiuhtlicue." Having said those words, she gave the child some water to taste, by putting the tips of her fingers in its mouth and said: "Drink, take this that must make you live on the earth, so you will grow and prosper" (Sa-hagun: p. 398). Thus the child was born anew, destined to serve the immortal gods throughout his life.

Blood

There has undoubtedly never been in the history of the world a people more preoccupied with blood. The Aztecs were possessed, obsessed by it, as if they had been subject to some magical enchant-ment. And there can be no doubt that for Bernardino de Sahagun, as for most of the Spanish chroniclers, that obsession was proof of a diabolical evil, that is, a pact with the devil. No other people have shown such a taste for bloody sacrifices—animals, especially humans, flayed, their hearts torn out, dismembered, burned. That civilized, refined people, who in many respects had achieved a degree of civilization superior to that of the Spanish conquerors, who cultivated the arts, philosophy, and poetry, could demonstrate, on the occasion of ritual festivals, extraordinary cruelty. Their reputation for cruelty would remain linked to their civilization long after it had disappeared, like a degrading mark, the sign of moral inferiority which did not cease, even today, to weigh upon the last survivors of the Indian nations.

However, when we look closely at the facts, the Mexican peoples never showed the kind of cruelty exhibited by the Romans in their circus games. The Indians' ferocity was not gratuitous. It was a sacred, mystical cruelty intended to please only the gods. In the hymn to the god of the sky, Tezcatlipoca, "our very human, very pious Lord, protector and defender, invisible and untouchable," it was his thirst for human blood that was expressed: "The god of the earth opens his mouth, for he has a great desire to drink the blood of all those who will die in that war. It appears the sun-god and the god of the earth, he whom we call Tlaltecuhtli, want to feast. They want to feed and provide drink to the gods of the sky and of hell, by inviting them to the feast of the blood and flesh of the men who must die in this war" (Sahagun: p. 304).

On the day of his birth, the male child was predestined by that baptism in blood, which connected him throughout his life to the insatiable desire of the gods: "Go to the battlefield," says the midwife on the day of the baptism, "go to the heat of the battles . . . your duty is to please the sun and the earth, and to give them food and drink" (Sahagun: p. 400).

In that cruel and magical world, man was but a supplier for the gods, and ritual cannibalism was the terrestrial symbol of their celestial or infernal appetite. Often, the final act of a human sacrifice was the dividing up of the victim's body among the dignitaries and priests. Sometimes, as in the Christian liturgy, the ritual act became pure symbol, as in the communion of the body of the god Huitzilopochtli in the form of a corn cake: "Those of Mexico," writes Sahagun, "who were the priests of the said [Huitzilopochtli] and were called Cal-pules, took four pieces of the body and an equal amount was taken by those of Tlalteluco . . . Everyone ate a piece of the body of this god, and those who ate it were unmarried men (bachelors), and they said that it was the body of the god called Teuqüalo [god is eaten]" (Bandelier: p. 176).

Blood and blood sacrifices were propitiatory, or expiatory, sym-bols which united men to their divine masters. In the civilizations of Central America, there was a curious mixture of devotion to and re-pugnance for blood cults. Among the Maya of Yucatán, and among the Tarascans of Michoacán, the sacrificial priests were of evil ap-pearance, painted or dressed in black, their hair tangled and sticky with the blood of their victims. They gave off an unbearable stench, as indicated by the name of one of them, mentioned in the *Books of the Chilam Balam*: Ah Teppanciz (Great Stench). Among the Aztecs, the priests of the cult of the Tlaloc gods were feared by all, especially during the festival of the month of *etzalqualiztli*, during which they indulged in furious, bloody abandonment, bringing to mind bacchic possession. Blood was the symbol of that mystical intoxication which enabled an encounter between men and their gods.

Blood flowed during religious festivals, the blood of sacrificed animals or men, blood that people drew from themselves as a sign of penitence. Even today certain survivors of Indian civilizations, such as the Tarahumaras or the Huichols, practice blood sacrifices in con-junction with their prayers. For the Indians, a religious act was above all tied to that letting of blood. To honor the devil, writes Sahagun, "blood was spilled in the temples by day and by night, killing (sacri-ficing) men and women in front of the statues of the "demons" . . . They also did it for devotional purposes on specially assigned (de-termined) days, in the following manner. If they wished to bleed (from) the tongue, they pierced the latter by means of the point of a knife, and through this orifice (hole) they passed a great number of thick straws, according to the devotion of each individual; some tied these straws end to end and then pulled them through the hole of the

tongue like pulling a string; . . . The priests also bled themselves
away from the temples . . . they took green (unripe) canes and maguey thorns (points) and, after having tinted them with blood which
they drew from their legs, they gathered all those thorns (or pricks)
and then went at night, naked, into the forest, wherever their devotion led them, and left them, seeped in blood, on a little bed (litter)
made of corn-leaves . . . men would also bleed themselves five days
before the main festival (of the month), which recurred every twenty
days. They would cut their ears to draw blood, with which they be-
daubed their faces, drawing lines of blood; the women made circles
(or rings), while the men drew a straight line from the brow to the
chin" (Bandelier: pp. 158–59).

Blood was more than a pact; it was truly the food of the gods.
"When they sacrificed a slave or a captive, his owner or master gathered the blood (of the victim) in a bowl (jicara), threw·a white paper
into it, then visited all the statues of the "demons" (gods), and
smeared this blood-soaked paper over their mouths; others dipped a
stick in the blood and painted the mouth of the idol (statue) with
that" (Bandelier: p. 159).

Blood was the sign of religious devotion, of man's humiliation
before his celestial or infernal masters. These mortifications, certainly very painful—Sahagun notes that the penitents drew the cord
through their tongues as many as eight hundred times—were the
Aztec people's communion in suffering. By reducing bloody cruelty
to a spectacle, Christian civilization distorted its profound truth;
bloody mysticism then took on something equivocal, suspect, as, for
example, in those statues of Christ covered with blood, in the Church
of Los Remedios in Mexico City.

For the Indians, blood and suffering sealed the common destiny
of men, their total submission to the gods. Even their wars were sacred, for their battles, before they determined one nation's power over
another, were waged to please the gods. The warriors killed in battle,
as well as sacrificed captives, were food for the sun, "which greatly

rejoiced and received much pleasure in tasting the blood of those who spilled it with valor" (Sahagun: p. 328).

Human sacrifices were objects of horror for the Spanish conquerors, who saw in them only a demoniacal perversion. How could they have thought otherwise? In their view, spilt blood fed neither the earth nor the sky, but was spilled in order to obtain earthly goods, for gold, for slaves, for the power of the king of Spain. The burgeoning European humanism of the sixteenth century could not recognize the magical virtue of that ritual, its cosmic cruelty.

Each god took his turn to receive his share of the feast. The festivals of the sun, of fire, of the Tlalocs, or of the serpent Mixcoatl (the Chichimeca serpent of the clouds), the festival of flowers, of the gods Huitzilopochtli, Tezcatlipoca, Teteo Inman, Xipe Totec—all these festivals were festivals of blood, full of that sacred horror which was at the very heart of the religions of Central America.

Each man owed a portion of his blood to the gods, as a sign of allegiance and submission to his destiny. Suffering was necessary for every act of daily life, as demonstrated by the ritual dedicated to the god of the merchants, Yiacatecuhtli, "the lord who guides." In front of their traveling canes, emblems of their god, merchants drew their blood "from their own ears, tongues, arms or legs. Then they offered incense" (Bandelier: p. 41); then when night had come they drew their blood for the god of fire: "They went into the courtyard, and they threw their blood toward the sky, by taking it on their fingernail; they did the same to the east, putting blood on their nails four times, as I have just said; and they did the same to the west; then they turned to the north, which they called the left hand of the world; then they turned to the south, which they called the right hand of the world" (Sahagun: p. 494).

Thus in the Indian universe blood was spilled every day; it flowed not for the possession of worldly goods, or to satisfy the appetites of some perverse king, but for the mysterious pleasure of the gods who had created the world and kept it alive. The blood of men flowed so that the equilibrium of the cosmos would never cease, so that the sun would return each day, so that fire, water, and corn would be provided. Blood flowed constantly from ritual wounds, from generation to generation, in order to protect the living from evil, and so that the incomprehensible destiny would come to be: "We do not know what God has determined," said the orator when a new king was elected. "But we await his decision" (Sahagun: p. 328).

Death

The obsession with flowing blood was also one with violent death. Among the nations of middle America, the obsession with death had been carried to such a degree that that is probably why the Conquerors from Spain viewed them as civilizations dedicated to misfortune and despair—and certainly also why they were so easily led to their demise. The Maya, the Toltecs, the Tarascans, and the Aztecs lived in a pessimistic anticipation of a catastrophe. *The Books of the Chilam Balam*, predictions of priests, mythical legends and tales—everything in them proclaimed the nearness of death. The Indian peoples lived the great philosophical themes with a keenness which no other civilization in the ancient world ever did. For them life was only a brief passage and nothingness ruled the world. But for the Indians those themes were not just philosophical ideas; they were a religion which gave meaning to every moment of their existence. Completely at the mercy of the gods, mortal men lived in somber devotion with a view to the supreme moment when they would once again be joined with their ancestors, in the timeless beyond.

When a child was born, he left the care of Ometecuhtli and Omechíhuatl, "the celestial woman and man [who were sometimes represented as a single bisexual being]," to come into this world, "a place of great evil and pain," "a place of hunger and thirst, of fatigue, of cold, and of tears" (Sahagun: p. 386). His true home was the House of the Sun, where he would go after he died, if he died in battle. The entire life of a young boy was led to prepare him for death, that moment he feared and desired at the same time.

Death was lurking behind everything. It was at the origin of beliefs and superstitions, as seen in the legend of the owl who announced the death of the Indian, which is known throughout Latin America. Sahagun even notes it: "They said that it was the messenger of the god Mictlantecuhtli, who came and went from hell, and for that reason they called it Yautequiua, the messenger of the god of hell" (Sahagun: p. 273). The obsession with death and the beyond is translated, even today, by the belief in "nagualism," that is, in the presence of guardian spirits residing in animal forms.

In the art of Mexico, death is constantly present, grimacing as on the *tzompantli*, the wall covered with the skulls of the tortured, grotesque as in the effigies of the festival of the dead or in the engravings of Posada, or yet ecstatic, as in the entrance of the warriors killed in battle into the House of the Sun.

The universe was made of death. The wind, the very soul of Quetzalcóatl, came from the four corners of the world, which were the boundaries of the resting places in the beyond: the east, the realm of the Tlaloc gods, was the origin of the *tlalocayotl* wind; from the north, the realm of the Mictlan hell, came the furious *mictlampa ehecatl* wind; from the west, realm of the evil Cihuapipiltin goddesses, the cold wind of misfortune and illness; from the south, realm of the Huitznahua goddesses, came the *huitzlampa ehecatl*, the dangerous wind. Surrounded by winds and death, how could a man be free? The entire world was inhabited by the dead, who lived alongside the living, sometimes helping them, often persecuting them. The three realms of death, as Sahagun describes them, the House of the Sun (the "Sky"), Tlalocan ("terrestrial Paradise"), and Mictlan ("Hell"), corresponded to the three stages of Indian cosmogony, a myth which existed on the entire American continent. Unlike the Christian religion, they did not imply a punishment, but only corresponded to a hierarchical division. Dedicated at birth to the gods of the earth and

the sun, the Aztec warrior, after his death, had to go to the celestial
resting place which was the one chosen for men killed in battle, for
captives immolated by the enemy, and for women who died in childbirth. After four years in the House of the Sun, the soul of the deceased returned to earth in the form of a bird with rich plumage.

Tlalocan, the place of abundance, where "there is much rejoicing
and coolness (comfort also), without any suffering," where "they
never lack green corn (ears of corn), calabash, wild amaranth seeds,
green pepper, tomatoes, green beans, and flowers," was the resting
place of "those who are killed by lightning, those who are drowned,
the lepers, those afflicted with pustules, the mangy, and gout-
stricken, and those with dropsy" (Bandelier: p. 193); they put blue
paint on the foreheads of those who died of these illnesses, they put
a few kernels of corn in their mouths, for these dead were leaving for
the land of eternal abundance, where "it was always summer and everything was green" (ibid.). The dead could then rest in the "grotto
of water" (Sahagun: p. 396), their faces turned toward the north.

Hell, Mictlan, was the place of katabasis. While reading Sahagun's account of it, one can't help thinking of the great mythical tales,
Gilgamesh, book 6 of the *Aeneid*, or even Dante. Those who died of
some disease, reports Sahagun, "be they lords, or chiefs, or common
people," went to Mictlan, "where a devil (demon) lived whose name
was Mictantecuhtli, . . . or Tzontemoc [he who lowers his head], and
also a goddess called Mictecacioatl, who was the wife of Mictlantecuhtli" (Bandelier: p. 190).

Then began the long voyage of the deceased. Armed with paper
amulets and water, he was to pass between many mountain ranges,
and over a road guarded by a snake and by a fabulous green lizard
called *xochitonal* (sign of the flower); then he had to travel over the
eight icy deserts, the eight hills, and face the "wind of knives," *itzche-
caya*, a wind "so strong that it carried stones with it and pieces of
(stone-) knives"; in order that the deceased could conquer that icy
and deadly wind, "they burned all the chests and weapons and all the
remains of the captives they had captured in war, as well as all the

clothes these had worn, saying that all these things were to go with the deceased (in question) in order to keep him warm in that passage, and thus protect him and prevent his too great suffering" (Bandelier: p. 191).

Then the deceased arrived at the great Chiconahuapan river, which evokes the Acheron river of Greek mythology. To go across the river of hell, "the natives used to keep and raise little dogs" with red fur, who were sacrificed, and who wore a red collar around their necks. When a dog had seen his master reach the river bank and had recognized him, he swam across the river, and carried him to the other side on his back. Then "when the dead arrived and stood before the devil who is called Mictlantecuhtli, they offered and presented to him the papers they carried, and bunches of candlewood (torches) and cones of perfume and loose cotton thread, as well as red yarn, a blanket, a belt if they were men, and the skirts and the entire bundle of clothes of a dead woman" (Bandelier: p. 192). After eighty days the remains of the deceased were burned, and the ritual was repeated each year for four years, at which time the funeral was then completed. After crossing the Chiconahuapan river, the deceased reached the realm of Chiconaumictlan (the Nine Hills), which was the end of his voyage.

These were the death myths of Aztecs, as related by Bernardino de Sahagun. Funeral rituals did not mark the end of a man's existence, but his culmination, his point of departure for a new life. The violence of life, the heat of battles, desires, and suffering were only a brief passage between the kingdom of the double god, both father and mother, Ometecuhtli, and the mysterious final resting place where, having gone through the doors of the House of the Sun, the entrance to Tlalocan, or the banks of the Chiconahuapan river, the soul of the deceased joined its ancestors.

Thus the Indian peoples of Anáhuac could join those who had truly engendered them, the first Toltec kings buried in the great city of Teotihuacán, those who had become gods. They could experience the ecstasy of life in the beyond, for, "according to what the ancients said, when men died, they did not disappear, but began a new life, as if they were awakening from a dream, and they were transformed into spirits or gods" (Sahagun: p. 611).

The Gods

The extraordinary richness of the Mexican myths was the source of Bernardino de Sahagun's feelings of horror and fascination. The religion of the ancient Mexicans, at the moment when the Spanish encountered it, was primarily a passion, and it was that which troubled and moved the evangelists. That people, who conquered and held the nations that surrounded it under its yoke, and who created one of the most refined civilizations of middle America, was also one of the peoples most devoted to its gods, entirely oriented toward the supernatural. Every gesture in life, every thought, seemed directed toward the gods alone.

The Aztecs' faith was violent and feverish, despite the somber portrait the first chroniclers gave of it. It was a faith expressed at every moment, in everyday life as well as during festivals. That faith was stronger than the instinct for survival or possessions. It was not by chance that Sahagun began his account with a description of the gods and the Indians' rituals. For supernatural forces held power and controlled destinies in the Amerindian world. And those forces represented the most serious danger to the Spanish colony.

Gods and myths were behind every event. There reigned a devotion, a mystical splendor over Mexico which was unknown to the West. As in the Mayan or Toltec civilizations, the shadow of fatality hung over the Mexicans. But in contrast, there was also exaltation, intoxication, sharing. The Indian gods were not inaccessible. They were not indifferent. They were very close, and were tied to the earth and to living beings through a pact of blood. They fed on the offerings, on smoke, on the bodies and hearts of victims. All that was living pleased them, everything was their due. Prayer was above all an exchange between man and the other world through which he sought to appease the gods and deflect misfortune from himself. As Sahagun reports, not without some mockery, if an Indian's wish were not fulfilled, he did not hesitate to reproach or insult the gods.

Just like men, the gods had their qualities and their faults. If Tezcatlipoca was the master of the "invisible," "the only being who knew how to direct the world," he was also a tyrant, unjust and cruel, "a sower of discord"; and, notes Sahagun, "they were afraid that whenever he trod on earth he caused wars, enmities and discords" (Bandelier: p. 25).

For the Spanish friar, the ambivalence of the pagan gods was incomprehensible. Tezcatlipoca, Huitzilopochtli, or the Tlalocs were "demons" who demanded a cult of "horrible cruelty" (Sahagun: p. 60). The *cihuacoatl*, the woman-snake, goddess of misfortune, whom Sahagun curiously associates with "our mother Eve," was a frightful demon who "screamed into the night."

For Bernardino de Sahagun, all the Aztec gods were demons who incited horror or mockery. The adoration of mountains, stars, or fire was a "great blinding," and the cult of the *tzoalli* (those effigies made of corn and bean dough) seemed to him to be "a child's game, for people without brains, rather than for men of reason" (Sahagun: p. 64).

The Indians' religious fervor was often the object of derision for the Spaniard of a rationalist Europe in the sixteenth century. Rituals and prayers were superstitions which condemned the Indians to the scorn of the Conquerors. There thus already appeared that distinction between Indians and "men of reason" which still endures today.

And yet those gods whom Sahagun discovered, both terrifying and nearby, masters of the Indians and subjecting them to their pitiless desires, those gods who were sometimes monstrous, sometimes unknowable—"spirit, air, and darkness" as the ancients described them—were living, with a strong and real life which disturbed the chronicler. That crowd of gods, some of them giants who presided over the genesis of the world, others hidden in the very folds of reality, the souls of trees, mountains, rivers, clouds, giving to every moment of the universe a beneficent or an evil direction, all of that was dizzying and admirable like a dual magic in the perceptible universe. It was the proximity of the supernatural which gave Amerindian thought its true power. Stripped of their gods, the Aztecs could not survive. Sahagun was surely the first to say as much: "Since all of that has ceased, owing to the arrival of the Spanish, and because the latter have torn down and abolished all the customs and all the laws the natives once had, to make them submit to the Spanish way of life, both for divine and for human things, being certain that they were barbarous and idolatrous, any government they once had was lost" (Account of the Author . . . , Sahagun: p. 578).

The proximity of the sacred, for the Aztecs as for the Tarascans and the Maya, was endlessly affirmed. Each day of the year was connected to a sign, that is, to a god. The reign of the stars and the gods was absolute, no one could escape from it. One of the strangest rituals described by Sahagun was that of the *mamalhuiztli*, the fire stick. "These people had particular reverence for and offered sacrifices to the *mastelejos* of the sky, who traveled near the Pleiades, under the sign of the Bull.[5] They made sacrifices and had ceremonies when they appeared again in the east, after the festival of the Sun." Sahagun then describes the cosmic ritual: "They called these three stars *mamalhuiztli*, and this is the name they gave to the sticks they used to light the fire, because, they seemed to think, there was some resemblance with the stars, and from there this way of producing fire came to them. For that reason they had the custom of burning the wrist of boys, in honor of those stars. It was said that whoever did not bear that sign, when he died, his wrists would be used in hell to light the fire, by turning them like a gimlet, as they do with pieces of wood" (Sahagun: p. 434).

For the Aztecs one of the most magical of all moments was the festival of Teotleco, "the arrival of the gods," in the twelfth month. "On the fifteenth day of this month," reports Sahagun, "the young men and boys enwreathed all the altars and oratories of the gods" (Bandelier: p. 60). On the eighteenth day there arrived "the god who had remained a bachelor" who was called Tlamatzincatl, that is, Tez-catlipoca. The festival took place on the last day of the month, "for on that day, they pretended the gods were all returning. On the eve [of that day], at night, they placed on a small mat [*petate*] a very compact little heap of stacked corn in the shape of a bone. On this heap the gods imprinted the sole of one foot as a sign that they had returned. All night the head-priest kept watch; he would come and go many times during his vigil to see whether the imprint was there. As soon as he saw the sign of the foot, he would shout: 'Our lord has arrived,' and at once all the priests of the Cu (temple) would blow cornets (horns), shells, and trumpets, and all other instruments they had then" (Bandelier: pp. 60–61). The Indians offered their gifts to the newly arrived gods. Many slaves and captives were burned alive on an altar named *teocalco*. "On top of the altar a young man was dancing, adorned with a switch of long hair with a tuft of rich plumes and a crown. His face was painted black with white lines . . . He carried on his back a plumage which was called vocalli (the shell of the caddis worm) with a dried rabbit on it. When they threw one of the slaves into the fire, he (the dancer) whistled by sticking one finger into his mouth, as is their custom (when whistling)." The dancer was accompanied by "another youth . . . dressed like a bat, with wings and all the rest to look like that animal" (Bandelier: p. 120). There was then a procession and prayers, and a strange game played by the priests, who wore paper stoles and ran around the bonfire where the captives had perished.

The terrifying beauty of the ritual carried out to await the gods shows the extent to which Aztec culture was connected to supernatural powers. Dedicated at birth to the gods Tlaltecuhtli and Tonatiuh, lords of the land and the sun, the young Indian also belonged to Tezcatlipoca. He was welcomed into the *telpochcalli* (the house of youth) "to start sweeping and doing other humble work in the house of our lord" (Bandelier: p. 195). At fifteen, his task was to obtain wood for the sacred pyres. The *calmecac*, religious colleges, trained "those who would become ministers (priests) of the idols." The

priests' role was also to serve the gods: they went to get wood, they
swept up, they collected maguey thorns for sacrifices. They also
learned songs "written in their books by signs; furthermore they
taught them Indian astrology, and the interpretation of dreams and
the counting of years" (Bandelier: p. 202).

Who were those gods who were so feared and so venerated?
There were a multitude of them: Sahagun counted seventy-six
temples in the city of Mexico. First there were the gods of rain, the
Tlalocs, who regulated fertility and rainfall. The Aztecs sacrificed
young children to them during the festivals of the first month, *atlacahualo*, and the third month, *tozoztontli*, then once again during the
sixteenth month, *atemoztli* (the falling of water). During the preparations for the festival, they cut out paper figures called *teteuitl*, which
were covered with drops of gum, and they made images of the mountains "over which the clouds formed" (Bandelier: p. 134). Some of the
figures were made of corn dough (*tzoal*), with calabash seeds for teeth
and beans for the eyes. They put those figures to death by tearing
out their hearts and decapitating them, and their flesh (*tepeme*) was
divided among the faithful.

The primary god of Anáhuac was clearly Huitzilopochtli, the
Hummingbird of the Left (the south), whom Sahagun calls "another
Hercules." That god, reports the chronicler, was portrayed with "the
head of a very ferocious dragon which emitted fire from its mouth."
He reigned in particular over Mexico/Tenochtitlán—the emperor
Montezuma wore his seal on his wrist—and was the hero of an epic
poem, the echo of which has reached us through the fragments Sahagun provides: Coatlicue, the goddess of water, was made pregnant
by a hummingbird feather which descended from the sky, and her
other children wanted to kill her out of jealousy. Huitzilopochtli, still
in his mother's womb, thwarted the treachery of his brothers, and on
the day of his birth he appeared "carrying a shield which was called
teucueli, with one dart (arrow); both were blue (shield and dart), and
his [Huitzilopochtli's] face was as if it were painted, and he wore on
his head a plumage of pasted feathers; his left leg was thin and also

feathered, and both thighs were painted alike in blue, as well as his arms" (Bandelier: p. 174). Then, with the help of a snake made of torches, called *xiuchcoatl*, Huitzilopochtli killed his sister Coyolxauh-qui, and cut her into pieces.

One of the most important festivals was devoted to this god, that of the fifteenth month, *panquetzaliztli*. At that time they erected his statue made of corn dough, while the priests of the god and of his "vicar," Paynal, "danced, winding around the temple courtyard." In front of the statue of the god and the image of the snake covered with turquoise stones, in the courtyard where the ball game (*teotlachco*) was played, they sacrificed captives to the image of two gods named Ama-pantzitzin ("clothed in paper"), and the captives' blood was spread over the playing field. There was then a mock battle between two factions, composed of slaves and warriors, symbolizing the battle be-tween Huitzilopochtli and his brothers. The battle ceased when Paynal arrived; then there were processions which ended with the sacrificing of captives and slaves. At the conclusion of the festival, the old men participated in the drinking of *matlaloctli*, the blue *pulque* [alcoholic beverage made of the sap of the maguey], and on the day of *nexpixolo* [the last day of the festival], when the souls of the victims had arrived in hell, everyone bathed and carefully washed their hair.

These prodigious rituals, every detail of which Sahagun consci-entiously describes, were the very ones which Pedro de Alvarado had witnessed when he ordered the terrible massacre in the temple court-yard in Tenochtitlán, which set the stage for the final destruction of the Mexican people.

For the Aztecs, Tezcatlipoca, the "smoking mirror," was the su-preme god of the sky. He was, writes Sahagun, "the creator of heaven and earth, and was all powerful; he gave to the living everything they needed, such as food, drink, and wealth. This said [Tezcatlipoca] was invisible, like darkness or air, and if he appeared and spoke to a man, he was like a shadow" (Bandelier: p. 178).

It was that universal god whom the Indians also called Yaotl, the

Enemy, most probably because of his magical battle against Quetzal-cóatl, the Feathered Serpent. It is he who is evoked in hymns: "Oh, our courageous lord! Under your wings we are sheltered, we are defended. You are as invisible and untouchable as the night, as the wind!" (Sahagun: p. 299).

The "very pious, very human" lord was surely confused with the Christian's God. According to Motolinia, he was venerated at Tex-coco, in the time of the king-poet Nezahualcóyotl, in an empty temple whose walls and ceiling portrayed a starry sky. The invisible and untouchable god was constantly present among men. "[Tezcatli-poca] was adored and prayed to by everybody and on all the roads and street crossings they put a stone seat in his honor, which was called Momuztli, and on this seat they put certain bunches of flowers in his honor and service, renewing them every five days, besides the twenty days' festival they celebrated for him" (Bandelier: p. 179).

This is surely what was most shocking to Bernardino de Sahagun in those rituals and festivals: the physical presence of the gods in the very midst of men. Songs and dances were not simply prayers or acts of thanksgiving. They were also magical scenes which materialized the mysterious forces of the other world. Thanks to those incantations, the gods descended, they mixed with men, they danced and sang with them. Motolinia reported that for the festival of fire on the day of *izcalli* six trees were erected, "as tall as the masts of ships." Then two women captives were sacrificed and flayed and the priests, wearing their skin and masks, came down the steps of the pyramid, while the people cried out: "Our gods have arrived! Our gods have arrived!"

In these cruel festivals the immolated victims were no longer mere mortals. Wearing the insignia and the robes of the gods, they were their "images," respected and venerated before being sacrificed. In the seventh month, *tecuilhuitontli*, the "image" of Vixtocihuatl, the goddess of salt, was immolated. In the eighth month, *uey tecuilhuitl*, the "image" of Xilonen, the virgin mother, goddess of the young corn, died while men and women took turns dancing. In the eleventh month, *ochpa-*

niztli, there was a magical, powerful ceremony: it was the festival of Teteo Inman, the mother of the gods; she who was called Toci, "our grandmother." In her honor, for eight days, people danced in silence, without songs or music, without moving their feet, "merely lifting and lowering their arms." The "image" of Toci then appeared and was taken to the temple "where she was to die, and nobody spoke nor coughed when they led her there; they all went amid great silence, although the entire town accompanied her" (Bandelier: p. 114). She was beheaded and flayed by the sacrificers. A priest who represented the god Cinteotl, the son of Toci, covered his face with the skin from her thigh, and another priest covered himself with the rest of her skin, and in turn became the "image" of the goddess. There was then a mock battle; the goddess pursued the participants, following a ritual which is still carried out today in the Nahuatl communities in the outskirts of Mexico City (in Milpa Alta, for example). At the end of the festival, the priest, the "image" of Toci, received offerings of feathers and incense which the Mexican people sent to the goddess.

The extreme complexity of the rituals was a symbol of magic: the goal of those gestures, repeated year after year, was transfiguration, when slaves and captives, through the power of sacred theater, became one with the divinities.

In the thirteenth month, *tepeilhuitl*, during the festivals dedicated to the highest mountains of Mexico, one man and four women were killed in the names of divinities. The man was Milnahuatl, "the image of snakes." The women were Tepoxoch, "flower of the mountain," Matlalcueye, "she with the blue skirt" (the name of the Tlaxcaltecan goddess of rain), Xochitecatl, "between the flowers," and Mayahuel, the "image of maguey," the goddess of *pulque*. Their bodies were eaten by the priests in the *calpulli* [the sacred field where the priests performed the fertility rituals].

In the seventeenth month, *tititl*, they celebrated the festival of the goddess Illamatecutli, also called *Tona*, "Our Mother"—probably an old form of the goddess Cihuacoatl (the woman-serpent), she who was later venerated under the name of Tonantzin, the miraculous Virgin of Guadelupe. During this ceremony a woman was sacrificed, and a priest danced around holding the victim's head in his right hand.

Quetzalcóatl represents the adventure of a man who became a god. "Quetzalcóatl, although a man," writes Sahagun, "was held as a god who, they said, swept the road clear for the gods of the water. This they supposed to be a fact because always before the rainy season begins there are heavy winds and dust clouds" (Bandelier: p. 26). Quetzalcóatl was the principal god of the people of Tula. In that city "he had a very high temple with many steps." His effigy, stresses the chronicler, was covered with blankets and "the face was very homely, the head long, and he wore a very long beard." According to the legend, in the time of his splendor Quetzalcóatl lived in palaces made of turquoise, silver, pink mother-of-pearl, and feathers. It was he who asked the Indians to do penance by scarring their legs using agave thorns, and showed them the art of cutting precious stones and melting down metals. He also taught hieroglyphic writing, and composed the first *tonal amatl*, the book of signs, the prophetic almanac.

The legend of this magician king, benefactor of the people of Tula, extended over the entire Mexican territory, and even beyond. He appeared in the Mayan cycle of Kukulcán (the Feathered Serpent), and also by the name of Yaxum, the Green Bird. Sahagun compares him to Hercules, then to King Arthur. But other Christian historians, such as Boturini or Sigüenza y Gongora, would later see him as a reincarnation of St. Thomas who came to America to spread the gospel of Christ.

The legend of the Feathered Serpent is undoubtedly one of the most ancient in middle America, linked at the same time to ancient animistic cults and to the discovery of the Venusian cycle of five hundred and ten days.

We already know how important the legend of Quetzalcóatl's return was in the conquest of Mexico. Four hundred years later the myth is still alive: in the region of Cuernavaca (the capital of Morelos state) don't they say that the soul of the revolutionary Emiliano Zapata, assassinated through treachery, returns when the wind blows?

For there is eternity in the myth: Quetzalcóatl is the dream of the golden age of the Indians when in his four palaces of the colors of the four parts of the universe there reigned the magician and artist king, surrounded by his feather dressers, *amantecas,* and by his four doctors, inventors of healing plants, Oxomoco, Cipactonal, Tlaltetecui, and Xochicaua. In his time the first veins of precious metals and turquoise were found not far from Tepoztlán, in the mountain called Xiuhtzone. Amber, crystal, and amythest were discovered. During the reign of Quetzalcóatl the solar and lunar-calendar, divided into twenty signs, was created, and the interpretation of dreams and the science of stars began.

Thanks to their king, the Toltecs lived in piety and justice. Men of that time were "tall, of greater height than those living today, and because they were tall they could run and had much endurance, and for that reason they were called *tlanquacemilhuique,* which means that they ran an entire day without resting" (Sahagun: p. 598).

However, Quetzalcóatl's glory and the good fortune of the Toltecs came to an end. "There appeared against them three necromancers by the names of [Huitzilopochtli], Titlacauan, and Tlacauepan, who played many tricks in [Tula]" (Bandelier: p. 180).

Quetzalcóatl fell ill, and Titlacauan came to see him, disguised as an old man, carrying a drink he claimed to be the elixir of youth. "You will . . . be like a young man," he said, "you will even become a boy again." The potion was actually the "white wine of the country (land) made of maguey (agave), the kind [of agave] they call *teumetl*" (Bandelier: p. 181).

The necromancer also bewitched the daughter of Huemac, the lord of Tula (since Quetzalcóatl was a priest and had no children), by showing her the phallus of a poor man who was selling pimento at a marketplace. To his great shame the lord had to give his daughter in marriage to the slave. To get rid of him Lord Huemac sent the slave to wage battle against the enemies of Tula, but the young man, who was none other than Titlacauan himself, assisted by his army of dwarfs, returned triumphant. He ordered a great feast during which, guided by magical music, many Toltec warriors fell into a ravine where they were turned into rocks.

Titlacauan increased his tricks against Tula: disguised as an old woman, he sold deadly amulets which made the people of the tribe go crazy. An ultimate trick brought the end of the hated city: disguised as a merchant, Titlacauan "made a tiny boy dance in the palms of his hands (they say this boy was Huitzilopochtli)" (Bandelier: p. 185). The bewitched crowd stoned the merchant and killed him, but his decomposing body carried a deadly stench, and became so heavy that they could not move it.

It was then that Quetzalcóatl departed for Tlapallan: "He ordered that all the houses of silver and shells . . . be burned, and he had all his other very precious things burned in the mountains or clefts." Then he left for Quauhtitlan, and there he asked his pages for a mirror. "Looking at his face (in the mirror), he said, 'I am old now'" (Bandelier: p. 187).

He continued on his way, preceded by many birds with rich plumage, and by his flute players. On a rock where he rested he left the imprint of his hands. "Looking back toward [Tula], he commenced to cry bitterly, and the tears he shed hollowed and perforated the stone on which he thus sat resting and weeping" (Bandelier: p. 187). He also left the impression of his buttocks on the rock. "He [Quetzalcóatl] on that occasion called the said place Temacpalco" (Bandelier: p. 188).

On the road to Tlapallan Quetzalcóatl encountered the necromancers who wanted to stop him. He said to them: "In no way can you prevent my departure, for I have to leave forcibly." "What for are you going there?" asked the necromancers. And Quetzalcóatl replied: "They came to call me and the Sun is also calling me" (Bandelier: p. 188). And Quetzalcóatl left, abandoning all his riches in the spring called Cohuapan. Then he went through the ranges of snow-covered volcanoes where his faithful dwarfs died from the cold, and he cried sadly in Tecamachalco. Farther on, on his route, he had a ball court built "made of square stones . . . and in the midst of the [court] he himself drew a mark or line, called tlecotl, and that where this line is the mountain appears very deeply rent (gashed)" (Bandelier: p. 189). Farther still he drew a cross on the *pochutl* tree (the ceiba tree, the symbol of the pillar supporting the sky in Mayan mythology) and on that place he built an underground palace called *mictlancalco* (the House of Hell).

He then arrived at the seashore, at the place which today is still called Coatzacoalcos (in Veracruz state); "he ordained a raft to be made of snakes of the kind which is called *coatlapechtli*; he entered it and sat down as in a canoe, and thus he left, navigating on the sea, no one knows how and in what manner he arrived at Tlapallan" (Bandelier: p. 189).

Thus ended the saga of Quetzalcóatl, who disappeared in the red land of Tlapallan, to the east of the universe, and whose return was awaited by the Indians of Mexico.

For Bernardino de Sahagun, the dream of origins was the one which joined those men and that earth to the vanished gods. The origin of the Amerinds was undoubtedly one of the most controversial issues in the time of the Conquest of the New World. For Father Beaumont (who was inspired by Father Brimilla Orinoco) the origin of the Indian race was unquestionably found in Noah's curse on his son Ham—which, in his opinion, explained the Indians' propensity for drunkenness. The idea of a Semitic origin for the American Indians was held by a number of historians, such as Sigüenza y Gongora and Boturini. The Indians themselves sometimes accepted the idea, for example the Cruzoob Maya of Yucatán, who identified with the "chosen people."

However, to the question posed about the Indians by Sahagun: "Who are they? Where do they come from?," they replied with the same strange legend. Before men, they said, a race of giants reigned over the high plateaus of Mexico; they created the "tumuli of earth which one still sees today and which seem to have been made by the hand of man" (Sahagun: p. 611).

Those giants, according to the historian Fernando de Alva Ixtlilxóchitl, were named *quinametin* by the ancient Toltecs, who "waged
many wars because of them, on the territory of what is today New
Spain."[6]

"Countless years ago," relates Sahagun, "the first peoples arrived
in this region of New Spain, which is almost another world. And,
having come by sea on boats, they landed on the northern shores.
And because they had landed there, they called it Panutla, actually
Panoayan . . . And from that port they began to walk along the
banks, looking always at the snow-capped mountains and volcanoes"
(Sahagun: p. 610). Thus the legend of the arrival of the first Mexicans prefigured the coming of the Spanish conquerors.

Those Indian peoples conquered the mythical kingdom of Tamoanchan. Then they continued their journey toward the east,
guided by their god, "whom they brought with them wrapped in a
cloth" (Sahagun: p. 611), and by Quetzalcóatl's four doctors, Oxomoco, Cipactonal, Tlaltetecui, and Xochicaua. They walked, and
"the Toltecs always preceded them" (Sahagun: p. 613). They founded
Xomiltepec and continued on their way. "And no one can remember
how long they wandered. They went off into a valley between the
mountains, where they all cried from fatigue and pain, for they were
very hungry and thirsty. And in that valley there were seven caves
where those people made their place for prayer" (Sahagun: p. 613).

It was then, according to Father Beaumont, that the "demon"
Huitzilopochtli gave the men a choice between two gifts, one
containing an emerald, the other two pieces of wood. The leader
Huitzon told those who chose wood that they had chosen what was
most precious: fire.

The separation of the Indian nations took place in that mythical
place: The Toltecs returned to Tula; the Michoaque, guided by their
leader Amimitl (Arrow of Water), went toward the west. The Mexica,
accompanied by related tribes, Tepanecas, Acolhuas, Chalcas, Uexo-
tzincas, Tlaxcaltecas, went toward the south. Before parting they
made offerings in the caves "and that is why all nations of this land

proudly say that they were born in those seven caves, and that their ancestors came from there" (Sahagun: p. 613).

The Kings

For the ancient Mexicans, there was no separation between men and the gods. The terrestrial world, with all its imperfections and injustice, with its splendor and passions, was the temporary image of eternity. The very organization of society was an imitation of the supernatural order. On earth, as in the other world, lords ruled over their servants and vassals. Ometecuhtli, the creator god, both man and woman, Mictlantecuhtli, the god of the Hells, and Yiacatecuhtli, the god of merchants, were lords who sat on their thrones, in their palaces, and who waged war or amused themselves just as mortals did.

The Mexican kings were their representatives on earth. The power those kings had received was of a divine nature. And at the time of the Conquest the Spanish had to measure themselves against that supernatural power. They were able to take advantage of the Indians' belief: the shameful chaining up, the torturing, the putting to death of the Mexican rulers were horrible and sacrilegious acts to the Indian people, acts which conferred superhuman strength upon the foreign conquerors. They were new gods who had come to bring a new order.

Until that time the Mexican kings had been considered above other men. They were venerated as idols while they were alive and adored as gods after their death. Among the Maya as among the Aztecs the kings' palaces were built near the temples. Among the ancient Purepecha, the cazonci[7] ruled over the three cities of Pátzcuaro, Tzintzuntzan, and Ihautzio, just as the god Curicaueri ruled over the realms of his brothers the Tiripemecha, at the four cardinal points.

The close association of power with the supernatural was expressed in the speeches which followed the election of the king in Mexico/Tenochtitlán. The orator, squatting in front of his master, wearing on his shoulder the knot of his cloak as a sign of submission, spoke in these terms to the new king: "Oh, Our very human and very pious Lord, very loving and worthy of esteem, more than all the precious stones and rich plumages! At present we have a great consolation and great joy, Oh Our very human Lord! For Our Lord God, thanks to whom we live, has given us a light and splendor similar to the sun, and it is you. He points to you with his finger, and he has written your name in red signs, and thus it is established above and here below, in the heavens and in hell, that you are to be Lord" (Sahagun: p. 322).

Replying to the orators, the king humbled himself. And, "squatting down, he turned his head to the one who was speaking, and during the entire discourse he didn't turn his head in any direction, but kept his eyes fixed on the speaker." Then he began to speak: "Our Lord God," he said, "has treated me with liberality and magnificence. Perhaps this is but a dream? Thus let the will of Our Lord God be done. Let it be so according to what has been ordered and decided by the lords who have elected me. What have they seen in me? Have they not done as someone who seeks a woman who can weave and spin? It is true, I do not know myself, I do not appreciate myself, and I can't say two true words. But I can say that my God has taken me from where I was living, in dung and refuse" (Sahagun: p. 329).

Bernardino de Sahagun doesn't hide his admiration for the oratory art of the Mexicans, their "marvelous language." For him, that legendary power, illustrated by such high moral qualities, was equal to that of the kingdoms of Antiquity: "They were," he writes in his prologue to book 6, "extreme in some things, very devout with regard to their gods, very jealous of their republic, very friendly to each other, very cruel to their enemies, human and severe to each other. I believe it was thanks to those virtues that they were able to create their empire, even though it did not last long. And now they have lost everything, as he who compares the contents of this book with the lives they lead today will clearly see" (Sahagun: p. 297).

The primary sense of the *tlaltoca amatl*, the book of the kings, was magic. The absolute lords of Tenochtitlán, of Tlatelolco, of Texcoco were more than men; they were essentially gods, and each of their gestures, each of their words, connected them to the other world.

Everything about them was sacred: justice, war, tributes, but also games—such as the famous *tlachtli*, the ball game, during which princes of rival peoples sometimes faced off in the courtyard of the temples (one of the most famous jousts took place between Montezuma the Elder, lord of Tenochtitlán, and Nezahualcóyotl, lord of Texcoco).

Food was also sacred: white corn tortillas, game, sea fish, *nequatolli*, a drink made of corn and honey, and especially cocoa, the true drink of the lords.

Residences were sacred; there were countless rooms in the palace where the government of the empire was carried out: a hall of justice, a war room, a room for the majordomos, a room for the cantors, and one for visitors.

The sacred nature of power was seen in the ceremonies that accompanied the election of a new king. The latter was led to the temple of Huitzilopochtli, where he was dressed in a dark green tunic decorated with drawings of bones, called a *xicolli*; he was given a gourd full of tobacco to snuff; then after fasting for four days the new ruler was invested by four senators who represented gods; the *tlacochcalcati* (the lord of spears), the *ticocihuacoatl* and the *cihuacoatl* (representatives of the snake-goddess), the *titlancalqui* (representative of Tezcatlipoca).

The magical splendor of the new ruler fully appeared in his regalia. Sahagun, like all the Spaniards, could not help being fascinated by such magnificence: he was in the presence of the expression of a power foreign to his own world, and the disturbing memory of the beauty of those half-gods is reflected in his account, illuminates it with a light of legend. One can't help thinking of the images of the *codex*, painted on sheets of agave paper or woven with feathers, in which lords and gods appear in all their mystical splendor.

Cloaks made of ocelot or jaguar pelts, decorated with sea shells

on a background of "clear azure water"; fawn-colored cloaks decorated with wheels, bordered with fringes portraying eyes; cloaks
decorated with three-footed vases, red and black, bearing "two
wings like those of butterflies"; fawn-colored cloaks embroidered with
butterflies made of white feathers, with an eye on each wing; cloaks
covered with flowers of white feathers. For all these cloths, "one must
note the talent of the women who wove them," writes Sahagun, "for
they create their motifs on the cloth while they are weaving them"
(Sahagun: p. 457).

The lords appeared before their supreme lord wearing their most
beautiful jewelry, feathers, gold, and turquoise: crowns, lip rings,
gold earrings in the shape of half-moons, with turquoise or sapphires
set in their nostrils, bracelets made of mosaics or feathers, garlands,
fans, mother-of-pearl necklaces, gold mirrors, bells. Sometimes they
had their faces covered with "mosaic masks, wearing wigs and gold
plumes" (Sahagun: p. 459).

It was during wars that lords showed off their barbaric splendor:
clothing, headdresses, emblems, and plumes gave them the appearance of the gods they represented.

The lords then wore a "helmet of very red feathers, which was
called a *tlauhquechol* (from a variety of quetzal), decorated with a border of gold and a crown of feathers, out of the center of which rose
a bouquet of quetzal feathers instead of a plume." Their bodies
were covered with "an armor of vermeil plumes which fell to mid-
thigh, covered with gold shells," they carried a shield encircled with
gold, covered with red, green or blue feathers, a drum decorated with
feathers and gold, and a shield made of jaguar skin scattered with
flecks of gold woven with golden threads.

"On their backs they wore green feathers in the shape of butterfly
wings, and they wore a sort of vest of yellow feathers called *tociuitl*
because they came from parrots, and that vest fell to their knees,
decorated with flecks of gold." They wore helmets made of gold or
silver, decorated with two plumes of quetzal feathers in the shape of
horns. They also held "a sort of banner made of quetzal plumes," or

"another sort of flag made of gold and silver." Some lords went into battle wearing on their backs "those types of emblems called *itzpapalotl* (the obsidian butterfly, symbol of the goddess-mother Cihuacoatl): this emblem was like the image of the devil, made of rich plumage, with wings and a tail like those of a butterfly, and its eyes, its feet, its nails, and its eyebrows and everything else were of gold, and on its head they put two tufts of quetzal feathers which looked like antennae" (Sahagun: p. 460).

The lords wore many other emblems, which Bernardino de Sahagun describes with admiring precision: the insignia of the *xochiquetzalpapalotl* (the butterfly of the precious flower); that of the *quetzal patzactli*, with a shield of green feathers; insignia of the *toxquaxolotl*, made of an armor of yellow turkey feathers covered with flecks of gold; insignia of the *zacatzontli*, of yellow feathers; the insignia of the *toztzitzimitl*, "a monster of gold in the center of the emblem;" that of the *xiloxochipatzactli*, in the shape of a feather helmet decorated with two gold eyes; insignia of the wheel; insignia of the sun; insignia of the *ocelotlachicomitl* jaguar.

Surely no other civilization had developed to such a degree a taste for costumes and for working with feathers. In this expression of the animal world—skins, ornamentation, tatooing, feathers—there was a hoodoo magic which the Spanish chronicler was unable to discover without feeling a mixture of horror and admiration. The ruin of the Indian kingdom in Mexico was also the destruction of that art of the body and of costume which turned warriors and lords into representatives of a supernatural world. Today—apart from rare vestiges in the Amerindian world—nothing remains of that magical art.

The People

In that magical civilization mortals were divided into classes, or rather castes, each of which played its role in the social structure. Beneath lords and priests were the warriors, chosen from among the nobility and raised in the *calmecac* (religious colleges) and in the *telpochcalli*

(house of youth). Put to the trials of battle, young men had to earn
the right to cut off their braid and receive the painting of courage:
yellow for the body, red for the face. The bravest among them re-
ceived the insignia of nobility, "large lip rings and leather earrings."
They became *quauhyacatl*, "the Eagle who guides" (Sahagun: p. 479).
They could ultimately become members of those elite corps which
Sahagun compares to "knights," and which bore the names of Eagles,
Jaguars, or Ocelots.

Bernardino de Sahagun expresses his admiration for the severe
education the Aztecs gave to their children, both girls and boys.
Dedicated to the gods, and particularly to the Sun and the Earth,
children had to toughen their bodies and lead a pure existence. In
book 6 Sahagun transcribes the exhortations of parents to their children teaching them moral virtues: how to walk, talk, dress, eat and
drink, wash one's body and face. How to beware of poison and sorcery. How to learn an honorable trade, "such as that of featherwork-
ing" (Sahagun: p. 344). For, specifies the chronicler, "nowhere did I
ever see anyone live off his nobility alone, nor from his rank alone."
The same advice was given to girls, who were to cultivate virtue and
give proof of devotion, humility, and obedience. They had to learn
to confront poverty, and to do that, no matter what their rank, they
had to know how to spin and weave, cook and grind cocoa beans.
They also had to learn to fight, and we know the role women played
in the defense of Mexico/Tenochtitlán when it was besieged by the
Conquerors.

But the Mexican empire was not just a warring empire. It was also
based on trade, and the *pochtecas*, the merchants, were in a certain
sense ambassadors and representatives of the power of Mexico beyond the borders of the empire.

The merchants were true agents of Mexican influence in middle
America. They were on the same level as the warriors and, reports
Sahagun, those who died on the road joined the heroes in the House
of the Sun (Sahagun: p. 500). Mexican history has preserved the
names of some of these merchants: we know that the market for par-

rot feathers was begun by Itzcoatzin and Tziuhtecatzin, at the time of king Quaquauhpitzauac; that the market for quetzal feathers was started by Cozmatzin and Tzompantzin, as well as the market for turquoise and jade; and that the market for gold jewelry was established by Tullamimichtzin and Miczotzigoatzin, in the time of king Quauhtlatoatzin. Those "consuls," as Sahagun calls them, celebrated the cult of Yiacatecuhtli, the god of merchants, with lavish and cruel rituals. The corporation of merchants worked within a code of honor and bravery worthy of that of warriors, and had an ideal of tolerance which might have served as an example to the Humanists: "Be careful, oh son, of offending anyone with your words or your actions. Be polite with and defer to everyone. Think, oh son, that if God has given you the goods of this world, you must not for that reason feel superior nor scorn anyone" (Sahagun: p. 495).

Artisans made up the largest part of the middle class, each belonging to a corporation which had its leaders, its tutelary heroes, its gods, and its rituals. In Michoacán, the Tarascan nation even established a system of representation of corporations which already evoked unions. Gathered around the king (the cazonci), the *uriecha* expressed the wishes and problems of the principal corporations: fishermen, bow makers or potters, painters, stonecutters, carpenters, goldsmiths, featherworkers, or hunters.[8]

Among the Aztecs each professional body had its own god, like the goldsmiths, who venerated Xipe Totec, or the diamond cutters, whose gods were their ancestors Chiconahui Itzcuintli, Naualpilli, Macuilcalli, and Cinteotl, and, as goddess, Papaloxahual. The featherworkers were of noble origin, and said that they descended from the Amantecas, the faithful of Quetzalcóatl, and whose god was Coyotl Inahual, the spirit of the coyote. The festivals of the featherworkers were magnificent; women danced intertwined, their bodies covered with multicolored feathers.

The marketplace of Mexico/Tenochtitlán reflected that hierarchized and ordered society; the emperor himself and his governors organized the market (the *tianquez*): "all things to be sold were put in order, each thing in its place, and officials were named, called *tian-quezpan tlayacaque,* who were in charge of the *tianquez* and for every-thing that was sold there, for each product or merchandise. One of them was responsible for setting the price of merchandise and to watch that there was no fraud between those who sold and those who bought" (Sahagun: p. 475).

The riches of his entire realm spread out under the eyes of the lord of Mexico/Tenochtitlán: cocoa, grain, pimento, honey, game, fish, fruit, cloth, paper, rubber resin, incense, pottery, feathers, jewelry.

That order, a symbol of the harmony and justice of the Mexican kingdom, reflected celestial order, and no one could act against it. Defrauders were severely punished, and thiefs and fences were sen-tenced to death.

Thus the harmony of that people was formed, each person as-signed to his task, according to a law which is difficult to imagine today: he who sold salt; he who polished stone mirrors; he who went into the mountains to bring back brooms, medicinal plants, or wood for the pyres; he who gathered tar; he who made wax or blue paint was completely ignorant of the art of his neighbor. Obeying their laws, however, was not a form of slavery, and we can imagine the happiness of that golden age, in spite of the cruelty of their wars and sacrifices. It was the happiness of a magical age, when time was not an inevitable and useless passage, but rather a connection to the wheel of the centuries, which carried out a mysterious and perfect destiny.

That order was fragile. Only the kings and priests had the power to perceive the turning of time. It was better to preserve the memory of that order that the god Quetzalcóatl, master of Tula, had be-queathed hieroglyphic writing to the Indians: "They knew and re-membered the things their ancestors had done, and they marked it in their annals, for more than a thousand years before, before the Span-ish came to this land" (Sahagun: p. 611).

Thanks to those books—books of kings, books of the Dead, chronicles, sacred almanacs, medicinal recipes, or inventories of the riches of the world—we can today relive a bit of that fabulous time.

But the balance of a civilization is precarious, and it takes very little to ruin it forever. The Indian world was as fragile as a dream, to which the dream of the oracles announced the end. Was it by chance that, as if foreseeing the abuses and pillaging which were soon to destroy the harmony of the Amerindian civilizations, in the time of Itzcóatl, "the kings and the princes who were ruling at that time decided together and ordered that all the paintings be burned so they would not fall into the hands of vulgar men who would treat them with scorn" (Sahagun: p. 611).

The memory of things past, the voice of the ancients gathered around Bernardino de Sahagun, is it not that which makes itself heard once again, raising up in the shadows of the present the splendor of a vanished world?

3   Mexican Myths

HEN CHRISTOPHER COLUMBUS WAS APPROACHING
the Antilles at the end of his first voyage he was not
just looking for a new route to the Indies or to
China. Like many of the voyagers of the Renaissance, he was in quest of the land of the Amazons,
that land inhabited only by women, warriors with long hair, fearsome
archers who guarded the entrance to the fabulous kingdom where
gold and all sorts of riches were in abundance. It was the myth of the
Amazons that guided the Conquerors toward the New World, where
the dangers they risked appeared to be worth the treasures they anticipated. It was that same myth of the Amazons which, following
the fall of Mexico/Tenochtitlán, led the terrible Nuño de Guzmán to
the west of Mexico, in search of what the natives themselves called
Cihuatlán, the Land of the Women.

For, oddly enough, in response to the old myth inherited from
the Orient and from Greece, there was the Aztecs' belief in Cihuatlampa, the House of the Sun, west of the world, the final resting
place of the Mociuaquetzques, the women who died in childbirth.

For us who live in the modern bath of geographical and historical
knowledge, the chimera of the Conquerors might appear difficult to

understand. It was indeed because of such misapprehension that the voyager Coronado attempted his mad expedition to the northwest of Mexico, and because of it that Cortés himself went as far as the shores believed to have been the California peninsula, and that the Portuguese gave its name—Amazon—to the longest river in the world.

Indeed, those mythical times began the history of New Spain. And, still through that mysterious law of balance, in response to the mythical island of the Amazons and Eldorado one found the mystical expectation of the Indian peoples, who saw those bearded and armored strangers as the messengers of their destiny—Quetzalcóatl, the magician prince of Tula, who had disappeared into the Atlantic Ocean on a raft of snakes, Kukulcán, the Feathered Serpent of the Itzás, or those Tepacha who came from where the sky met the sea, to bring their message of destruction to the people of Michoacán.

The surprise we experience today before that confrontation of mythical legends, upon which the outcome of the greatest armed conflict in the history of humanity would depend, must not cause us to ignore the reality of the situation. When the Spaniards set foot on the American continent, they were not all that different from the peoples they sought to subdue. Despite the technological progress of the Renaissance, men continued to live in a universe in which the fabulous was mixed in with the real, a universe in which possibilities and limitations seemed constantly to shrink in the face of what was observed.

The New World, at the time of its discovery by the Europeans, was the favored place of myths. In discovering those fabulous kingdoms, those civilizations of dazzling richness, the Spaniards also invented another dimension for man, which evoked the golden age of myth, in a time which preceded and yet justified rational knowledge. The fascination felt by the great chroniclers of the sixteenth and seventeenth centuries—Motolinia, Olmos, Diego de Landa, Diego Duran, Beaumont, Sahagun, and Acosta—was a fascination for dreams and myths. The strength of myths was also in their logic, in their architecture. Those strange peoples lived their beliefs, not in the absurd disorder which the Spanish wanted to attribute to savages, but in a coherence and harmony which seemed, to the witnesses of the final moments, worthy of ancient history. All those who later wrote on the mythical past of the Indians, from Sahagun and Acosta to Boturini and Clavijero, would draw the same comparison, sometimes establish the same relationships: the Aztecs, the Maya, the Purepecha were the Romans or the Greeks of the New World, and their gods, their legends were the expression of the same sort of paganism.

What was extraordinary in that meeting between the two worlds was there, in the myths. Upon discovering the complexity of the Amerindian civilizations, the Spaniards at the same time discovered a world in which all modern thought—human sciences, history, the sciences of language—was in embryonic form. That mythical universe was not just fable; it was a universe of new forms: the myths that were found in varying forms throughout the American continent were also monuments, artistic creations. They were at the heart of Indian religion, at the origin of knowledge.

Let us look first at the Indian myths. They are those which the Spanish chroniclers reveal to us with the combination of wonderment and horror they felt in the presence of a cruel force. For they were not dealing with a vague superstition, but with a complex construction which they found again and again among most of the civilizations of middle America. They were truly dealing with the beliefs of a people.

The Four Directions of the World

For the Aztecs, as for the Purepecha and the Maya, the world was square, and each of its four sides was symbolized by a color, a tree, an animal, and a guardian spirit. For the Maya, the guardian spirits of the compass points were important gods: these were the Bacabs, bearers of the Ahcantun stones ["the sacred four stones" at the corners of the earth]: in the north was the white Bacab (Zacal Bacab), in the south the yellow Bacab (Kanal Bacab), in the east the red Bacab (Chacal Bacab), and in the west the black Bacab (Ekal Bacab). In the center of the square was the color Yax, jade green. The origin of this division of the world into compass points and colors is undoubtedly cosmogonic. It brings to mind the ancient Chinese representation of the world where to each compass point there was a corresponding color and a vital organ (*tsang*): lungs, heart, spleen, liver, kidneys. Among the Maya, this division is related to the first observations of the stars, without any doubt the most ancient heritage of the cultures of middle America: monuments of the Mound Builders (in the southeastern United States), Toltec or Maya pyramids. This division is certainly linked to the creation of calendars, the architectural culmination of which appears in the pyramids of Teotihuacán, Uxmal, and Chichén Itzá. One finds the same division in the genesis myths of the *Books of the Chilam Balam*:

—The first man was Ah Canul. The white tree *uaxim*, the *ixculun* tree, the *chacah* tree are his little hut . . .
—The red flint stone

is the stone of the red *Mucencab*.
The red ceiba tree of abundance
is his arbor,
which is set in the east.
The red bullet-tree is their tree.
The red zapote . . .
The red-vine . . .
Reddish are their yellow turkeys.
Red toasted corn is their corn.

The white flint stone
is their stone in the north.
The white ceiba tree of abundance
is the arbor of the white *Mucencab*.
White-breasted are their turkeys
White lima beans are their lima beans.
White corn is their corn.

The black flint stone
is their stone in the west.
The black ceiba tree of abundance
is their arbor.
Black speckled corn is their corn.
Black tipped camotes are their camotes.
Black wild pigeons are their turkeys.
Black *akab-chan* is their green corn.
Black beans are their beans.
Black lima-beans are their lima-beans.

The yellow flint stone
is the stone of the south.
The ceiba tree of abundance,
the yellow ceiba tree of abundance,
is their arbor.
The yellow bullet-tree is their tree.
Colored like the yellow bullet-tree are their camotes.
colored like the yellow bullet-tree
are the wild pigeons which are their turkeys.
Yellow green corn is their green corn.
Yellow-backed are their beans.[1]

According to Ignacio Bernal, the origin of this myth of colors is perhaps found in the distant Olmec civilization, the first to build cosmographic monuments, and to associate jade with the east. Among the Maya, one of the last manifestations of this symbolic system of colors appears in the litany of the Papatun (the Breakers of Stone, inventors of corn) assembled in Tusik by Villa Rojas in 1913. On the other hand a Huichol myth reported briefly by Peter Furst[2] also associates the symbolism of colors to the discovery of corn: guided by ant-men, a young man encounters Tatei Kukuru Uimari, the Mother of Corn, in the form of a bird who, after reassuming her human form, presents to him her five daughters, who represent the five varieties of corn: red, yellow, white, blue, and black. He takes the daughter of

blue corn, the most precious (she who is the color of jade or turquoise) as his wife, and takes her back to his mother's house. The
latter mistreats her and forces her to flee. After an interval of four
hundred years, the same myth is told in the *Histoire des règnes de Colhu-
acan et de Mexico*, in which the hero Quetzalcóatl, disguised as a black
ant, steals a few grains of corn from some red ants which he takes to
Tamoanchan.[3]

The great genesis myths are those which are found in a corresponding form among many different civilizations: from the Caribs to
the Aztecs, even including the seminomadic nations of the north.
The creation of the world is linked to its destruction, as seen in the
Olmec myth of the jaguar devouring the world and in the Aztec myth
of the five suns. One finds the same theme of destruction through
flooding in Father Francisco Ramirez's *Relation*. Moreover, the Puré
myth provides a possible key to the symbolic division of the world
into "left hand" and "right hand," designating the south and the north:
When the gods decided to rebuild the world for the fourth time, they
"ordered the god of hell to put all of that in order. His wife having conceived, she gave birth to all the plants and trees, such as they are. All
of this, according to what was told, came from between the legs of a
goddess whom the gods had put on earth, whose head was in the west,
her feet facing east, one arm pointed north and the other south. And
the god of the sea held her head, and the mother of the gods her feet,
and two other gods each held an arm, so that she would not fall."[4]

Creation-Destruction

In ancient Mexico the creation of man and that of nutritive plants
seem tied to the idea of a preliminary destruction. After several fruit-
less attempts which resulted in the creation of an imperfect man—
without legs, as in the Texcoco myth,[5] without joints and without
gender, as in the myth of the ancient Purepecha[6]—the gods sentenced their creature to death in a flood. Among the Huichols, the
creation of woman came after the flood: there was a black dog that

accompanied Watakame in his voyage for survival, then, shedding its animal skin, the dog became his consort.[7]

Among the Carib Indians (the Waunana of the Colombian Choco) the myth of the flood is at the very center of religious rituals: in order to protect the world from ultimate destruction, men had to pray to Hewandama, the creator god, in front of a balsa-wood canoe, the symbol of salvation.

For most of the peoples of ancient Mexico the creation of objects and elements useful to men expressed the idea of a tearing away from the natural order. It was most often the ruse of an animal which enabled the discovery of a secret which would enable man to dominate nature. To conquer water, fire, nutritive or medicinal plants, to acquire techniques, man had to make a pact with things and animals, that is, establish a magical alliance between the real and the supernatural.

The myth of the ancient inhabitants of Texcoco relates the ruse the hero Quetzalcóatl used to steal corn from his guardians, the ants. In the *Books of the Chilam Balam*, a bird, the green woodpecker, helps man capture the precious seeds enclosed in the rock.[8]

The possession of water was also a threat of destruction, as told in the Aztec myth of Tlalocan:

The ancients of this land believed that all rivers came out of a place they called *tlalocan*, which is like terrestrial paradise, the place where a god named Chalchihuitlicue reigned; and they also said that the mountains built upon it are full of water, and their outer walls are made of earth, as if they were large water vases, or like houses full of water. And when the time will come, the mountains will shatter, and all the water contained in them will flow out, to annihilate the earth.[9]

Living on the earth, man made a pact with the masters of water, the most powerful of the gods. For the ancient Maya, water was at the center of the cross, symbolized by the color of jade. It was there that the ceiba tree, the pillar and the vault of the sky, was raised.

Certain Mayan codices (the *Codex Borgia* for example) illustrate the theme of creation-destruction: the earth animal (the jaguar of the

Olmecs) gave birth to the quadruple tree of the world, portrayed by the famous cross of Palenque. In Aztec symbolism Tamoanchan, the kingdom of Quetzalcóatl, is represented by a broken tree.[10] In the *Codex Florentinus,* and in Sahagun's book, the tree appears "inlaid with breasts" in the center of Xochiatalpan, the "Land of flowered water," which nourished children who died at a young age.

Water myths have survived in most of the indigenous cultures of Mexico. Among the Mazahua the "Master of Water" took a young girl and brought her to his cave. After he sent her away, she gave birth to the aquatic animals.[11] Among the Purepecha of the Tarascan meseta, the origin of water appears to have been associated with the ritual sacrifice of children, as in the cults of the Nahuatl Tlalocs.[12]

The discovery of fire was the same sort of stolen secret. The most ancient rituals of pre-Columbian America appear to have been created around fire, or hearthstones. The old fire gods (the Aztecs' Huehueteotl) and the Purepecha's god Curicaueri evoke the same connection between men and the one whom contemporary Huichols call Tatewari, our grandfather. Apu, the first shaman, leader of the fabulous creatures who preceded men on the earth, stole the fire hidden in the heart of the wood. Another Huichol myth recorded by Peter Furst[13] tells how fire was concealed by the opossum (an animal still considered sacred by the Huichols), which was cut into pieces by the animal-demons who were guarding it; having magically returned to life, it picked up its pieces and managed to steal the flame, that little piece of wood where "Tatewari flourished." The myth of concealed fire is found in many indigenous cultures. Among the Mazahua, it was the *tlacuache* (the coati) that stole it using its tail, which henceforth had no fur. For the Tepehuas, the fire myth was associated with the flood. After the great inundation man dared to transgress the interdict of the gods and cooked his food; a first messenger who was sent shared his food with him. But a second one obeyed his orders. The first messenger was transformed into a vulture which ate dead prey; the second was turned into an eagle who fed on living beings.

As for man, he was changed into a monkey whose head was in the place of his rump.

Creation myths were sometimes simple transpositions of reality. Fertility myths, which inspired fertility rituals, associated giving birth with natural riches. Sahagun thus mentions the goddess Chicomecóatl as being another Ceres. It appears that certain goddesses of carnal love or of medicine, Xochiquetzal, Quilaztli, Toci, and Tlazotéotl, were avatars of the mother-goddess.[14] Temazcalteci and Yaoltici, the midwives, ruled over the mysterious *temazcal*, the Aztec steam bath which represented the maternal womb. According to a myth told by the anonymous author of the *Histoire du Méchique*, Quetzalcóatl and Tezcatlipoca, metamorphosed into snakes, caught the divinity of the earth (*tlaltecutli*) by the feet and hands, and having quartered him, divided his body into the sky and the earth. From the terrestrial part flowers and all nutritive plants then sprang forth. This brings to mind the Purepecha myth of the genesis of the world, as reported by Father Ramirez: the goddess of hells who, held down by her feet and hands, was forced to give birth to all the plants of the earth. The goddess Cuerauaperi is still venerated today as the very expression of the power of nature, under the name of *Kuerahpiri*, the creator spirit.

Myths of Katabasis

It is clearly in Amerindian cultures that the old myth of a descent into hell has remained most alive. In his essay on the origins of the Russian popular tale, Vladimir Propp reveals the transposed tale of shamanic initiation rituals in folklore: the ogre is the officiant, the little hut in the forest is the initiate's place of reclusion, and the sensation of fear that runs through the tale is the anguish of the adolescent who must attain adulthood. Most Amerindian myths do in fact follow this model and even go beyond it, for they explicitly describe the voyage the apprentice shaman must pursue into the other world, into the land of the dead. The tale of katabasis is given in detail in Sahagun's *History* (based on the oral tradition of the *Codex Florentinus*): the voyage of the soul toward Mictlan, the subterranean world, reminds us of the great mythical poems, the voyage of Gilgamesh, the myth of Orpheus, or book 6 of the *Aeneid*. In the course of that long and difficult adventure, the soul of the deceased encounters a series of trials: it crosses the river Apanoayan, the mountain ranges, the eight frozen regions; it confronts the *itzehecayan* wind of rocks, and on the banks of the black river encounters the lizard Xochitonal (perhaps a representative of the goddess-mother). Finally, on the back of a dog it must go across the great river *Chiconahuapan* before arriving at *Itzmictlanapochalocan*, the home of *Mictlantecuhtli*, master of hell. This fabulous voyage evokes the one the soul of the dead had to undertake to *Xibalba*, the mythological hell of the Quiché Maya, as related in the *Popul Vuh*.[15] The soul had to cross the five rivers of blood, dust, and thorns before arriving at the crossroads, symbols of the four colors and the four directions of the world, and confronting the trials of the "houses": the house of shadow, the house of stone knives, the house of cold, the house of the jaguar, and the house of the vampire.

Although the mythology of the ancient Purepecha is little known to us, owing to the loss of the first part of the *Chronicles of Michoacán*, the repeated allusions to the road traveled by souls of the dead indicate a belief in the voyage of the soul after death. A myth about the creation of tobacco, provided by Cruz Refugio Acevedo Barba, demonstrates the currentness of this belief among the Tarascans of Michoacán: an orphan, tired of having his harvest stolen by a young girl, follows her to a cave. Having fallen asleep through magic (or by a drug), the young man follows the girl in his dream to the other world. The girl hides the young man under her skirt, and gives him hair as a talisman. But the four brothers of the girl find him, and pretending to take him with them to look for wild honey, they shoot him with an arrow and kill him. In despair, the girl embraces his body, and from their union there emerges the first tobacco plant, which is to make the world rejoice.[16] A Tzotzil tale of Chiapas, told by Jacob Pimentel[17] also associates the voyage to the other world with a dream: a hunter kills an armadillo, a subterranean animal. That night he falls asleep in the house of a rich landowner, and is witness to a trial in the other world, in the course of which he is judged for crimes his dog committed.

It is undoubtedly in Huichol mythology that one finds the tale of shamanic initiation told most clearly: we follow the wanderings of the shaman Mara'akame through the lands of the other world, to the realm of the sun, where Tatewari, Our Ancestor, the first shaman in the world, reigns. The initiatory voyage of the apprentice shaman is truly a katabasis, a descent into hell: he crosses the region around the mountain range and arrives at a path which splits: the path to the left leads to punishment, reserved for Huichols who had sexual relations with the Spanish; the other path, under the watch of the black dog, the first companion of Watakame after the flood, leads to the tree of life, Xapa, laden with sexual organs, which feeds the souls of the dead. For the initiate the goal of this voyage is to obtain the help of Kauyumarie, the divine deer, the ancestor of men, in order to bring back the *uru kamé*, the rock crystal, symbol of the soul of the dead, the substance of their bones and life.[18]

The descent into hell is the expression of the cosmogonic system of pre-Columbian America, in which the universe is divided into three levels: sky, earth, and hell (or the underworld). These three kingdoms are symbolized by three forms of life: the bird, the tortoise or the snake, and the mole or the armadillo. In this tripartite system the underworld is obviously of greatest importance, for it is the place from which men emerged. The voyage to hell is thus a return to one's ancestors, to one's origins. The theme of emergence is found throughout middle America, among the Hopis of Arizona and the Pueblos of New Mexico, for whom the *kiva* is the symbol of man's subterranean birth; among the Maya, a natural well, or *cenote* (Uuc Yabnil, seven waters, later known as Chichén Itzá), was the conquering faction's (the Itzás) mythical place of origin. The origin of the Chichimeca peoples is an emergence myth which also evokes seven springs or caves. Jacinto de la Serna's *Treatise* provides a shamanic illustration of this theme of the birth of men: among the terms used by the ancient Aztec *nahualli* (sorcerers) to designate the woman's uterus is the expression "the seven caves," which reminds us of the legend of Chicomostoc.[19]

Emergence myths can perhaps be associated with the ancient theme of the earthly animal whose open mouth expels living creatures, a theme that is found in the artistic expression of many Central American peoples, including that of pre-Incan Peru.

Thus the initiatory voyage the shaman takes to the realm of the dead is the completion of a cycle. For the Huichol Indians, the world of the dead was the place where the sexual act took on its complete meaning. The descent into hell is a return to the entrails of the earth, to that underworld where life assumed its first form. This belief in the meeting up of dead ancestors and future souls found its complement in the regular and all-powerful movement of the stars, upon which man established his rhythm of life. It was no coincidence that when the ancient Maya invented their calendar, they accorded it with the rhythm of the planet Venus, whose cycle and heliacal setting and rising symbolized the life, death, and rebirth of the god Kukulcán.

Metamorphoses

The Amerindian myths of transformation do not seem to belong to the same cosmogonic system. Some of them are even directly inspired by the myths and fabulous tales which came from Europe: *Cinderella* and *Tom Thumb* among the Mazahua, or the Yaqui tale of the Dead Stepmother, modeled on the story by the Grimm brothers. Yet the theme of metamorphosis is strongly present in the mythology of the ancient Mexicans: there is the *nahual*, that animal-magician who is mentioned in Sahagun's book.[20] According to Molina [an early missionary who published the first Nahuatl dictionary], the *nahual* (from the Nahuatl verb *nahualcaqui*) was the one who entered hidden. One might naturally make a connection with the name of the Maya *balam*, which designated both the jaguar and the diviner priest, whose origin would be the same: from the verb *bal*, to be hidden. In the beginning the *nahual* was a sorcerer, a shaman, that "owl-man" mentioned in the *Codex Florentinus*, able to change his appearance. Huichol myths tell of the battle that Tatewari, Our Ancestor, the first shaman, had to wage against the magician Kieri, an adept in black magic and datura, who tricked his rival by metamorphosing himself. The magical duel is also the theme of theomachy, in particular in the legend of Quetzalcóatl, as told by Father Sahagun: the Toltec hero confronted the god Titlacaoan (Tezcatlipoca) and his necromancer's ruses, in a combat in which they changed their appearance.[21] Nagualism is at the heart of the religious beliefs of the ancient Mexicans, as is shown in the legends of the Nahuatl tradition, and in certain supernatural facts reported by the chroniclers (Francisco de Saliedo, for example). Metamorphosis is sometimes an element of a religious system, as among the Yucatecan Maya, where the sorcerer Bird (*Uayom chich*) designates an avatar of the Feathered Serpent, Kukulcán. It is often linked to a punishment for the transgressions of interdicts, as illustrated in a passage from the *Chronicles of Michoacán*[22] in which the men of the village of Xaracuaro were changed into snakes after eating that animal. A contemporary legend from the Tarascan village of Cheranastico portrays an old man punished for having ignored the same interdict.[23] Metamorphosis sometimes appeared as an evil spell, explaining the origin of evil: in a Tepehua tale, a witch who ate children is sentenced to be burned alive in the village oven. When the inhabitants open the oven door, the ashes that fly out are immediately transformed into mosquitoes, bees, and wasps that sting the men.[24]

In the theme of metamorphosis one finds the ancient myth of the werewolf, the *lobison*, so widespread in Spanish and Portuguese legends. It is a European tale which one sees in the Chinantecan story of the woman with two souls:[25] a man, attacked by a jaguar, cuts off one of its paws; he then discovers that the jaguar is his own wife.

The theme of vampires, so common in Europe (the Greek *broucolacos*) is practically unknown in Mexico, except in a clearly acculturated form, as in the Mazahua tale of the woman who flies off every night in the company of her mother secretly to drink the blood of children.[26] The very strong presence of bloody rituals dedicated to the gods surely explains the absence of the vampire in Mexican folklore. Huitzilopochtli, Tezcatlipoca, and especially the bloodthirsty Xipe Totec reveal the predator instinct that gives myths their strength. The most striking example of this is undoubtedly that of the goddess-mother Cuerauaperi, who, according to the belief of the ancient Purepecha, "took hold" of the spirit of her victims, "entered" into them, and partook of their blood.[27]

A diluted variation on the theme of metamorphosis and the *nahual* appears in the many man/animal associations of Amerindian folkloric tales: it is sometimes the union of a woman and a snake, as in the tale of the supernatural "lightning" snake in the folklore of the Mixe Indians of the northwest of Oaxaca,[28] or in the Kwawxochipixkeh, the lover/demons of contemporary Nahuatl folklore.[29] A strange example of this proximity between man and animal is shown in a tale of Mazahua folklore which brings to mind the beliefs of medieval Europe: a snake takes the place of a baby, sucks the mother's milk, and to calm the child, gives it its tail to suck. The husband discovers the scene, and when he kills the snake, his wife also dies.[30] Another example of the alliance between man and animal is found in the theme—probably unique in Mexican folklore—of the wild child. In a contemporary tale of the Purepecha of Uripicho (Michoacán), regarding the origin of honey, two children who have been abandoned by their mother are taken in by a lionness (a cougar) who raises them in her den. Later some hunters kill the adoptive mother, and the two brothers flee into the forest, where they discover wild honey and learn how to hunt. Then one of the brothers opposes the arrival of Christ in the form of a jaguar, and kills him. But the new religion enters into him through the magical powers of a chameleon who gives him the formula of prayer.[31]

The ogre is a variation of the werewolf theme, common in Mexican folklore. Characteristic of the mythical interpenetration of America and Western Europe, the theme of the ogre encountered that of the underworld: these are the tales of the "metis" folklore of Juan Oso (the Bear), or the tale of the *Green Bird*, found as far away as Texas. In this tale a young girl named Luisa goes to the House of the Sun, where an ogre lives. In search of the fabulous bird she goes as far as the moon, which is itself an ogress. The wind that pursues her is also an ogre. It appears that the ancient gods of the Aztec pantheon survived only in their predatory form.[32]

The old woman who ate children seems more linked to indigenous mythical bases: among the Tepehua, it was the old Tijasdaka-nidaku who concealed a newborn and had it cooked to prepare tamales (corn bread filled with meat).[33] R. H. Barlow has recorded a similar tale from the Nahuatl of Guerrero.[34] In the *Chronicles of Michoacán* the character of the old evil one is a goddess: Aui Camine, the gods' aunt, descends from the heavens, wearing a coarse weed skirt and, using her magic, changes a newborn into a mole, has it cooked by its mother, and gives it to its own father, the lord Hopotacu, to eat. Through this augury, the gods signify the coming destruction of Yzipamucu which will bring about the unification of Michoacán.[35]

The character of the old evil woman is very common in the folklore of middle America: she is the famous Llorona, a mixture of pre-Hispanic themes and European legends which is found in the creole regions of Mexico: Jalisco, Querétaro, and San Luis Potosí.[36] She is the Tule Vieja, in Central America and Colombia, dressed in white and walking backward to trick men. In Yucatán she is the X-Tabay, the ancient goddess of death by hanging. She is the Aztec's Coatli-cue, the lunar aspect of the goddess-mother, the "white woman" Father Sahagun mentions.[37]

Popular Tales

In Mexico, the popular tale is the result of that fusion of cultures which expresses the freest form of a myth, that is, the combination of a belief in the supernatural and a lesson in common wisdom. In the animal fables the most frequent hero (the one whom ethnographers call a "trickster") is the weak animal who opposes the strength or the meanness of its enemy. These are the countless tales of the coyote; the coyote and the rabbit, the coyote and the coati, the coyote and the mole, etc. In a typical tale, found in Jalisco, the coyote wants to eat young pigs, but their mother protests, under the pretext that they have not yet been baptized. The ceremony takes place with the coyote acting as godfather. He is immediately pushed into the water and beaten with a stick.[38] Other heroes play a role in these popular tales: the agouti among the Maya of Quintana Roo, the coati or the raven among the Nahuatl of Guerrero. The racing motif is one of the most frequent: a race between the grasshopper and the coyote (Mazahua), between the cricket and the puma (Tarahumara).

Many tales are inspired directly by European folklore: *Blancaflor*, whose heroine changes into a mermaid, *Cenicienta* and the *Pulgarcillo* of the Mazahua, which are simple transpositions of *Cinderella* and *Tom Thumb*. *Tata Juan*, from Tarascan folklore, seems to have been inspired directly by the *Thousand and One Nights* (*The Voyage of Sinbad*).[39] In the *Madrasta muerte* (The Dead Stepmother) the Grimm brothers' tale is entirely adapted to the shamanic beliefs of the Yaquis.[40] But most of the characters in popular tales have neither roots nor borders, as in the countless adventures of Pedro de Urdemalas, a character who has become typically Mexican despite his picaresque origins. Other heroes have found their place in the folklore of the New World: Juan el Flojo (the Lazy One), a modern adaptation of Apuleius's *The Golden*

Ass; Juan Cenizas (inspired by Perrault's *Puss in Boots*); Chico Miserias, who can trick the devil; *Alonso Zonzo,* who accumulates blunders; Juan Huevon (the Idiot), who manages to kill giants and marries the king's daughter; Juan Borrachales, the drunk who is tricked by his wife, who pretends to be dead (inspired by the *Thousand and One Nights*); or Queveo (Mon Diu! Que veo!), the typical fool; and finally Don Ca-cahuate, both naive and clever, the hero of Mexicans who emigrated to the "north."

In their purest form myths, not unlike tragedy, are perhaps the most important moment in the troubled history of Mexican civiliza-tion. The cement of dreams, the architecture of language, made of images and rhythms which respond to and harmonize with each·other through time and space, their wisdom is not of that which can be measured on the scale of the everyday. They are concurrently reli-gion, ritual, belief, phantasmagoria, and the primary affirmation of a human coherence, the coagulating strength of language against the anguish of death and the certainty of nothingness. Myths express life, despite the promise of destruction, or the weight of the inevitable. They are without any doubt the most durable monuments of men, in America as in the ancient world. This living force of myths is surely that which struck the Western traveler most in the first moments of his encounter with the Indians of Mexico, when that architecture was still intact, in all its magnificence and inner truth. It is that strength which animates the great books of Mexican legend—the *Codex Floren-tinus*, Father Sahagun's *History of Ancient Mexico*, the *Chronicles of Michoa-cán*, and the mysterious *Books of the Chilam Balam*.

Despite the disaster of the Conquest, despite the destruction an-nounced by auguries, that force has never ceased to exist. It still vi-brates in the work of Agustin Yañez, in the poetry of Gilberto Owen and Octavio Paz. It is that force above all which runs through the burning and solitary expanses of the writing of Juan Rulfo, like a sacred shiver. In the silence of *El llano en llamas*, in the violence of *Pedro Paramo*, one perceives the circular movement of time, the cruel harmony of chaos, the irony of the most ancient dreams of man.

It is in the rituals of the ancient Mexicans, as Bernardino de Sahagun describes them, that we find the greatest evidence of that
absolute of human creation, the living strength of myth:

This celebration was called Ixneztioa, which means "to search for good
luck" (fortune). It was their belief that on this festival all the gods were
dancing, and therefore all the natives who danced were dressed in diverse
fancy costumes; some impersonated birds, others different animals; some
represented the bird called "tzinitzcan," others butterflies; some dressed like
drones, others like flies, still others like beetles; some carried on their backs
a sleeping man, who, they said, represented sleep.[41]

4 Nezahualcóyotl, or the Festival of Words

THE POETRY OF THE WORLD surely does not show us a more contradictory, more mysterious poet than the one above, one who can instill (in us who read his songs at a distance of five hundred years) such fascination, blending the delight of an exalted and vibrant language with the anxiety of ambiguity, the impression of an uncertain, fugitive, and sometimes dazzling meaning like a reflection, a dream. It is, I believe, the primary charm of poetry to give the lesson of mirage, that is, to show the fragile and vibrant movement of creation, in which the word is in a certain way human quintessence, prayer.

Despite the abyss of time and the destruction which today separates us from the great Nezahualcóyotl, the "half-starved coyote," also called Yoyontzin, "he who ambles along," lord of the Acolhua people of Texcoco, if we can read these songs, hear them as if they were coming to us accompanied by the rhythm of drums and bells, with the shimmering plumes and masks, in the intoxicating perfume of copal, if their music and words can still move us, in a time when the pagan

This chapter was previously published as an introduction to *Chants de Nezahualcoyotl*, translated by Pascal Coumes and Jean-Claude Caer (Obsidiane-Unesco, 1985).

festival is only a distant remembrance in our unconscious memory, it
is perhaps mainly because of that contradiction, that uncertainty.

This Nezahualcóyotl, whom the first post-Conquest chroniclers—
Sahagun, and especially Fernando de Alva Ixtlilxóchitl, himself a de-
scendant of the lord of Texcoco—depict as the most just and the
most elevated lord of his time, but also as a profligate and domineer-
ing man who didn't hesitate to put Cuacuauhtzin to death in order to
marry his wife, but who on the other hand dictated the most accomplished code to govern his people and undertook works to protect
them from floods and to provide them with drinking water, enabling
them to survive on the banks of the saltwater lake: what was he really
like? An enlightened despot, the protector of the Acolhua people,
heir to the Toltec culture, a poet who transposed the words of the
ancient religious and warrior rhythms into the realm of lyric poetry,
a philosopher who imposed the symbolic cult of the unknown god,
Tloque in Nahuaque, master of the near and the far,[1] the creator of all
things, for whom, against the aggressive polytheism of the Aztecs,
Nezahualcóyotl had a temple raised decorated only with one starry
sky. But Nezahualcóyotl was also an ambitious politician, a lover of
power and of earthly pleasures, and like all the lords of Anáhuac, a
great provider of human victims for the altars of Huitzilopochtli, Tezcatlipoca, and the Tlalocs. There is something excessive and baroque
in the portrayal of the prince/poet which makes one think of the
Western Middle Ages, of the Frankish or Scandinavian kings, and
perhaps even more of the great Oriental princes in the time of Cyrus.
There was the same absolute military power (the Triple Alliance
which extended his kingdom from Guatemala to the deserts of northern Mexico, with the exception of the Mayan zone and the kingdom
of the Tarascan king, Zuangua); there was the same ostentatious
pomp, the same unspeakable cruelty exercised over the enslaved
peoples, and especially the same religious zeal, which inspired the
lord's every action and dictated his every word.

And yet that ostentatious and incantatory poetry which nobles
from the colleges (*calmecac*) recited in the king's court, surrounded by

the solemnity and the pomp of ritual festivals, thanks to Nezahualcóyotl takes on new meaning for us, a new grace; the only living
voice of that world destroyed by the Spanish Conquerors, this poetry
is also that of a simple man, who forcefully tells us the most moving
and truest things of everyday life: the fragility of friendship and love,
the passing of time, the insolent beauty of youth, its passion, its
ephemeral triumph, and always, that world sentenced to death and
destruction, under the watch of the god who created it:

> Dress yourself in flowers
> In flowers the color of the ara of the lakes,
> Brilliant as the sun,
> The flowers of the raven,
> Adorn yourself here on earth,
> Only here.
> It is thus
> Only for a brief moment,
> The flowers, for a moment,
> we have readied them:
> Already, we carry them to the god's home,
> To the home of the Fleshless.

What this tells us, without emphasis, but with all the symbolic
splendor of the Nahuatl language, in that musical and alliterative
rhythm which made it the most creative and most melodious language
of Indian America, resounds in us with the disturbing depth of a
prophecy. While he sings his hymn to youth and love, and makes us
hear, in his words, the rhythm of the Indian festival and its magical
power, Nezahualcóyotl is a young man, the prince of a powerful and
prosperous people, the equal of Montezuma Ilhuicamina, lord of
Mexico/Tenochtitlán, and of Totoquihuatzin, lord of Tlacopan [Ta-
cuba], chief of the fearsome warrior groups of Eagles and Jaguars, the
gods' representative on earth. He was thus the most famous and most
beloved of the poets of the Aztec aristocracy, he who truly invented
the elegy, as is stressed by José Luis Martinez in his beautiful biogra-

phy of Nezahualcóyotl, and who created the first Mexican literature, by separating it from collective myths and purely religious hymns.

And yet it is not glory or triumph that moves us here, but rather the doubt we can perceive in the songs of Nezahualcóyotl. We can indeed once again note the pessimism of the Indians of the high plateaus, of their obsession with death and the world of the "Fleshless." We can once again evoke those prophecies which troubled the history of all the Mexican nations, threatening the powerful of the land precisely when they were at the height of their glory. Moreover, doesn't Don Fernando de Alva Ixtlilxóchitl attribute to his illustrious ancestor the terms of a prophecy which at the time ran through all of middle America, from Yucatán to Michoacán, announcing that "the Lords will finish their reign; then the magueys, even young, will have large trunks, and the trees, even young, will bear fruit."[2]

There is all of that in Nezahualcóyotl's poetry, but there is above all a personal anxiety, an interrogation of himself and of the world which is the unique realm of literary creation. What touches us and moves us even today in that poetry from beyond time is the feeling of doubt which troubled that man and that civilization, already preparing them for the death that was coming. Scarcely fifty years after these songs were sung, after the festivals and oratory jousts during which each person confronted another by means of poetry and hymns, while musicians beat their drums and blew their trumpets, and while feathered dancers spun in the courtyards of palaces, death and destruction had come from the other side of the world. Less than fifty years after that cruel and poetic civilization had ended, its songs were covered by the anguished silence of the Conquest.

Today, despite the silence and the gulf of time, as if through a miracle, we can again hear the voice of Nezahualcóyotl, and in his voice the echo of a vanished art and faith, the murmur of a ceremony of the senses and of a festival of words. Gold, turquoise, jade lip rings, weapons made of obsidian, feather headdresses, and paper kites, flower garlands—all the symbolic beauty of that world joins in that festival, in that dance of life, in the intoxication of copal and the blood of the victims flowing over the earth.

Listening to these songs, one has the illusion of again hearing the obsessive rhythm of the drums and bells, the noise of dancers' feet pounding the ground, their bodies possessed by the gods, while warriors confront each other in portrayals of combat, warriors who bear the extraordinary names of the divinities of the sky and of heroes of the earth: Montezuma, the "Lord with a Furrowed Brow," Itzcóatl, the "Obsidian Snake," Citlacoatl, the "Snake of Stars," Cuauhtecohuatzin, the "Spread-Winged Eagle," Huitzilopochtli, the "Hummingbird Down," or Acamapichtli, the first king of Mexico, the "Stick of Commanding in his fist."

But beyond the festivals of song and of the gods, we hear a melody full of melancholy and truth, and it is that song which we continue to hear, the precious words of doubt:

> Not forever on earth,
> only a little while here.
> Though it be jade it falls apart,
> Though it be gold it wears away,
> Though it be quetzal plumage it is torn asunder.
> Not forever on earth,
> only a little while here.[3]

5 The Barbarian Dream

THE ORIGIN OF CIVILIZATION IS BARBARISM. Rather, it is because civilization opposes barbarism that it takes shape, is able to assert itself. The Egyptians, the Greeks, the Romans, then the Franks and the Saxons could dream of a world in which barbarians, those nomads who threatened their borders, would be definitively removed. They, too, were destroyed by the very ones they despised.

We can imagine how fascinated the sedentary peoples were by those barbarians who represented the end of their civilization. It was a fascination in the presence of the unknown, but also, surely, in the presence of a dreamed-of freedom, and the manifestation of a secret desire that would abolish order and legality. For policed nations, barbarian peoples lived naked and free, in anarchy, without constraint, unaware of decency or religious and moral prohibitions. The civilized man's scorn for the barbarian has as corollaries admiration, envy, a sort of repressed aspiration.

The barbarian is above all a free man. A nomad, he appears held by no social organization or rules. Above all, he does not appear to be attached to any form of work whatsoever. This is a long-lived image of the original predator, to whom man is instinctively connected; he is constantly wandering, finding sustenance in hunting, pillaging, and war. He knows only the earth he pounds with his feet, and his horizon has no boundaries. He has no land or country; his home is wherever he sets up camp, for a season, a night, or only a moment of rest. Having no possessions, he knows neither fear nor envy. Living constantly with uncertainty, he has no fear of death, and the hardships of his wandering existence do not allow him to be wrong about himself or others. Friendship, the trustworthiness of his fellows are his only values, and those values are unshakable, steeped in adversity and tribulations. In a barbarian society each man is his own master, owing no tax nor tithe, able to take care of himself. He must simultaneously be a warrior, a doctor, a priest, and the head of his family. He must never know the weaknesses and vices of policed men, and his body must be equal to the pitiless landscape which surrounds him; resistant to fatigue and inclement weather, able in combat and quick to flee, endowed with hearing, sight, and smell comparable to those of wild animals, guided by an infallible instinct. For the barbarian the intelligence of the civilized man could only be a weakness. On the contrary, the speed and exactness of his reflexes, his immediate awareness of danger are guarantees of his survival. Reason and conscience cannot be his guides. His notion of good and evil is instinctive, without hesitation or ambiguity. The barbarian is not immoral; he is beyond all morality, in that sort of original purity which is at the legendary sources of life.

The nomadic barbarian did not define himself in relation to the civilized man. The very characteristic of the barbarian nations of North America was in space: to be more precise, in the immensity of the lands they occupied. When the Spanish arrived in the sixteenth and seventeenth centuries, the agricultural policed empires of Mesoamerica appeared to be enclaves in that great expanse. Beyond the limits of the vassal realms of the Triple Alliance of Mexico/Tenochtitlán, of the empire of the Purepecha cazonci Zuangua, there began a wild, uncultivated land which went from the Atlantic to the Pacific and extended as far as the Great North, that is, a territory more vast than all of Europe. Desert America, peopled with nomadic barbarians, included the largest part of the Spanish colony, from the Rio Lerma to the sources of the Rio Grande, and from the coasts of Texas to those of California. The barbarian nations were countless. Nations such as the Guachichiles and the Pame, and the Cora of the Mesa del Nayar, and simple warrior factions to which the Spanish gave whimsical names: Cueros Quemados, Coje Piedras de Chihuahua, Bocas Negras, or Come Perros de Jimenez. It was a countless population the Conquerors found upon their arrival, a true dust cloud of nations which were perhaps proof of the breaking up of ancient rural societies from the East who became predators out of necessity and following the development of weapons. A dust cloud of nations with strange names, almost all of which are gone today: Acaxee, Ahome, Chinipa, Guazapari, Hiaqui, Huite, Mayo, Nassa, Nebome, Opata, Papago, Parras Pima, Sauaripa, Seri, Sicuraba, Sinaloa, Sisibotari, Tarahumara, Tegueco, Tepehuane, Temori, Varohío, Xixime, Zoe, Zuaque, in the north-west, Ape, Arigame, Bobota, Canome, Catujane, Chacahuale, Chinipa, Chinguaguane, Concho, Cora, Cocoyome, Conejero, Cuampe, Hueiquechale, Huichol, Guazapari, Guazarachi, Gualaguise, Ihio, Joxica, Julime, Jano, Jumia, Mescal, Milixae, Mamite, Ocane, Orejone, Otaquitanome, Pajalme, Panana, Pamate, Pauilane, Parchae, Papule, Pastaloca, Sibolo, Suma, Supi, Temori, Tinti, Tocho, Tilixae, Tzonpanale, Toboso, Tubare from the central desert, and farther north, the Piro, Apache, Lipan, Chiricahua, Gileño, Mimbreño, Faraone, and the Comanche, Penateca, Taovayace, Tanimu, Juacane, Ovae, Xaraname, to the peoples of the East, the "Texas," Ais, Assinai, Olive, Nacogdoche, all of them untamed, indomitable, and "the best archers in the world."[1] Out of scorn, fear, and derision, the Conquerors gave those barbarian nations insulting nicknames: *desnudos* [the naked ones], *infieles* [the pagans], *gandules* [the rootless], *borrados*, or *rayados* ([the scarred ones] because of body painting or tribal scars).

The barbarians were free, they lived in space. They lived in caves, in huts made of branches, sometimes in pisé houses. Having for the most part no knowledge of agriculture, they had no sense of land ownership. Their realm was one of hunting, which changed with the game they sought. The progressive disappearance of the bison led the Apache, Comanche, Utah, and Paiute hunters to the regions where new prey was found: horses, mules, and the cows of the Spanish colonists. A countless, moving group, the barbarians from the north and northwest lived in a permanent state of war, which was both the reason for their power and the cause of their demise. If due to their weapons and mobility they were at first invincible, their incessant rivalries, their inability to form alliances, and their savagery subsequently rendered them easily open to corruption and to the isolation of a modern world.

The Chichimeca

It was the Chichimeca who began the barbarian dream of Mexico. If we know only very little about the Chichimeca nations—since nations as different as the Otomi Pames, the Uto-Aztecan Huichols or Guachichiles, and the Athapascan Apaches are all grouped under that name—at least we are certain of the ancientness of their civilization. The Chichimeca came from the north and formed the ethnic reservoir out of which emerged most of the tribes which were to form the rural societies of Mesoamerica. The first chroniclers, and particularly Fernando de Alva Ixtlilxóchitl and Fernando de Alvarado Tezozomoc, tell of the same legend of Aztlan and the seven caves of Chicomostoc out of which came the eponymous heroes, founders of the principal Mexican civilizations: Xelhua, Tenuch, Ulmecatl, Xicalancatl, Mixtecatl, Otomitl. The same legend, told by the Lienzo de Jucutacato [an early-seventeenth-century painting on canvas found in Michoacán at the end of the nineteenth century] and by the principal Spanish chroniclers, Motolinia, Beaumont, and Duran, associates the ancient Purepecha with the myth of emergence from Aztlan. As for the *Chronicles of Michoacán*, it confuses the Uacusecha, the last to arrive

on the site of Lake Patzcuaro, with the Chichimeca. Having undoubtedly come from the north, the Uacusecha, the "Eagles," a barbarian
people living from the hunt and from war, settled on the banks of the
lake, conquered the fishermen/farmers who were living there, and out
of their alliance in the thirteenth century one of the most powerful
empires of middle America was born, one which came to an end in
1530 with the death of the cazonci Tangaxoan Zincicha at the Spanish stake. The founding of Tzintzuntzan and Patzcuaro shares the
history of the establishment of Tenochtitlán in that it was the culminating moment of the barbarian peoples, those Chichimeca who were
as capable at warfare as in the hunt, one which enabled the emergence of the most civilized societies of Mexico. From their nomadic
origins, there nevertheless remained an aggressive and warlike character in the nobility who dominated neighboring groups. The very
origin of the barbarian peoples who came from the north to conquer
the rural nations of middle America gave its character to that "arid"
civilization which then merged with the more fertile regions.

Origins

In Mexico, the barbarian dream began with myth. The origin of the
Aztecs of Mexico/Tenochtitlán and that of the Purepecha of Tzintzuntzan are found in that northern desert, that legendary Aztlan—
Aztatlan, the land of cranes out of which came, at the beginning of
the historical era, in year One Reed, the first inhabitants of Chicomostoc. The famous *Crónica mexicayotl*, by Tezozomoc, places the origin of the Mexican people in that wild country where the Chichimeca
reigned: *Yancuic Mexico*, New Mexico, a desert and hostile land which
at the time of the Spanish Conquest became a dreamland, Eldorado.
Aztlan, "which is in the middle of the waters," was above all a mythical land, the place of emergence, associated with the ancient themes
of genesis and the flood. The seven caves of Chicomostoc, from
which the seven *calpulli* were born, at the time evoked the seven cities
of Cibola [similar to Eldorado], places of mystery and fortune, all the

more dazzling in that they rose out of the poverty of the desert. The first voyagers could not miss the relationship between that myth of emergence and the subterranean sanctuaries (*estufas*, or *kivas*) of the Pueblo Indians.

Having emerged from the desert of pre-birth, the Chichimeca nation left the maternal breast to set out on a voyage which led it to its promised land. During that exodus, the Aztecs (people of Aztlan) were guided by their divine hero, the great Tetzahuitl Huitzilopochtli, the Hummingbird of the Left (the south) who taught them the art of war and how to wield the bow and arrow. The *Crónica mexicayotl* sketches a realistic portrait of these first barbarian migrants, in which one can already recognize the Chichimeca described by Father Tello or Father Andrés Perez de Ribas: "And there, in Quinehuayan, the rock is called Chicomoztoc, for it is pierced with holes in seven places, open caves on the steep mountain; and the Mexicans came out of there and brought their wives with them when they left from Chicomoztoc, in couples. This place was frightful because countless ferocious beasts lived there: the *cuetlachtl* bear, the *ocelotl* jaguar, the cougar, snakes, and Chicomoztoc was filled with agave thorns and weeds. And since that place was very remote, no one knew where it was. Thus those who came from there to here spoke of it, those who are called the *teochichimecas*. Thus when they left from there to come here: everywhere there were forests, mountains, canyons, everywhere were cactus, green reeds, thistle, agave, weeds, *cuilotales* [a kind of bush]. For when they came here, they came on foot, and the prey they shot with their arrows and ate were deer, rabbit, ferocious beasts, snakes, birds. They came here wearing their leather loincloths, and they fed on everything they could find to eat. For it was here that they had been summoned by he whom they were carrying, their burden, he whom they adored."[2]

The Chichimeca *teomamas* ["godbearers"], carrying their god Huitzilopochtli on their backs enclosed in a chest, walking from their place of origin toward the unknown lands of the south, symbolized the walk of the barbarians toward the sites of the future empires. On the high plateau of Anáhuac they founded the city of Tenochtitlán, at first as a group of four: "A person by the name of Iztac Mixcoatzin, a second person named Apanecatl, a third called Tetzcacoatl, and the fourth, a woman called Chimalma."[3] Then came the alliance of the Thirteen Lords, who founded the city, dividing it into four parts which corresponded to the structure of the universe and was connected to the creation of the ancient calendar of the mother-civilizations of the northeast. At its birth, the city of Mexico/Tenochtitlán was the symbol of the four parts of the world: Moyotlan (San Juan), Teopan (San Pablo), Tzocualo (San Sebastian), and Cuepopan (Santa Maria la Redonda). In his chronicle, Fernando de Alva Ixtlilxóchitl designates as founder of the Toltec, Mexican, and Acolhua lineages "a first king named Chichimecatl, who was the one who led them to the New World where they settled."[4]

The Chichimeca *teomamas*, crossing mountains and deserts while carrying their god, evoke the "Ancestors of the Road" in the *Chronicles of Michoacán*; they also evoke the war festivals of the Purepecha religion, during which the gods were led to battle, carried on the backs of the *thiumencha* priests. The first Uacusecha nomads to arrive in the region of Zacapu, the warriors of King Ticatame, were also guided by their god Curicaueri, whom they carried on their shoulders.

The Hunters

The *Chronicles of Michoacán*, the story of the founding of the Pure empire by the Uacusecha (called "Chichimeca" throughout the book) is one of the most precious documents on the arrival of the barbarian migrants at the beginning of the historical era. Those men, who spoke the Pure language, whose origin is very mysterious, through their customs, religion, and war techniques indeed had something in common with the other nomadic tribes who peopled the center and the west of Mexico. Nomads, living essentially from hunting and gathering, the Uacusecha reached the Michoacán territory around the middle of the thirteenth century, under the command of their king, Ticatame. The first king was thus truly the chief of a barbarian people who had no knowledge of agriculture. His military strength, bolstered by the superiority of Chichimeca weaponry—perfected bows and arrows, undoubtedly a knowledge of poisons—as well as by battle tactics, intimidation, faking, aggressiveness, enabled that chief of a minimal tribe to take over the seignories of the sedentary peoples of the region of Zacapu. The Uacusecha's advance into the Michoacán was thus unstoppable. Carrying the ancient god Curicaueri, whose return was perhaps awaited by the sedentary Purepecha, the troops of Ticatame spread the same terror as the Chichimeca warriors of Mixton would do two hundred years later. The behavior of those mysterious invaders was the very portrait of the barbarian warrior who would dominate the north of Mexico until the eve of modern time. Arrogant and cruel, he imposed his law on those he dominated, and his religious faith accepted no compromise: "There was one thing [Ticatame] wanted to tell [the Zizanbanecha]. 'Tell your Masters, as they already know, that as I and my people go into the mountains to gather wood for the temples and I make arrows, I go to the fields to give food to the Sun, and to the celestial gods and those of the Four Quarters of the world; also to Mother Cuerauaperi with the deer which we shoot. I make the salve to the gods with wine after which we drink in his name.'"[5] The ritual of a *salva*—the offering of the first hunt—to the gods on the hunting grounds evokes the most ancient propitiatory rituals—practiced both by the nomads of the north (Comanches, Apaches, Sioux) and by the semi-sedentary tribes of the Mayan plain—the survival of which among the Aztecs has been noted.[6] The warning not to take the deer meant for the gods, and the ignoring of that warning by Ticatame's brothers-in-law, which led to war, shows well the nature of the confrontation between the culture of the sedentary farmers and that of the nomadic hunters, which was to give birth to the Pure people. One might assume the existence among that barbarian warring faction of a cult of deer perhaps similar to that practiced by the Huichol Indians of Nayarit.[7] The legend told in the *Chronicles of Michoacán* of Cupanzieri, who was changed into a deer after his death,[8] perhaps gives evidence of a cult of the deer ancestor identical to that of many barbarian nations of the north and the northwest—Mayo, Yaqui, Pima, or Parras—as described by Father Perez de Ribas, all of whom practiced a cult of deer heads associated with peyote rituals.[9]

The "Desnudos"

In the portrait of the Uacusecha, those violent and virtuous people who were the first to arrive, everything evokes the Chichimeca culture as it was described by the Spanish witnesses: it was a society reduced to a clan, whose chief exercised his authority over his extended family. Those of the Eneani, Uanacase, Zacapuheti, and Aparicha lines probably formed endogamic groups, as opposed to the indefinite populations of the sedentary seigniories in which exchanges and mixtures were easier. One of the vestiges of this clan structure appeared at the time of the first institutions which favored the unification of the empire: the king (later called cazonci, under the growing influence of the Nahuatl world) was surrounded by the *quanguariecha* nobles, elite warriors most probably dedicated to the cult of the god Urendecuauecara, *"dios del lucero"* [god of the Morning Star], that is, of the planet Venus, and whom the king considered as "his lords."[10] Until the fall of the empire, the *quanguariecha* were chosen exclusively from among the lineages of the Chichimeca invaders, thus insuring the purity of the line. The kings themselves were chosen from the family of the first Conqueror, Ticatame, which was connected to the supreme god Curicaueri through a pact whose "stone of power" (the obsidian matrix out of which sacrificial knives were made) was the unique symbol. Therefore the *Chronicles of Michoacán* comes to us as the single original Indian document consecrating the value and nobility of the barbarians, and celebrating the beneficial alliance of the nomads and the sedentary peoples.

Other cultural traits connected the Uacusecha and the barbarian peoples of the north. Like the nomads of the desert zone, the Uacusecha were primarily hunters and gatherers. When King Tariacuri wanted to put his son Hiquingare and his nephews Tangaxoan and Hiripan to the test, he sent them into the mountains so they could gather their thoughts in solitude and learn to "eat the grasses." His nephews wandered for a long time before their uncle found them, and the *Chronicles of Michoacán* describes their gathering wild plants; they ate "weeds, the kind that are called *apupataxaqua* (chayote leaves), *acumba, patoque, coroche,* and *zimbico,* even one called *sirumata* (hemp to make ropes). There were none that they did not eat."[11] Fasting and the trial of solitude in the mountains were rites of passage among nomadic societies. Similarly, the *Chronicles of Michoacán* sketches the portrait of a society with a limited familial structure, monogamous, living without slaves, which was undoubtedly the one which dominated Michoacán until the time of Tariacuri (around 1370–1450). The Uacusecha society, at the beginning of the conquest of Michoacán, does not seem very different from those of the warriors from the north, the *teochichimecas,* the *zacachichichimecas,* those "men of wood," monogamous, virtuous, and combative, whom Father Sahagun evokes in his work.[12]

One of the characteristic traits of the barbarians was nudity. As opposed to the prudish civilization of the Spaniards, the *desnudos,* as the Conquerors called them, were symbols. Those hardened warriors who went nude in the harshest climates symbolized the virile force and the purity of Eden. It was they, and not the subjects of the great Mesoamerican kingdoms, who would engender the theme of the noble savage. It was also they who symbolized the indigenous myth of the Golden Age, as transcribed by the *Chronicles of Michoacán:* we have the portrait of the virtuous heirs of Tariacuri—Hiripan, Tangaxoan, and Hiquingare—whom the *Chronicles* oppose to the decadent chiefs in the time of the last kings of Michoacán, Zuangua and Tangaxoan Zinchicha: "Look, you chiefs, those who were Masters of the Chichimeca were raised in great poverty." The extravagance of costume and ornament (jewels, lip rings) was synonymous with lies and corruption: "Now you are chiefs with large lip rings which stretch your lips so that you seem more important. It would be better for you to put on masks, for you put on airs with such large lip rings. You all wear skins, never leaving them off or undressing yourselves but always going about in skins. You will never take any captives. If you were the valiant men that you ought to be, you would take them off, and you would put some blankets on your naked backs when you work. You would take your bows and arrows, put on your war jackets, for that is the way your God Curicaueri does."[13]

Many of the Spanish chroniclers were struck by the physical beauty of those men who lived nude, and whose hair fell to their backs. The wild appearance of the barbarians, their agility and their resistance to fatigue, rather than making them supermen, connected them to the animal kingdom. The Guachichiles, the Coras, the Seris, the Tepehuanes, and later the Apaches and the Comanches, were believed to be close to nature. Speaking of the Seris in the *Cartas Anuas*, the Jesuits of the eighteenth century emphasized the animal-like aspect of the Indians: they were "light without the encumberment of clothing" and "naturally fit for the hunger, the thirst, the heat, and the fiery sands of this land."[14] For Father José Ortega, it was the very nature of the land and the climate that kept the Indians in their wild state, in "their barbarism made naturally from laziness."[15] The scorn most of the Spanish Conquerors felt for the *gandules*, the *desnudos*, was based on their conviction that the Indians did not truly belong to the human race. It was that belief which justified the war "of fire and blood," slavery, and the despoiling of the Indian land. And religious figures did not escape such prejudice. The Jesuits felt the Seris had to be exterminated: "Until their entire race is extinguished," they wrote in 1753, "there will be no possible hope for tranquility or lasting peace."[16] According to Father Perez de Ribas, the barbarians were "stupid animals," who through their nudity and violence evoked man after the fall.[17]

The Best Archers in the World

What is striking in these early portraits of the barbarians is the savagery of their warring societies. Living nude, young boys were trained at a very young age to hunt and wage war, and to wield arms. According to Sahagun, the Chichimeca were truly *tamime*, "that is, bow and arrow shooters."[18] The dexterity of the Indians of the barbarian nations was a subject of amazement for the Spanish Conquerors. In the hands of the Chichimeca that archaic weapon, constructed from primitive materials (rope made of vegetal fibers, arrowheads of obsidian or flint), could rival the perfected weaponry of the Spaniards—arquebuses, crossbows with grappling hooks, cannons. In fact, in the sixteenth and seventeenth centuries the Chichimeca bow achieved an unequaled perfection, as Paul Kirchhoff and José de Jesus Davila Aguirre have pointed out: the arrow was made of an *asta* (shaft) of reed, light and straight, upon which the *anteasta* (the head) made of hardwood was mounted. It carried a point of barbed stone, which was tied down with tendons (often ritually extracted from the back of human victims) and with a glue extracted from the root of wild orchids (*chautle*). The fiber cord was fixed to the bow only at the last moment to prevent its being strained.[19] The power and dexterity of the archers was astonishing: "They are so adept at archery," wrote Antonio de Ciudad Real, "that before the arrow reaches its target, another is already leaving the bow, and another, and yet another. And they are so adept and aim so well that if they aim for the eye and hit the eyelid, they say that was a bad shot." The power of the bow as wielded by the Chichimeca and the making of it had a sacred connection. The same chronicler adds: "All the Chichimeca, men, women, and children, are warriors, for they all help each other in making bows and ammunition, and it is remarkable that each Chichimeca nation distinguishes itself by its arrows, in the shape and the mark they bear, so that, just as they differ in their languages, they also differ in the appearance of their arrows. The first, second, and even the third shot from a Chichimeca bow have such force that their effect is almost equal to that of an arquebus, since with one arrow they can pierce right through an entire steer, and we have seen arrows go through four layers of coats of mail and nail a soldier's thigh to the two sides of his saddle."[20]

The power of the Chichimeca bow was so fearsome that in the Nayarit wars [the wars which, near the end of the sixteenth century, led to the conquest of the western highlands] the barbarian warriors (Coras, Tecuals) could make a mockery of the firearms of the Spaniards, "which were often like fireworks which did no more harm than emit the noise of an explosion."[21] The use of natural poisons, known throughout the north and northwest of Mexico, made this weapon even more fearsome. Poisoned traps were set on enemy paths: "They had great knowledge of all sorts of herbs and roots," writes Sahagun, "of their qualities and virtues, and of the most poisonous which immediately killed people."[22]

The *Chronicles of Michoacán*, the tale of Uacusecha warriors, sketches a portrait of the bellicose virtues exalted among the first invaders of Michoacán. Ticatame, Sicuirancha, and Pauacume, wandering in the still wild mountains of northwestern Michoacán, were then only chiefs of a nomadic tribe looking for new hunting grounds, moving around while carrying their god Curicaueri, going to war with the sedentary tribes. When Vapeani and Pauacume finally discovered the banks of Lake Patzcuaro, there was a veritable cultural exchange that took place between the fishers/farmers of Uranden and the Chichimeca predators. The sedentary Indians discovered the taste of wild game, and the hunters that of fish. Other things were learned from the Chichimeca: the art of tanning skins, the wielding of a bow, battle tactics, and above all, the monotheist cult of Curicaueri, the god of fire. As among the peoples of the north, each Chichimeca faction had its own distinctive arrow, and Ticatame had no difficulty recognizing the deer that his brothers-in-law had wrongfully taken for themselves.[23] The art of archery was carried to its highest level, long after the settling down of the Uacusecha. When King Tariacuri sought an alliance with Zurumban, lord of Tariaran Harocutin, there was a feat of archery that sealed their friendship. Noticing a hummingbird perched on a flower, Zurumban challenged Tariacuri: "Shoot it, sire! Since you are a Chichimeca. Shoot it." And faced with Tariacuri's dexterity which enabled him to stun the bird without even hurting it, Zurumban cried out: "You are indeed a Chichimeca for this bird is not easy to shoot for it is so small. How can anyone compete with you? You do not miss a shot, and no one can compete with you."[24] The very appearance of the Purepecha kings, as described by Cervantes de Salazar and by Father Beaumont, evokes the barbarian splendor of the war chiefs from the north, such as the Sinaloa Sisibotari, described by Father Andrés Perez de Ribas: "He was handsome and still young, wore a long cloak attached at his shoulder like a cape, and his loins were covered with a cloth, as was the custom of that nation. On the wrist of his left arm, which holds the bow when the hand pulls the cord to send the arrow, he wore a very becoming marten skin."[25]

Barbarian Myths and Religions

It is certainly in its conception of the cosmos that the Chichimeca civilization differs most from the cultural theocracies of middle America. Here again the *Chronicles of Michoacán* is a precious document for understanding the religious rituals of the nomadic tribes at the beginning of the historical era. The *Chronicles* provide a vast quantity of details on the rituals and beliefs of the Uacusecha Chichimeca. Although the loss of the first part of this document prevents an exact reconstruction of Purepecha cosmogony and its calendar,[26] it is nevertheless possible to note some general traits of a religion common to most of the wandering nations of the desert zone, the "Arid Culture" Paul Kirchhoff speaks of.[27] These traits are: the cult of arrows, in relation to a solar cult; the division of the world into Four Quarters, symbolized by four colors; stellar cults, particularly of Venus and the Pleiades; ritual war; cults of deer; the cult of sacrificial stones, and of the obsidian matrix; the cult of the eagle; ritual anthropophagy and the cult of bones; rituals of incense and tobacco pipes; hallucinatory rituals, sometimes the use of drugs such as peyote, mushrooms, or datura; the importance of prophecies and dreams, which often resulted in messianic movements; and the continuation, throughout most of the barbarian zones, of the "holy war" against the Christian invaders, perhaps as a continuation of ritual wars. These are the traits which characterized the barbarian nations up to modern times, and which differentiated them from sedentary societies. They enable the reconstruction of a religious entity, the chief characteristic of which was mystical, which for a long time thwarted the efforts of the Conquerors and the Christian missionaries.

The Sun

The sun was probably the primary divinity among most of the barbarian nations of the north and northwest. The Chichimeca, reports de Alva Ixtlilxóchitl, "had no idols: they called the sun father and the earth mother."[28] In the region of Acambaro, the Chichimeca (Pames, Guamares), along with the Otomis, practiced a cult of the sun-god. Farther north, the Tepehuanes, the Coahuilas, the Apaches, and the Comanches practiced a cult of the father-god, the sun, to whom they offered blood, incense, and tobacco.[29] The Aztec cult of the sun, perhaps inherited from their barbarian past, is described by Father Sahagun.[30] The young warrior was consecrated to the sun during the ceremony of the *tepochcalli* (the house of youth), in the course of which he committed himself to "give food and drink to the sun and the earth with the blood of his enemies." Tonatiuh, the sun-god, was "he who walks in splendor" and the Aztecs also called him the "heart of the sky."[31] In Nayarit, the cult of the sun was associated with ritual war and with the wielding of arrows. The Coras of the Mesa del Nayar were directed by a great priest named Tonati, guardian of the idol Tayaoppa, father of the living, venerated in the form of a white stone once given by the sun and deposited in the place called Toacamota, to whom the Indians offered arrows instead of prayers.[32] In the *Chronicles of Michoacán*, one finds many allusions to a solar cult, associated with war rituals, probably representing the religious heritage of the barbarian Uacusecha.

The Cult of Arrows

The relationship between the solar cult and arrows is an important aspect of the Chichimeca cultures from the north. Torquemada, referring to the lost work of Father Andrés de Olmos, tells of a legend of the creation of the world among the people of Texcoco which perhaps provides a key to this relationship. According to the legend, man was born from an arrow sent by the sun, which pierced a hole in the earth, out of which came the first creature.[33] The genesis of the world as described in the *Codex Chimalpopoca* associates the arrow with the division of the world into colors and directions: "A yellow eagle, a yellow jaguar, a yellow snake, a yellow rabbit, a yellow deer. Shoot an arrow into Huitztilán (toward the place of thorns, to the south), into Huitznahuatlalpan (toward the ground without thorns), into Amilpan (toward the irrigation field), and into Xochitlalpan (the flowering land), and there you will shoot a red eagle, a red jaguar, a red snake, a red rabbit, a red deer. And when you have finished shooting arrows, put the bow in the hands of Xiuhtecuhtli, the lord of fire, [also called] Huehueteotl, the old fire god."[34] The cult of arrows is probably connected to the worship of the obsidian or flint matrix used to make sacrificial knives. The divinity itself was present in the stone knife, which then symbolized supreme power, sealed by the exchange of blood between man and his celestial masters. In the *Chronicles of Michoacán* this cult is forcefully present. When King Tariacuri hands power over to his son Hiquingare and to his nephews Tangaxoan and Hiripan, it is in the form of that stone—the *padra*, the hard stone from which the sacrificial knives of the god Curiacaueri were made: "I want to give you a part of Curicaueri. This is one of the stone knives that he carries with him, and you will wrap it in blankets and take it there, for it is for him that you will bring wood, that you will establish a camp and build an altar where you will place this knife."[35] It was that stone, symbol of divine power, that Zizispandaquare, the son of Tangaxoan, hid from his half brother Ticatame, so that he might reign as absolute master of Michoacán. It was undoubtedly the same stone that the barbarian Acaxees of Sinaloa revered in the form of a "large knife of natural flint, which they venerated so that the flint points of their arrows would never fail."[36] The rapport between man and the sun thanks to messages from arrows appears in the barbarian rituals of the Aztec festival of fire, *Toxiuhmolpilia*, the festival of the end of the cycle during which an enemy warrior (*otomi*) by the name of Xiuhtlamin (according to Garibay, "he who shoots an arrow into the fire") was sacrificed on Uixachtlan, where the new fire appeared.[37]

The *Chronicles of Michoacán* confirm the Chichimeca cult of divine arrows: when King Ticatame is threatened with death by his brothers-in-law, the Masters of Zizaban, he cries, "Very well, let them come. I have four kinds of arrows and they shall have a taste of them, especially of those that have black, white, red, and yellow flints called *hurespondi*. I, likewise, shall sample the sticks that they fight with to see what they taste like."[38] Arrowheads, dedicated to the sun (*hurhiata*) and associated with the colors of the four quarters of the world, had their ritual characteristics. It was those same arrows that King Tariacuri gave to his heirs as a sign of power, in order to assure them victory in battle: "These arrows are the gods. With each one of them, our god Curicaueri kills, and he does not release two arrows in vain."[39] The sacred character of arrows, messages from men to the sun and the celestial divinities, was one of the most important themes in the religion of the Cora and the Huichol Indians of Nayarit. To pray to the solar idol, tells Father Ortega, "they all brought arrows wearing pearl necklaces and feathers, so that the chief priest would offer them in their name."[40] Like sacrificial knives, the flint arrowheads were parts of the gods. The Sicurabas of the Carantapa mission worshiped idols "in the form of large flint knives which they used to make the points of their arrows, where, according to what they said, the demon had made a pact so they would be victorious in their wars."[41] The same arrow cults were reported by missionaries of Coahuila at the end of the eighteenth century; in Nayarit, the cult of the god Tajadsi was carried out by offering "handfuls of arrows" in which were found a large arrow portraying the god himself.[42] When the chief priest Tonati of the Mesa del Nayar surrendered to the viceroy in Mexico City, it was in the form of a sacred arrow that he brought his submission.[43]

Fire

Curicaueri, the supreme god of the Uacusecha Chichimeca, whom they carried with them and who guided them in their long exodus to Michoacán, was one of the most ancient evidences of a cult of fire. Among the Aztecs, Xiuhtecuhtli, the lord of fire, known also as Huehueteotl, the old fire god, is proof of a similar cult, which undoubtedly became secondary following the settling of the Mexica, and the development of agrarian rituals. Among the Purepecha, Curicaueri was he who was "engendered high above," the one whom the gods of the sky sent to earth for men to serve him, with the smoke of the sacred pyres and blood sacrifices. Men owed him "straps and hatchets" to carry wood, and "work in the field and war squadrons." Curicaueri was the one who "made his flames in the center of the house of the chief priests, the one for whom the pyres continuously burned." The festival of war, Hantsinansquaro, was a stellar ritual dedicated to the god of fire, the symbol of life at the end of the Venusian cycle. The prayer transcribed in the *Chronicles of Michoacán* is one of the rare testimonies to that cult: "Thou God of Fire who hast appeared in the midst of the houses of the chief priests, perhaps there is no virtue in this wood which we have brought to the temples or in these fragrances which we have here to give thee—receive them, thou who art called primarily Morning of Gold and thou Urendecuauecara, God of the Morning Star, and thou who hast the Reddish Face. See how contrite the people are who have brought this wood for you."[44]

The cult of the new fire, associated with the cycles of the universe, was clearly the symbol of one of the most ancient religions of middle America, a trace of which we discover both among the Aztecs (Cuecaltzin, the "flame of fire" and Yxcocauhqui, "the yellow face")[45] and among the Maya, who venerated Kinich Kakmo, the Ara of fire, god of Izamal. The god of fire and war, Curicaueri received his tribute of perfumes and smoke, and when they took him with them, the Uacusecha wrapped him up to protect him from the cold. In the north, the Taovayace Comanches practiced a cult of fire, and the Pueblos of New Mexico kept a flame constantly burning in their *kivas*.[46] The Indians of the Parras mission associated the ritual sacrifice of a deer with the cult of fire. The bones and blood of the deer were thrown into the flames, the smoke of which symbolized union with the world of the deceased.[47]

Festivals of War

The major rituals in the religion of the ancient Purepecha of Michoacán were the "festivals of war," Cuingo, Hicuandiro, and Hantsinansquaro. These violent, bloody festivals were related to the rituals of the "flowered war" of the Aztecs, but the Purepechas' ritual was so strong and so elaborate that we might assume an influence of the Michoacán civilization over Anáhuac. In fact, we probably have evidence here of a trait common to the two cultures which strongly suggests the reality of a nomadic Chichimeca civilization predating the founding of the sedentary empires. The most important of these festivals was Hantsinansquaro, associated with the cult of the new fire and probably with the cycle of Venus (the "heliacal" rising of the planet). Hantsinansquaro (perhaps from the verb *uantsikuarhani*, to turn) was a cosmic festival celebrating a change linked to the calendar: "The priests who carry the gods on their backs, and play the trumpets in the high temples, after looking at a star in the sky, build huge fires in the houses of the chief priests."[48] The prayer of the priest Hiripati was addressed to the god Urendecuauecara, whose other name, Khuangari, designated the star itself.[49] The festival of Hantsinansquaro brings to mind the cults of the god Kukulcán among the Maya, in which the return of the stellar god was celebrated after his long hiding in Hell, or yet the legend of the Toltec god Quetzalcóatl, as told in the *Anales de Cuauhtitlan:* "The ancients said that he was converted into this star which appears at dawn; thus, according to what they say, Quetzalcóatl appeared when he died; and for this reason they called him the Lord of Dawn."[50]

Warriors

The war festivals were festivals of fire and blood. The ritual war waged by the Uacusecha Chichimeca against the four borders (which corresponded to the four quarters of the universe, Guachichiles to the North, Mexicans to the East, Cuitlatecas to the South, and Nahuas to the West) was primarily a war to feed the gods. The captains went to battle covered with their ornaments, carrying feather standards (the *punguarancha,* the gods of the feathered war). War was part of the divine order that reigned over the world from its beginning: "This is what they told our god Curicaueri when they begot him— that he go with his Captaincies in formation by day, that our Goddess Xaratanga should go in the midst, that the First Born Gods should go on the right hand and the Gods called Viravanecha on the left. All shall go by day, in the place appointed to each one, with the people from his village.[51]

Wars, in the time of King Tariacuri, were waged routinely by the barbarian nations: they were wars without mercy, *a fuego y a sangre,* like those waged by modern armies against the rebels of the north at the end of the nineteenth century. Tariacuri drew the battle plan on the ground and attacked by surprise, seeking to frighten the enemy with the ferocious appearance of the warriors and with their war cries. We think of Antonio de Ciudad Real's description of the Chichimeca warriors: "They are like ferocious lions, and make such terrible and fearsome cries that they are enough to disturb and disconcert many people."[52]

Their speed and the element of surprise made them invincible warriors: "They are like rapid eagles," writes Father Ocaranza, "who take advantage of the darkness of night or the early hours of the day."[53] The battle techniques of the Uacusecha were similar to those of the barbarians from the north and northwest: the Xiximes, "the most ferocious, inhuman, and rebellious nations,"[54] the Seris, who attacked by surprise, the Apaches, who were terrifying by their appearance and their war cries.[55] It was those battle techniques which enabled the warriors of the god Curicaueri to take hold of the Michoacán territory in less than two centuries, from the investiture of Tariacuri (around 1380) until the death of Zuangua upon the arrival of the Spanish in 1520.

Anthropophagy

Ritual anthropophagy seems to have been a dominant characteristic of the barbarian societies of the northwest, particularly among the mountain peoples of Nayarit, Sinaloa, and Sonora.[56] The Xiximes, the Cazcanes, the Guachichiles, the Zacatecans, at the time of the Mixton wars, were anthropophagous.[57] Although the anthropophagous rituals of the Mexicans and the Purepecha in the time of the great empires had reached the heights of cruelty, it would be presumptuous to compare the nomadic societies which practiced animal sacrifices to the sedentary theocratic nations which favored human sacrifices. Here, again, the *Chronicles of Michoacán* is a precious document on the anthropophagy rituals of the ancient Purepecha: the sacrifice of the priest Naca, told in a burlesque style, demonstrates the banality of anthropophagy; slaves and captives were immolated and eaten by the victors, and their bones were kept as trophies.[58] But it was in the very formulation of anthropophagy that its religious significance appears. At the time of war festivals, the *Chronicles* tell us, the gods "were hungry," and men were their "food." Through the sacrifice of captives on the altars of Curicaueri and Xaratanga, the Uacusecha sealed an ancient alliance with the gods, and substituted themselves for the gods in mystical transfiguration. Sacrificing victims was more than an honor: it was a ritual participation in a mystery in which the divinity, the sacrificer, and the victim were as one.[59]

One of the rituals associated with anthropophagy was the Hunis

Peraquero (or Unisperanscuaro) festival (the festival of bones). It is described in the *Chronicles*: during this festival the lords and the priests gathered in the house of the chief priests and prayed before the bones of the victims sacrificed on the altars, while evoking the story of the battles. The cult of bones was widespread among the peoples of the north and the northwest, among the Tepehuanes, the Ahomes, and the Coras of Nayarit, who venerated a skeleton named Mexe which represented the ancestor of men.[60] The cult of bones might be associated with the cult of trophies—the heads of the conquered, skulls, scalps, the origin of the practice of "scalp-hunting." The cult of bones, human trophies, ritual anthropophagy, and human sacrifices were the dominant characteristics of the religions of middle America, expressing the proximity of death, and the mystical union with the divine forces through the drama of war.

The Eagle

In middle and northern America the solar cults frequently seem associated with the cult of the eagle. Among the Indians of Nayarit, Sonora, New Mexico, and Arizona, eagle feathers were used to decorate the dancers in the solar rituals, or to embellish sacred arrows. The eagle, a predatory bird par excellence, was the symbol of the nomadic peoples living from the hunt and from wars, inhabiting the most arid and the wildest regions of the American continent. The very name of the faction that conquered Michoacán in the twelfth century is symbolic: the Uacusecha, the Eagles. This name brings to mind the definition de Alva Ixtlilxóchitl mentions regarding the Chichimeca: "The appellation and name of Chichimeca was given them at the beginning, for it is a word unique to this nation which means eagles."[61] The symbol of the eagle, which one discovers in the warrior order of the Aztecs, has a more precise meaning among the Uacusecha. The priests of the god Curicaueri gathered in the House of the Eagle to stand watch and to pray before battles. The major gods of the Pure pantheon were "Royal Eagles," which ruled over the "small Eagles." In honor of the supreme eagle, Curicaueri, warriors were painted yellow, the color of fire, and wore bird feathers which symbolized fire and the sun: eagle, white crane, and parrot feathers. At the time of the fall of the Pure empire, at the time of the cazonci Zuanga, the number of prophecies and auguries increased. A young slave woman belonging to the lord Uiquixo (whose name evokes Tzintzun Uiquixo, the hummingbird of the left, that is, the Mexican god Huitzilopochtli) was taken by "a white eagle, whistling and bristling his feathers, and with a great wart over large eyes which indicated that he was the God Curicaueri."[62] It was that same whistling of an eagle, the omen of war, which King Tariacuri had resounded in the mountains around Patzcuaro before launching the final attack against his enemies.

"Perfume Pipes"

If *copal*, or American incense, was widespread throughout the American continent, tobacco had a more limited usage. The Caribs, peoples of Central and South America, were probably at the origin of tobacco rituals, and particularly of the pipe in shamanic ceremonies. In North America, the tobacco pipe was found among most of the nomadic nations. It symbolized the barbarian culture, tied to practices of sorcery and to war rituals. It is a cultural trait that was found as an exception among the sedentarized Purepeca of Michoacán, which gives proof of their connection to the barbarian nations of the north and northwest. The *Chronicles of Michoacán* indeed mention the *canutos de sahumerios* (perfume pipes), the use of which was still unknown by the Spanish chroniclers, and which appeared clearly in the illustration of the festival of justice, Yzquataconscuaro (or Uazcuata Conscuaro).[63] Among the Uacusecha, as among the nomadic peoples of the north, the tobacco pipe was reserved for religious rituals, and for war councils. The relationship with the barbarian rituals is obvious: tobacco smoke (*andumucua*), like the smoke of incense and of pyres, was meant to communicate with the gods. Tobacco smoke symbolized prayer in the nomads' shamanic rituals. The description of the ritual among the Mimbreño Apaches (New Mexico) even asserts a connection with the mythology and the cosmic calendar of middle America: "small puffs of smoke, supposedly representing clouds, are blown to the cardinal directions by priests using pipes."[64] The Texas Comanches observed a similar ritual, offering clouds of smoke to the sun, the earth, and to the chief gods.[65] Other peoples, such as the Pimas and the Yaquis, used tobacco smoke only in the secret of shamanic curing ceremonies, during which the pipe was used to blow or breathe on the sick person's body.[66] But among most of the barbarian peoples, as among the ancient Purepecha, tobacco smoke was associated with war ceremonies, and sealed a mystical pact with the gods before battle. Father Perez de Ribas reports that to commemorate victories "the principal chiefs and sorcerers gathered together in the house, or under the chief's canopy; they lit a fire and sat down around it; then they lit some pipes of tobacco, which they had prepared, and they invited each other to smoke those offerings. When they had completed that ceremony, the Indian who had most authority among them stood up, and then began to intone his oration."[67] At a distance of one hundred leagues and one hundred years, that is the portrait of the festival during which the Purepecha chiefs sat smoking as they listened to the chief priest Petamuti speak. Among the Varohíos of Sinaloa, war councils followed a similar order: "They had their meetings while celebrating in their fashion with pipes of tobacco, which they smoked. Then, intoxicated by that barbarian smoke, and by the fire that Satan had lit, they delivered many speeches full of rage and anger."[68] Similarly, the Nebomes, at times of war, "as a sign of war sent each other pipes of tobacco which they were accustomed to using."[69] Common rituals of smoke clouds, associated with little balls of perfume thrown into the sacred fire to obtain the gods' mercy during war, emphasizes the connection between nomadic and sedentary cultures, their obvious coming together, the best example of this being the civilization of the ancient Purepecha.[70]

Dreams, Auguries

Most of the Amerindian cultures fed on dreams. Among the Inca, as among the Aztecs, dreams were considered to be true voyages of the soul outside the body, during which men could know the future and receive divine warnings. It was those dreams, along with auguries, which disturbed the Indian world when the Spaniards arrived, and rendered it so vulnerable. Dreams held a privileged place among the Aztecs: during the festival called Ixnextioa, reports Sahagun, dancing men had the power to transform themselves into gods, among whom was included the god of dreams, in the form of a sleeping man whom another man carried on his back.[71] The vision of a poet like Neza-hualcóyotl, permeated with melancholy and doubt, is very near to that of the Spanish baroque poets Góngora and Calderón de la Barca.

In the *Chronicles of Michoacán*, the unique book about the Pure culture, the importance of dreams appears with the greatest force. The history of this people seems to be a history of dreams. The ascent to power by King Tariacuri's nephews Tangaxoan and Hiripan was determined through a dream, in which the major gods of the Uacuse-cha, the god Curicaueri and the goddess Xaratanga, appeared to them in the forms of "a lord painted black" and an old woman "with gray hair in places" and announced their reign to them. Caracomaco, the lord of Querecuaro, succeeded in attaining power despite his lower-class origins, by forcing the doors of a dream. Night after night he slept on the steps of the temple of Querenda Angapeti, in Zacapu, until the god's wife, Pevame, noticed him and helped him obtain the insignia of royalty.[72] It was also a dream that told the Pure people of their coming destruction, when the slave of Uiquixo witnessed the final gathering of the gods on the mountain of Xanoato Huacío, near Patzcuaro.[73]

Among the barbarian peoples of the north and northwest, dreams had a mystical significance, which was accentuated at the time of the Spanish Conquest. After a period of tolerance toward the newcomers, bearers of new technology and a new religion, there began the era of rebellions, of resistance against the invaders. Apart from the Cazcanes and the Coras of the Mesa del Nayar, who had a veritable clergy, the barbarians' religion had no hierarchy and was often reduced to familial cults and shamanic ceremonies. It is in this context that one must view the origin of the role of dreams. Dreams and visions affirmed a relationship between the divinity and man which was absolutely contrary to the strongly hierarchical structures of the Church of the first Christian missionaries. Shamanic ecstasy signified the individuality of faith, revelation, an immediate relationship with the forces of the beyond. It was upon that ecstatic relationship with the divine world that the identity of the barbarian peoples was built, where each man could, thanks to the gift of his dreams, merge into the other world.

The Dreamers

Prophets and seers appeared in moments of trouble. During the insurrection of the barbarian nations against the Spanish invaders, it was the *hechiceros* (the sorcerers) who inspired the Chichimeca of Maxorro and Tecamaxtli, the Zuaques of Taxicora, the Tepehuanes, the Tarahumaras. Among the Coras of Nayarit, it was the "old Indian of Tenerapa" who promised immortality, resurrection, rejuvenation, and the punishment of the Spaniards. Among the Xiximes, the "sorcerer" appeared with the traits of a young man and was armed with a bow and held "two arrows in his hand, carrying a stone idol a half-ell tall, who spoke all languages." The same young man appeared to the Acaxees, bearing "a crystal like a mirror on his stomach" and uttering "irresistible" words.[74] In their visions, the barbarian insurgents discovered the ancient myth of Teopiltzintli, the child-god of Tzenticpac, who had vivified the Chichimeca of Mixton and Ixtlahuaca: "Each time they saw him, he appeared to them in the form of a child who spoke to them, taught them, answered their concerns and consoled them in their afflictions, and let them know that in the sky there was a god with great power, that this lord had created the sky, the sun, the moon, the stars, trees, mountains, rocks, all that was visible and invisible, and that the sky was of silver, and that there were many precious feathers and stones, and a Lady who never grew old, and she was the sovereign virgin, and thanks to her men had received their flesh."[75]

The visions of the priest-gods already enabled the mixture of beliefs which would later produce Messianism.[76]

Among the nomadic peoples of the north, dreams played a determinative role in the armed struggle against the Spanish and Anglo-American Conquerors. There were the dreamers who appeared alongside the great war chiefs and sometimes took their place: the brother of Tecumseh, the Navajo Popé who led the revolt of the Pueblos in 1680; Tamucha of the Utahs who in 1850 announced to the French that the Indians were soon going "to sweep out all the colonies from the frontier";[77] and the shaman Noch-ay-del-klinne, also called the Dreamer; and the sorcerer/warrior Pionsenay of the Chiricahuas of Cochise.

Dreams and Hallucinations

The visions of the nomadic warriors from the north were sometimes the product of hallucinogenic drugs. Drugs were part of the shaman's techniques, either for curing ceremonies or for war rituals. It is somewhat difficult to measure the importance and extent of hallucinogenic drugs in the cultures of middle America, as most of the Spanish chroniclers described them under the general term of *borracherias*, or intoxicants. Regarding the Chichimeca, Father Sahagun notes that "they were the ones who first discovered and used the root called *peyote* and ate or drank it, taking it instead of wine, and they did the same with plants called *nanacatl*, which are bad mushrooms which intoxicate like wine."[78] It is completely probable that the use of psylocibin mushrooms, peyote, and datura (*ololiuhqui*), at the origin of shamanic ecstasy, had spread into all the cultures of Mesoamerica, and that it played an important role in war rituals and human sacrifices.[79] But it was above all in the cultures of North America that hallucinatory rituals were significant, undoubtedly owing to the role they played at the time of the wars of insurrection. The testimonies of the Spanish historians unanimously stress the importance of those rituals and the prophecies they encouraged. Among the Acaxee Indians, reports Father Perez de Ribas, the ritual ball game (the *tlachtli* of the Mexicans) was celebrated on a field (*batey*) where there was "on the one hand an idol in the form of a man, and on the other, the very renowned root among the Indians of New Spain called peyote. This root, although it is medicinal, is also used in many superstitions which the Holy Tribunal of the Inquisition must sometimes punish."[80] To a certain extent it was the belief in auguries and dreams, and the use of peyote, which established the spiritual unity of the barbarians, and set them against Christianity. In Nayarit, the Tonati, chief priest of the cult of the sun in Taocamota, celebrated a peyote ritual: "Next to him they placed a dish filled with peyote, which is a diabolical root," writes Father José Ortega.[81] The Indians of Parras, for the ritual of the deer heads dedicated to the sun, ate "the weed called peyote, which makes one lose one's reason and creates diabolical thoughts in dreams."[82] Intoxicants played a determinative role in the Indian wars north of Mexico at the end of the nineteenth century. Alcohol made of mesquite, the *mexcal*, the *tiswin* of the Apaches (or the *tesquino* of the Tepehuanes), peyote, datura, hallucinogenic mushrooms were the ingredients that enhanced the Indians' exaltation and comforted them with an idea of their invulnerability, as hashish did during the Arab wars. But it is especially a continuity with the mystical wars of the Uacusecha that appeared in that valorization of fanaticism. The last visionaries of the modern world, the Apaches, Comanches, Pawnees, Sioux, and Arapahos, when confronted with the violence of the European Conquest, found strength in an illusion of immortality to wage a hopeless battle.

The "Hechiceros"

The unity of the barbarian peoples was found not in politics, but in magic. Magic, in connection with war rituals, gave the chiefs' power a sacred value. For the Spanish Conquerors, the barbarian nations lived beyond what was human, ignoring the laws and the dictates of conscience. For the religious figure Diego Muñoz, the Indians could "be considered as monsters of nature, because in their customs they are so different from men, and because their intelligence is comparable to that of the beasts." He adds: "They have neither kings nor lords . . . nor law, nor any religion."[83] For the Spanish Conquerors an authority based on magic could have no human value.

The role of the *hechiceros*, or sorcerers, in the barbarian wars is symbolic of the rupture between the Indian and the Christian worlds. Originally, the sorcerer/healer was the founding hero of the nations. Such was the role of the Toltecs' Quetzalcóatl, who was beaten by his rival Tezcatlipoca in a magical duel. Xólotl, the god/king of the Chichimeca, guided his people from the kingdom of Aztlan to the caves of Tenayuca, accompanied by his wife Tomyauh and his son Nopaltzin. The *Crónica mexicayotl* evokes the magical ties which from the beginning joined the Chichimeca people to the god Tetzahuitl Huitzilopochtli, he who "spoke to them, advised them, and lived among them."[84] It is possible to see, in the war rituals of the Mexicans and the Purepecha, the continuation of a nomadic tribal organization, in which the war chief was accompanied by a seer/healer. The *Chronicles of Michoacán*, a unique document written from the Chichimeca point of view, informs us of the survival of the organization of ritual war. Festivals of war, the Festival of the Arrows (Uazcuata Conscuaro) or the Festival of Bones (Unisperanscuaro) portrayed a magical ritual around the chief priest Petamiti and the Hiripati diviners:[85] harangues, bloody sacrifices, the smoke of incense and tobacco, prayers and offerings were preparations for war, and gave birth to a mystical exaltation comparable to that of the *hechiceros* during the insurrections against the Spanish Conquerors. During the festival of justice, says the *Chronicles*, "with all the chiefs and principals the chief priest would stand up. Taking his staff or spear he would tell the people the entire history of their ancestors, how they came to the province and the wars they fought in the service of their gods. The narration lasted until nightfall."[86] That was the role played by the barbarian *hechiceros,* as described by the chroniclers: "preaching and speaking great sermons and speeches before the members of the tribe."[87] The importance of the "sorcerer" was evident in those "speeches" which preceded battles, in which the virtues of the ancestors and faith in victory were exalted. Battles were not fought to obtain land, but to feed the gods, in a mystical union with the other world. Such also was the role played by the *quanguariecha,* the "knights" of the Pure monarch, in which one can see a religious order rather than a military hierarchy, as among certain nomadic peoples of the north.[88] The portrait of the first Uacusecha kings, virtuous and mystical, evokes the Chichimeca barbarians, so distant from the 'qualities and vices of civilized peoples.

It was during the colonial era that the role of the *hechiceros* appeared with the greatest strength. The names of most of these "sorcerers," instigators and sometimes organizers of rebellions, have been forgotten today. Some of them were reported by the Spanish historians: Guaxicar, the "leader" of the Indians of Guaxacatlan; the priest-god Cuanemeti, representative of the god Teopiltzintli at Ixtlahuaca; the "bishop" of the Acaxees; the "king" Juan Cocle of the Tarahumara rebellion of 1606; the "bishop" Hernan of the Tobosos; Nacabeba, the rebel chief of the Indians of Matapan. Most of the barbarian rebellions of the northern states of the Spanish colony were the work of visionaries, sometimes combining messianic themes with shamanic cults. The "sorcerers" preached war, the only means of returning to ancestral values and beliefs. Many of the chiefs and "sorcerers" were Christians converted by the first missionaries who later returned to their own religion after being horrified by the Spanish and the bad treatment and despoilment inflicted on them by the soldiers. Among the Zuaques and the Teguecos of Sinaloa, the insurrection was directed by Lanzarote, Nacabeba, Taxicora, at least the first of whom was baptized. The Tepehuanes, the Guachichiles, and the Vallaguaniguaras (or Borrados of San Cristobal) were commanded by chiefs who had returned to their original faith (the *capitan* Samora,

Martin Chico); their exhortations against the Christians were all the more violent for their having been converted. The "apostates" would leave a legend in the barbarian wars, a legend which was to continue in the Apache wars of the North American frontier with the renegades.

The primary reason for their rebellion against the Christian religion was their attachment to traditional values: Father Perez de Ribas, speaking of Cabomeai, chief of the Nebomes, saw the cause of his rebellion in "the memory of the ancient barbarism in which he had been raised."[89] Likewise, the Seris went to war "tricked by their desire for freedom and so as not to be subject either to laws or to religious instruction."[90] Intertribal vengeance sometimes played a role in the insurrections, as in the Mixton wars when the chief Don Christobal, leader of Xalixco, exhorted the neighboring nations to join together to conquer the Spanish "and to kill all those who spoke the Mexican language."[91] In Nayarit, the Tonati himself, after his surrender to the Spanish, was removed from his office during the rebellion of 1721 by a *hechicero* who organized the resistance against the Conquerors. The origin of revolts was sometimes found in an augury, as reported by Father Tello: in Tlaxicoringa (Huaynamota), during a ritual dance, a gust of wind carried away a calabash (perhaps associated with the cult of peyote), and old women prophesied that the same wind would sweep away the Spaniards. Thus began the bloody Mixton war.[92] We are reminded here of the auguries and visions which haunted most of the American societies upon the arrival of the Spanish, and also of the prophecies which gave birth to the greatest Indian insurrections: the formation of a triple Indian kingdom at Oaxaca, the fabulous apparitions of the Virgin at Cancuc in Chiapas, and the miracles of the talking Cross during the Cruzoob war in Quintana Roo at the end of the nineteenth century.

The Holy War

The "holy war" (a term coined by Philip Wayne Powell),[93] which inspired the barbarians to rise up against the Spanish, was the expression of a desperate outburst against the threat of death which the Conquerors, starting in the seventeenth century, brought to the nomadic societies of the north and northwest. It was an outburst against the despoiling of the lands on the part of the Tarahumaras, the Mayos, the Yaquis, and the Seris, and against slavery and forced labor on the part of the Chichimeca peoples of the mining regions. But it was an even greater outburst against the destruction of their religion and traditional values. The role of the "sorcerer" is explained by that total equivalency of war and religion which was one of the philosophical foundations of Indian cultures in the Mexican west, as seen best in the elaborate war festivals of the ancient Purepecha. As in those festivals, it was religious faith which sustained the barbarian peoples' struggle against the Christian invader. It was indeed a holy war, on both sides: for the Spanish Conquerors, the Indians were "infidels," the "gentiles" in every respect comparable to the Muslim enemies of the war of reconquest. The war waged upon them by the soldiers of the king of Spain was just, for it was above all a matter of "converting the very barbarous and cruel Chichimeca people to the holy Catholic faith and to the service of Your Majesty."[94] For the barbarians of the north and northwest, the Spanish invader was the absolute enemy, less because he belonged to a different race than because he practiced an exclusive colonization and professed a religious ideology radically opposed to that of the Indians.

What is striking in the history of the Christian mission among the barbarians is the Indians' change of attitude toward the missionaries. Their initial contacts, at the end of the sixteenth century, were by and large favorable, and many Chichimeca, moved by the arrival of the new gods—and undoubtedly by auguries—followed the example of Ocelotl, the chief of the warloving Totorames, who kneeled down to kiss the hoof of Nuño de Guzmán's horse, or yet the example of Pantecatl, the son of the chief of Acaponeta, who, persuaded that the Spanish had come "from where the sun rises" to accomplish a prophecy, accepted his baptism as a submission.[95] But the bad treatment by the *encomenderos*, the pillaging of food reserves, and the slavery practiced systematically by an army that considered it to be compensation for a nonexistent salary, caused revolt to break out.[96] The Spanish priests then appeared as accomplices of a tyrannical power. The rebellion of the Indians of the Cuinao valley, then the Mixton war, and the general league of the Chichimeca nations were not only directed against the Spanish colonists, but also expressed a rejection of the Christian doctrine. Many of the Indian leaders, baptized by the missionaries upon their first encounters, later rejected the Christian religion and incited their people to revolt. Don Christobal, chief of Xalixco and then the apostate chiefs of the terrible war of the Peñol de Nochistlán, Don Francisco Aguilar and the Zacatecan Don Diego Tenamaxtli, initiated a long series of battles against the Christians and their Indian allies. Thus the rebellion of the Zacatecans was led by former converts: Don Juan (chief of the Chalchihuites), Don Christobal de Amanquex, Don Francisco de Sombrerete, Don Juan de Avino, lieutenant of the Zacatecan chief Tzayn. The rebellious Acaxees of the Sierra de Topia were led by a "magician Indian, sorcerer, great speaker who resembled Simon Magus," who called himself "bishop" and celebrated baptisms and marriages. During the rebellion of the Sierra Gorda, the Indians burned all the churches. In 1585 the first revolt of the Indians of Nayarit against the missionaries brought on by the presence of Spanish colonists on Indian land, burst forth with significant iconoclastic violence: Father Francisco Gil and Father Andrés de Ayala were killed in the Guaynamota convent and their heads were burned, then put on display "as a sign of victory, an ancient and diabolical custom among the Chichimeca."[97] The terrible revolt of the Tepehuane Indians (in 1616) was incited by a mysterious Indian from New Mexico who preached war against the Spanish in order to liberate them from those who were subjugating them.[98] The revolt of the Indians of Nayarit, at the beginning of the seventeenth century, was led by an "apostate" by the name of Don Alonso de Leon, and the Tepehuanes gathered around a Tarahumara Indian who called himself "king" under the name of Juan Cocle and who preached the destruction of the missions. In 1644 the confederation of "seven nations" (Toboso, Cabeza, Salinero, Mamite, Julime, Concho, Colorados) was inspired by an apostate Toboso chief, Geronimo Moranta. The revolt of the Tarahumaras in 1646 was led by Teporaca, whom Father Alegre called *Indio ladino* (convert), and that of the Indians near Monterrey was led by another *ladino* named Nicolas el Carretero (the Carrier).

Southeast of the colony, most of the rebel movements, in Chiapas in particular, were led by spiritual figures who were opposed to the Christianity of the Spaniards, and who preached the return to ancestral traditions. These were the movements that resulted in the "Indian wars" of the frontier, against the Yaquis of Juan Jusacamea (called Banderas), and against the Apaches of Victorio and of Cochise, in a climate of extreme violence and fanaticism.

Barbarians vs. Christians

The rejection of Christianity which motivated the barbarian rebellions was foremost a violent and desperate assertion of Indian identity. Through their customs and beliefs, through their very conception of the world, the barbarians were diametrically opposed to the Christian civilization. Most of the Indians' grievances against the Spanish priests were a result of their pagan tradition: polygamy, nudity, the incineration of the dead, the use of body painting and tatooing, long hair and jewelry, festivals of intoxication, ritual dances and the use of hallucinogenic drugs. But the rupture with the missionaries was above all the result of the fundamental contrast between the religious concepts of the Indians and those of the Spanish Conquerors. Polytheism, blood sacrifices, and zoomorphic cults formed the very essence of Indian religiosity. Those who, in the early days, had added the new divinities of the Christians to their ancestral pantheon could not, however, accept the exclusion of their own gods, a symbol of a defeat on the military level which they had not yet truly experienced. The rejection of the new gods thus occurred with the brutality of a political rebellion. The Coras of Guaynamota who initially converted rose up at the end of the sixteenth century, "persuaded by the

Devil that they had no need of God, that it was not He who fed them, but rather their own idols."[99]

The very doctrine of Christianity, its notion of charity, its cult of peace, and profession of love were completely foreign to the philosophy of the barbarian peoples in which war, blood sacrifices, and a mystical identification with the forces of the other world were valued. The message of love and justice brought by the first missionaries, in which the moral concepts of the Renaissance were expressed, could only be met with incomprehension, then with distrust as time went on and the words were contradicted by the brutality of the military Conquerors, despoilers and keepers of slaves. The *Chronicles of Michoacán* convey the incomprehension, and the rancor, very well: "What? Must we live according to the things that the Spaniards have invented to annihilate us? For the lords who are now our own have brought with them prisons, jails, and tortures through ferocious dogs devouring their victims smeared with grease,"[100] exclaimed the counselors of the last king of Michoacán.

But even more than the contradictions and the incomprehension, it was the strongly clerical character of the new religion which made it so foreign to the barbarian nations of the north and northwest. For the nomadic Indians of the desert zone, as for the Yucatán Maya and the Chiapas Tzendals, religion was above all a revelation. It implied neither dogma nor doctrine, and was truly subject to no clergy. An indissociable mixture of myth, usages, and shamanic rituals, it was practiced in tribal or familial cults communicating with the other world through dances and visions. It was above all a religion of ecstasy, as Mircea Eliade describes it.[101] A syncretic religion, it allowed man, whoever he was, to attain the supernatural. Furthermore, it was never separate from the real world, since it expressed the identity of the clan, the tribe, incorporating the simplest acts of everyday life. Out of all that came the profound rupture which, beginning with the first encounters, separated the Christian missionaries from the indigenous spiritual leaders. Religious authority, in seeking to substitute itself for the power of the Indian rulers and war chiefs, and in imposing a foreign morality, could only incite scorn or hatred. Among the nomadic peoples of the north and northwest, unlike the theocracies of middle America, religion was not an authority exercised by clerics, but a supernatural power linked to original myths, in which man participated wholly with empassioned vigor. The rationalism and morality of the Christian missionaries could lead only to failure, to rejection. The destruction of the values and religious symbols of the Indians was the occasion for revolt in most barbarian societies. "Why don't our gods become angry? Why do they not curse them?" exclaimed the Purepecha after the Spaniards destroyed the altars of their gods.[102] The same destructive furor took hold of the barbarian rebels after the Conquest. Churches were burned, holy icons were desecrated and destroyed, Spanish priests were assassinated, and their remains were displayed as a sign of triumph. These revolts sometimes broke out abruptly, and were quelled just as quickly. Most often they degenerated into true wars against the Spanish invaders and the Christian missionaries, as in the alliance of the Zuaques and the Teguecos, led by Nacabeba and the apostate Lanzarote, in the war of the Sierra Gorda (in 1600), or in the revolt of the Conchos, led by an Indian who "had proclaimed freedom of conscience so they might live as they were accustomed to, without observing the Catholic religion."[103] The continual violence of the Indian rebellions culminated in the Tepehuane insurrection in 1616, in the Pueblo uprising in 1680, and in the sacrilegious furor of the Lacandóns, as described by the bishop Casillas of Guatemala: "They killed and captured many people, and they sacrificed children on their altars; they tore out their hearts, and with the blood they annointed the images which were in the church, and at the foot of the cross they sacrificed others: then, having accomplished these acts, they began to say and proclaim: Christians, tell your God to defend you."[104]

Messianisms

It was the violent and irrational character of the Indian religions that contrasted them most to the Christianity of the Conquerors. In most

of the revealed religions of Indian America, the priest was more than
an intermediary, he was himself a god. Through his body and voice
it was the divinity itself which was present and spoke. It was that
belief, blended with Christian themes of incarnation, which was at
the origin of messianic movements among the Coras, the Tepehuanes, as well as the Tzendals of Chiapas and the Maya of Quintana
Roo. The Tepehuane war of 1616 erupted in a climate of magic and
exemplary fanaticism. An "old Indian" apostate from New Mexico
preached holy war while promising immortality and rejuvenation for
all those who would fight against the Spanish invaders. He also appeared to the Xiximes, but in the guise of a young man, and to the
Acaxees as a warrior with a "crystal like a mirror in his stomach,"
proffering "irresistible" words.[105] Father José de Arlegui tells the legend of that mysterious Indian, "or better to say a demon dressed like
a barbarian," who went from village to village and stirred up the Tepehuanes around the city of Durango. His speech was "so reasonable
in its words, and so efficacious in moving the saddened souls of the
Indians that they had scarcely heard him when they immediately became very angry at the Spanish, hating the law they were being
taught and the way of life that had been imposed upon them."[106]
Inspired by a sort of mystical frenzy, the Tepehuanes' prophet became
a veritable Messiah: "That miserable man assured them that he was
the son of God, and as such they adored him, and knew him by no
other name." He promised ultimate victory over the Spaniards, and
that the Tepehuanes would then be able to take their wealth, their
grain, and their livestock. The war was inspired by the blindest fanaticism: "They believed to such a degree that they would be resus-
citated that they threw themselves on the points of the Spanish
swords, on their spears, and with a barbaric courage they even walked
right up to the barrels of the blunderbusses."[107] The Indian wars of
the seventeenth century, in the southeast as in the north of the
colony, show the extent of the Indians' violence, fanaticism, and faith
in ultimate victory over the Spaniards and in the immortality of their
warriors. The rebellions of the Zapotecs of Tamaculapa and Oaxaca

were tied to a vision which expressed a true messianic belief: a new god enclosed in a *petate* was to appear on the main square of Antequera (the city of Oaxaca) to chase away the Spanish and bring about the advent of three indigenous kings who would put an end to slavery.[108] The rebellion of the Maya of Bakhalal at the beginning of the seventeenth century was the Indians' challenge to the king of Spain, combined with messianic cults. The account Father Cogolludo gives of it provides the first description of the ritual of the *misa milpera* which has survived to the present: "One of those apostates was their priest of idolatries, who said mass for them, and he celebrated it with their food of tortillas and their drink of pozole."[109] The account Father Ximenez gives of the rebellion of the Tzendal Indians of Cancuc in 1712 clearly shows the messianism which inspired the Indians, and their rejection of the Spanish clergy.[110] The cross which descended from the sky in Cancuc, surrounded by "many lights," already evoked the speaking cross and the rituals of the Cruzoob Maya of Quintana Roo in the nineteenth and twentieth centuries: the *indizuela* [derogatory: "little Indian maid"] who interpreted the words of the Holy Virgin and of Saint Martha already evoked the "pythonesse" of Tulum at the time of the Cruzoob Mayan insurrection in the nineteenth century. The cult was organized around the "chapel" (statues and cross hidden by a *petate*), which was the model for the future Balam Na of the insurgents of Chan Santa Cruz. The chief of the rebels was a *ladino* apostate named Don Sebastian Gomez de la Gloria, who was surrounded by his "majordomos," his cantors, and a "secretary" who transcribed the words of the *indizuela*. Fanaticism and messianism inspired revolt, using mystical revelations and the proclamations of the Indian woman by the name of the "Very Holy Virgin who is enclosed in this *petate*." These proclamations incited holy war, and caused the Indians to be confused with the first Christians, as they would later be during the war of the Castes: "Now there was no longer a God nor a King, and they had to adore, believe, and obey only the Virgin who had descended from the sky . . . And they were to kill the priests and the pastors as well as the Spaniards, the metis, the negros, and the mulattoes so that only the Indians would remain on that land."[111] It was the same mysticism which at the end of the eighteenth century would animate the Maya of Cisteil, grouped around Jacinto Canek, wearing the blue cloak of the Virgin of the Conception, who announced to her faithful that the Spaniards' weapons "now have no more power against us."[112] In the north and northwest of the colony, Indian insurrections followed each other in the same climate of magic and fanaticism. The rebellion of the Jano-Suma-Jocome league of the high Bacuachi was led by the Indian Buchaurini, who proclaimed "that he was god, that he had created everything, and that he no longer wanted them to sell corn to the Spanish nor to be Christians, and that it was better to burn all the Spaniards, then they would live better, and there would be water in abundance on earth."[113] If we refer to the definition of messianism given by Maria Isaura Pereira de Queiroz, the "paradise on earth" and "collective redemption,"[114] most of the Indian wars of Mexico starting in the sixteenth century and continuing until modern times have messianic movements at their origins. As in the mystical wars of the plains Indians of North America, the influence and notoriety of the barbarian religious chiefs was diffused with an ease and swiftness which proved the depth and necessity of those movements: indeed, in many cases there was a veritable founding of new religions. From the uprisings of Mixton and Jalisco to the final episodes of the Apache war, that is for nearly three hundred and fifty years, Indian insurrections followed one another, year after year, nation after nation, like the same dream of violence, magic and death.

The "Despeñolados" [Those Who Hurled Themselves from Cliffs]

Year after year, nation after nation, barbarian rebellions were crushed by the armed Spanish forces, then, after independence, by the Mexican army. The religious chiefs (hechiceros) were executed without a trial during the often arbitrary and cruel repression that aimed for the extermination pure and simple of the Indian bravos. For the nations who entered into that total war defeat meant death, since the very goal of their revolt was definitive victory and the expulsion of the Spanish oppressors. The first war of the rebellion against the colony, and one of the most violent, the Mixton war, shows the degree to which the Indians' involvement was total. At first there was rebellion against the abuses by the *encomenderos*, and war, supported by auguries and religion, became all-encompassing; it was a "Chichimeca" war, in which the entire population participated, including women and children.[115] The battles took place with a mystical and savage anger, with the insults and curses of the Spaniards responding to the war cries and cannibal frenzy of the Indians of Juchipila: "And around ten or eleven o'clock in the morning, the enemy appeared around the City (Guadalajara) wearing their feathered ornaments and carrying bows, clubs, rondaches, and spears, armed with all sorts of weapons, and they were so great in number that they circled over a half league around the City, and one could see only enemy Indians with painted bodies, nude, looking like the devil."[116] To the fanaticism of the barbarians inspired by their *hechiceros* and war chiefs, going into battle intoxicated with wine and peyote, there responded the religious frenzy of the Spanish attacking the Peñol de Nochistlán, led by the miraculous apparition of a white knight in whom they recognized the archangel Saint Michael or the knight Santiago [Saint James].[117]

The desperate violence of the battles of the Peñol de Nochistlán was the same that distinguished most of the barbarian wars until the capitulation of the Apaches in 1880. The insurgents, faced with the power of the armed strength of the Spanish (allied with their traditional enemies, the Tarascans of Michoacán, Mexicans from Mexico or Tlaxcala) had no other recourse than to barricade themselves in the natural fortresses of the *peñoles* where they sustained a terrifying siege. In the Peñol de Nochistlán, sixty thousand Indians were besieged by the army of the viceroy Don Antonio de Mendoza. Their determination to die was unanimous. To the exhortations of the Spaniards, the chief Don Diego Tenamaxtli replied "that they did not want to surrender, nor make peace, that they were on their lands, and that the Spanish should return to their own and there they would have peace."[118] The seizing of Peñol de Cuina took place in a savage blood-bath, while the Indians committed suicide so as not to be captured. The Indians, seeing they were lost, "began to kill each other and to throw themselves into the void, and they killed their own children by throwing them against the rocks, a terrible thing to see, and in that way more than four thousand Indians, not counting the women and children, were killed or committed suicide."[119] Deprived of water and food, terrorized by defeat, the Indians of Nochistlán also threw themselves off cliffs and died in great numbers. Suicide was the only recourse of the Indian peoples faced with the arrival of the foreign Conquerors: when he learned of the imminent arrival of the Spanish soldiers of Cristobal de Olid, the cazonci Tangoxoan, the last king of Michoacán, dreamt of death, and his dignitaries sought to lead him along: "Sire, have copper brought and we shall put it on our backs and let us drown ourselves in the lake."[120] The cruelty of the *encomendero* Pedro de Bobadilla led the Indians of Culiacán to revolt and to suicide: "He had hounds, and as if he was hunting wild beasts, he hunted men and cut them into pieces. And seeing this cruelty worthy of hell, all the people of the province of Culiacán rose up and the Indians of the plains and of the coast set fire to their villages and their supplies, and after killing their children because they could not take them with them, they took refuge in the mountains."[121]

Suicide concluded the terrible war of the Tepehuanes when the fighters, persuaded that they would be resurrected, waged an assault on the Spaniards' spears and arquebuses. The same desperate violence occurred in the final confrontations between the barbarians and the civilized, during the wars to exterminate the Apaches and Comanches at the end of the nineteenth century.

Thus the holy war of the Chichimeca and the barbarians from the north seemed to find its continuation in the Indian wars of the Pawnees, the Arapahos, the Sioux, and the Seminoles. One might imagine a relationship between the Chichimeca and the barbarian insurrections of the sixteenth and seventeenth centuries and the messianic movements of the North American Indians.[122] The "dream dances" (or "powwows") of the Iroquois, the "ghost dances" of the Oglala Sioux, the "sun dances" of the Kiowas, in which rituals blended with shamanic themes and with the use of peyote, strangely recall the *mitotes* (dancing festivals) and the preaching of the barbarian *hechiceros*. The same themes inspired them: the promise of immortality or rejuvenation, the ultimate triumph of the Indians over the whites or the metis, shamanism, visions and trances, as well as the use of peyote and tobacco toward magical ends. The presence of "seers" and "dreamers" alongside the great Indian leaders of the North American plains—Pontiac, Tecumseh, Wovoka—recalls the *hechiceros* of the barbarian wars alongside Tzayn, Maxorro, Macolio, and the Apache Martinillo. Among the barbarians, ritual dances, shamanism, and peyote seem to have played an important role, especially during the Chichimeca League of 1561,[123] which was seen again in the nineteenth century among the last nomadic insurgents against the Christian order. After 1810 the holy war was particularly violent and desperate. Pushed by the North American colonists, who were supported by a modern army, and retreating before the military expeditions of the Mexicans, the Apaches resorted to the tactics used by the Chichimeca: they took refuge in the inaccessible mountains of the Sierra Madre, and survived with the help of pillaging. Against the superior strength of modern weaponry they pitted the fanaticism of the "Path of Netdahe," "death to the foreigners," a declaration made by their ancestors upon the arrival of Coronado in New Mexico. The Netdahes, warriors of the fearsome band of Chiricahuas, rallied together most of the war chiefs who made the history of the final Apache resistance: Juh, Zele, Nanay, Loco, Kaah-Tenny, and probably Geronimo.[124] It was a mystical war, a war without hope that pitted the last nomads in that world, heirs of the tradition of the hunter/gatherers, against the soldiers of the most powerful and most technically advanced nation in the modern world. That war was much more than a confrontation of races or peoples: it was truly a conflict of ideas and cultures, in which a primitive society that valued physical strength, courage, and religious devotion fought an unequal battle against a materialist society concerned only with money and success. The representatives of North American society, practicing a policy of extermination through the intervention of agents such as John Clum, were themselves aware of the significance of that war, as we see expressed in the disillusioned words of the military surgeon James Roberts: The Indians would "become civilized just as soon as they became money lovers."[125]

As for the Chichimeca of Cuina, of Nochistlán, and Juchipila, it was indeed a total war, without mercy. To the "Path of Netdahe," glorified by Cochise, Juh, and Victorio, there responded the total war of the North American general James Carleton in 1862, and the policy of extermination of the governor Joaquin Terrazas, who proclaimed the war *sin paz*—a modern version of the war *a fuego y a sangre* declared by the first Spanish Conquerors. In 1862 General James Carleton would send to Colonel Kit Carson an order of war against the Chiricahuas which was the equivalent of a true slaughter: "All Indian men of that tribe are to be killed whenever and wherever you can find them. The women and children will not be harmed, but you will take them prisoners."[126]

As for the barbarian rebels at the time of Spanish colonization, death was the only outcome for those last nomads who had become outlaws through the force of events. Illness, malnutrition, and poverty struck down the last warriors, decimated the ranks of the Comanches of Katum'se and Sanaco, the Lipans, the Tonkawas, the Gileños, Chiricahuas, and Mescalero Apaches. The chiefs disappeared one after the other, in a glorious death like Victorio, or assassinated through treachery like Loco, Manuelito, or Mangas Coloradas, carried off by the flu like Tahza, or by smallpox like the Mescalero Apache, Santana. Reduced to a handful of "half-armed and even worse dressed savages," according to John Clum,[127] those who had been the most feared warriors on the frontier had to seek refuge in Pa-Gotzin-Kay, the "Stronghold Mountain of Paradise," in the Sierra Madre to the west of Casas Grandes, which was the sacred place of their origins. It was there that Victorio died in 1880, killed by a

Tarahumara mercenary of the troops of General Terrazas, and it was there that Juh ended up, having fallen from a rock, in a doubtless accidental death, which recalls that of the *despeñolados* of the Chichimeca rebellion.[128]

Thus ended the barbarian dream, which began with the intoxication of a holy war against the invaders, and became, in the course of centuries, a symbol of despair and death. The dream of another world, another time, it leaves an indelible mark on us. More than nostalgia or remorse, there is the disturbing feeling of knowing a civilization has been lost forever. It is not by chance that the epic of the last nomads touches our imagination so much. Those cruel, free, and proud men, hardened warriors, virtuous and mystical, attached to their territories, to their forests and to their rivers "as to their own parents,"[129] those whom the traveler Zebulon Pike could still describe in 1807 as men who were "perfectly independent in their manners,"[130] unaware of the pettiness and the vices of the civilized nations, do they not continue, even today, beyond their death, to question our institutions, our laws, our faith, indeed, our entire culture?

6 Antonin Artaud, or the Mexican Dream

MEXICO IS A LAND OF DREAMS. By that I mean a land made of a different truth, a different reality. A land of extreme light, a land of violence, where essential passions are more visible and where the mark of the ancient history of man is more easily perceived, just as in certain legendary lands—Persia, Egypt, China. Why are there dreams? What makes Mexico one of those privileged places of mystery, of legend, a place where the very moment of creation still seemed close when already, inexplicably, the other supreme moment, that of the destruction of that world, was about to occur?

Is it the very physical nature of the land, a land of volcanoes, deserts, high plateaus so close to the sky and the sun, a land of exuberant jungles, of desert plains, of cliffs, canyons, and deep valleys? The virgin quality of the nature in that New World—as opposed to the ancientness of the lands of Europe, formed by man, subjected to his use sometimes to the point of sterility—this is surely the very principle of that dream: during the romantic period, notably in the work of Chateaubriand, virgin nature was the central theme of dreams: in the New World where man was in harmony with nature, all was possible; everything seemed more beautiful, much truer.

161

Man, too, gave birth to a dream; the man of the indigenous societies of the highlands. A dream in which the nomadic savage, the
hero of the novels of Fenimore Cooper or Chateaubriand, was contrasted to the Aztec and the Inca, servants of their solar gods,
builders of prodigious monuments, legendary heroes of the peoples
sacrificed by the Spanish Conqueror to his fever of gold, then abandoned to slavery and despair. It was a romantic image, as well, one
which fascinated generations of readers of novels and tales of voyages
in the last century.

It was legend above all: the magical power of names, gestures,
and the gods, the mystery of lost civilizations, taking with them into
the abyss of oblivion all the power and knowledge of their founders.
At the heart of that mystery was an instinctive fascination caused by
the magician-peoples and their cruel rituals combined with an admiration inspired by their artistic and cultural development. Mexico is
probably the country in the New World where the childlike and romantic, idyllic notion of the "noble savage" was disproven, thanks to
the tales of the explorers and the works of the abbot Brasseur de
Bourbourg and of Michel Chevallier. Europe then discovered the
New World for the second time, its prestigious past, its architectural
treasures, and the extraordinary seductive power of its living folklore.
In the nineteenth century France spontaneously rediscovered the
path of dreams; and Napoleon III, emperor of the French, heir of an
adventurer, had the crazy dream of a Mexican epic which would
establish in the New World an extension to his empire and a counter-
balance to the commercial empire of the United States. The dream
of Napoleon III was above all, I believe, a Mexican dream, that is,
the dream of new strength. Other dreams have traversed the history
of Mexico, certainly more generous than the dream of the Conquerors, the extravagance of Napoleon III or the adventures of Iturbide [a
general who proclaimed himself emperor of Mexico in the early
1800s]; the dreams of a better world envisioned by the first Spanish
evangelists, such as Bartolomé de Las Casas, who were moved by the
beauty and the innocence of the Indians, victims of the cruelty of the

colonists who exploited them; there was also the vision of Don Vasco de Quiroga [first bishop of Michoacán], the abnegation of Fray Jacobo Daciano [who founded a monastery in Michoacán in about 1540], but also the impossible dream of Boturini [an Italian missionary], his idea of a history of New Spain in which the memories of Greek classicism are blended with Aztec and Toltec myths; or yet the purely oneiric thesis of Don Carlos de Sigüenza y Gongora on the Phoenix of the West, St. Thomas the Apostle confused with the legendary figure of Quetzalcóatl.

But those dreams and adventures which have traveled across Mexico from the time of the Conquest have not been gratuitous manifestations of the imagination. One must above all, it seems to me, bring them closer to the power of dreams which is at the very heart of pre-Columbian civilizations: prophetic dreams, dreams in which men encounter their gods, in which they receive their consecration to exercise power over other men, as we've seen in the *Chronicles of Michoacán* and in those great mystical texts of Indian America, the *Books of the Chilam Balam*. Thus to the Spanish Conquerors' wild dream of gold and new lands responded the indigenous peoples' dream of and obsession with the end of the world and their anguished wait for the Return: the return of the men wearing white, the masters of the earth, which had been announced by the Mayan prophets, Ah Kin Chel, Xupan Nauat, and the Chilam Balam; the return of Quetzalcóatl awaited by Montezuma and the Mexicans, from which Hernán Cortés profited so well.

What is most strange about that flow of dreams which has traveled across Mexico, is that it covered all centuries, producing in a continuous manner those explosions of the irrational, of illusion, and even of the absurd: eddies of the baroque as in Boturini or in Don Ramon de Ordonez y Aguiar, the author of a curious book entitled *Historia de la creacion del cielo y de la tierra*, in which Quetzalcóatl is identified with a brother of St. Thomas and the masters of Culhuacan [one of the main towns of the valley of Mexico] with the descendants of the Canaanites of Palestine; collective eddies, as in the adventure of

Mariano, the Indian king, or in the rebellion of the Cruzoob Maya of Quintana Roo. The power of dreams led to the contemporary age in what one might call a renaissance of the irrational.

Mexico—like Gauguin's Tahiti—has probably been the favored place of the dream of paradise lost. In France, in the work of Brasseur de Bourbourg and thanks to the observers who accompanied the French intervention in Mexico, we have had the first revelation of that magical power and of the Indian imaginary that fascinated readers, as if the minutest facts of the marvelous adventure of the Conquerors were blended with the mysteries and secrets of primitive peoples. It is surely that latest phase of the Mexican dream that we are experiencing at present, after the novels of D. H. Lawrence, after Jacques Soustelle's *Mexico,* after the dark, almost mythical tales of Juan Rulfo.

It was the discovery of the ancient magic of the conquered peoples that gave new value to the contemporary indigenous world and which has enabled the Mexican dream to be perpetuated. The dream of a new land where everything is possible; where everything is at the same time very ancient and very new. The dream of a lost paradise where the science of the stars and the magic of the gods were as one. Dreams of a return to the very origins of civilization and knowledge. Many poets have had that dream, both in France and in Mexico. And it is no coincidence that this dream attracted one of the most well-known seekers of dreams, the surrealist André Breton, to Mexico. But one of the first to express that dream, a mixture of violence and mysticism, surely the first to experience it, was the poet Antonin Artaud.

On February 6, 1936, Antonin Artaud landed at the port of Veracruz. He was forty years old. Following Artaud's disastrous experience with surrealism and his excommunication by André Breton, who sentenced him for treason; following the failure of his attempts at theater and film; following his romantic disappointments with Genica Athanasiou, and his being stricken with increasingly ill health owing to his use of drugs, Europe had become a living hell for him. He fled, and chose to go to Mexico in an attempt to attain the dream of his life, the dream of a new existence in a country whose hidden forces and imaginative power were still intact. In *El Nacional Revolucionario* of July 5, 1936, he wrote, "What I came to do in Mexico":

> I came to Mexico to look for politicians, not artists.
>
> Here is why:
>
> Up to now I have been an artist, which means I have been a *manipulated* man.
>
> In truth the question is this:
>
> Contemporary European civilization is fragmented. Dualistic Europe can offer the world only a frightful dusting of cultures. To make a new unity rise up from that dusting has become a necessity.
>
> The Orient is completely decadent. India sleeps while dreaming of a liberation which will appear only after death.
>
> China is at war. The Japanese of today have proven to be the fascists of the Far East. For Japan China is but a vast Ethiopia.
>
> The United States have only succeeded in infinitely multiplying the decadence and the vices of Europe.
>
> All that is left is Mexico and its subtle political structure, which, after all, has not changed since the time of Montezuma.
>
> Mexico, that precipitate of innumerable races, is like the crucible of history. It is from that precipitate, that mixture of races, that it must derive a unique product from which the Mexican soul will emerge.

In this same article Artaud adds: "I came to Mexico to look for a new idea of Man." That "new idea of Man" was what the poet would pursue during his entire stay in Mexico, increasing his articles, letters, lectures, meetings, in a quest to ease his suffering.

But in truth Artaud's break with Europe was not yet consummated. The trip to Mexico and the Mexican dream were born in part out of the fascination felt passionately by the artists of the surrealist movement at that time for the cultures they called "primitive" and in part out of their wish to revolt against European ideas. We must remember that Jorge Cuesta was in Paris in 1928 and that he met with the heads of the surrealist movement; and we must remember the reverberations of surrealist ideas in Mexico—e.g., the publication in 1928 of a study on André Breton's *Nadja* by Jaime Torres Bodet; and the publication, in the journal of Salvador Novo and Xavier Villaurrutia, *Ulises*, of a selection of the poetry of Isidore Ducasse; and, in 1929, of a study on Paul Eluard by Jorge Cuesta.

When Artaud arrived in Mexico City he had, he said, "a virgin mind, which doesn't mean without preconceived ideas." In another article, published in *El Nacional* of June 3, 1936, Artaud, speaking of the Mexican revolution, explained the meaning he gave to the word revolution: "renaissance of the pre-Cortesian civilization." But his dream did not prevent him from perceiving the fragility of that interpretation, for he said, "In Europe there is an anti-European movement, and I fear that in Mexico there is an anti-Indian movement." Later, in the very name of the revolution, Artaud spoke out against the Marxist doctrine of the instructors of the Tarahumara Sierra, as well as against the danger of acculturation posed by the Jesuit missions.

But Artaud's faith in a new Mexico was shaken by the difficulties of his life in Mexico City. Lodged in a questionable house in the "Roma" district, without money, practically without food, and, in addition, desperately in need of drugs, Artaud in truth did not find the Mexico he sought. He found it only in books, in the objects exhibited in the Palace of Fine Arts, and occasionally in the works of Ortiz Monasterio, "the technician of sculpted stone" and in the painting of Maria Izquierdo. Artaud somewhat harshly said: "There is no Mexican art in Mexico." Even the works of Diego Rivera seemed "impersonal" to him, influenced by Europe, and what was more serious for Artaud, "materialistic." Artaud concluded: "We are far from the powerful solar brilliance of original Mexican art."

Thus Artaud seemed increasingly to close in on himself, to forget the world of modern Mexico and to follow his dream of a return to the golden age of the Aztec empire. In the three lectures he gave at the National Autonomous University of Mexico on February 26, 27, and 29, it was a condemnation of Marxism as well as a condemnation of surrealism as "a negative attitude" that provided the central theme for his talks; and he presented his concept of a magical theater, a sort of link between rituals and signs, as in Mexican mythology: "The gods of Mexico," said Artaud, "are the gods of life prey to a loss of strength, to a vertigo of thought."

This obsession with nothingness and death, joined to the supreme expression of a life made of cruelty and violence—Artaud found it all, completely, in Mexican myths; it then became for him the treasure that, without any doubt, had to be revealed to the Mexicans themselves, who were living cut off from their own past, and to the entire world in order to annihilate the evil power of materialism.

One of the most surprising things Antonin Artaud did while he was in Mexico was to write his *Open Letter to the Governors of the State*, published on May 19, 1936, in *El Nacional*, in which the poet seems to take up the surrealist ideas that had inspired, some ten years earlier, his *Letter to the Dalai Lama*. In the former letter Artaud tried to move the official powers and to make them feel the urgent need of the indigenous cultures, cultures which were, according to Artaud, "for the living": "Yes, I believe in a force sleeping in the land of Mexico. It is for me the only place in the world where dormant natural forces can be useful to the living. I believe in the magical reality of these forces, as one might believe in the healing and beneficial power of certain thermal waters. I believe Indian rituals are the direct manifestations of these forces. I do not wish to study them as an archeologist nor as an artist, but as a sage, in the true meaning of the word; and I will attempt to allow my entire consciousness to be penetrated with their healing virtues, for the good of my soul."

Such was the profound meaning of the "revolutionary message" Artaud wanted to deliver to Mexico. And in 1936 it was indeed revolutionary; Vicente Mendoza wasn't to establish the Folklorist Society of Mexico until two years later, and the idea of an Indigenist Institute was still far in the future. Was Artaud's appeal heard? It is difficult to say, but it appears that after having written his text, the poet became increasingly self-absorbed, focused on his dream of a Red Earth, where one might find the secret of "hidden forces," of "that force of light which turns pyramids on their foundations until they are placed on the sun's magnetic line of attraction." The cult of the sun, yin/yang dualism, medicine from plants, magical auguries, sacrifices, the religion of peyote—for Artaud all of that was the expression of the very heart of his dream, and it gave birth to a vision so powerful that it seemed completely to erase the daily reality of Mexico.

It was at that moment, at that point in the dream, that *A Voyage to the Land of the Tarahumara*[1] appeared, probably at the end of the month of August 1936. Did Antonin Artaud really go to the Tarahumara Sierra? His most faithful Mexican biographer, Cardoza y Aragon, speaks of an official anthropological mission organized at that time by the Palace of Fine Arts for the National Autonomous University of Mexico—since the National Museum of Anthropology did not yet exist—and states that Artaud left for the Sierra on that mission. Curiously, one finds no mention of it in the University archives, and the director of the Fine Arts museum does not even seem to remember Artaud's name. If we have no doubt that Antonin Artaud truly went to the land of the Tarahumara, he must have gone there alone, or more exactly, without any official aid. The difficulties were enormous. At the time, the Chihuahua-Creel train was certainly working, but to arrive in Norogachic, at the bottom of the canyons, there were obstacles. Artaud was ill, weakened by drugs; in addition, he spoke neither Spanish nor the language of the Tarahumara. At that time Norogachic was, like most of the Tarahumara villages, under the protection of the Jesuit mission, and it is difficult to imagine how Artaud, an apostle of paganism, could have communicated with the Indians, much less attended the peyote ceremonies.

We must therefore return to the dream, to the waking dream Artaud had of the petroglyphs of the "mountain of signs," and of the peyote rituals, the dance of Tutuguri and Ciguri of which Carlos Basauri speaks in his *Monografía de los Tarahumaras* published in 1922. It was that same dream of a return to the "Race of Lost Men," that dream of the Land of the Magi Kings, of the rituals of the Kings of

Atlantis, and of the search for what Artaud called a "Primeval Race." For Artaud that race was the people who had knowledge of the secrets of the creation of "Primal Numbers," as Pythagoras did, where men expressed male and female powers with the points of their headbands, which were sometimes white, sometimes red; for, explained Artaud, "the Tarahumara are obsessed with philosophy; and they are obsessed to the point of a kind of physiological magic; with them there is no such thing as a wasted gesture, a gesture which does not have an immediate philosophical meaning. The Tarahumara become philosophers in exactly the way a small child grows up and becomes a man; they are philosophers by birth" (p. 10).

In that dream, with the most violent expression of reality, Artaud discovered all his old obsessions, in a sort of incantation that combines memories of Plato, the Tibetan *Bardo Thodol*, and the story of Heliogabalus. In Norogachic, said Artaud, "I saw . . . the [ritual] of the Kings of Atlantis as Plato describes it in the pages of *Critias*" (p. 64). That ritual, during which an ox was sacrificed to an accompaniment of music and matachini dances, became, in Artaud's vision, the living proof of a communication with the beyond and of the memory of the Atlanteans, gathered together in the same "fabulous and prehistoric source." For Artaud every element, every sign, confirmed that intuition: the Tarahumara were connected to the cabala tradition by signs engraved on the mountains; they were heirs to Judaism through their legends that told of "the appearance among the Tarahumara tribes of a race of fire-bearing Men who had three Masters or Kings who traveled toward the Pole Star" (p. 60). The Tarahumara people were thus the expression of that "ancient and very complete science which the absurd language of Europe has designated: UNIVERSAL ESOTERISM." Here are the symbols found on the objects and clothes of the Tarahumara: the anserated cross, the swastika, the double cross, the large circle with a dot in the middle, the two opposing triangles, the three dots, the four triangles at the four cardinal points, etc.

Thus wandering through the "mountain of signs," absorbed in his exalted vision, at each step the poet saw a drawing, a form, a relief which were so many signs to him: "This inhabited Sierra, this Sierra which exhales a metaphysical thinking in its rocks, the Tarahumara have covered it with signs" (p. 16). In the shapes of the rocks Artaud saw the body of a man who was being tortured, or a naked man leaning out of a large window whose "head was nothing but a huge hole" (p. 14), or the breasts of a woman. He saw the same rock repeated eight times, projecting two shadows on the ground. He saw trees that had "deliberately been burned in the shape of a cross" (p. 16); others which bore "spears, trefoils, or acanthus leaves surrounded by crosses." Tormented nature seemed to indicate the ancient agreement between man and the gods; and it was that agreement that Artaud called Science.

But it was in the Indians' dancing that Artaud found the center of his dream, in that trance which liberated the "hidden forces." Did Artaud really witness the dances of the Tarahumara? He had surely read the writings of Carlos Basauri on the dance of the Tutuguri, in which one finds the description of young goats tied to the ground in the form of a cross, while the blood of the victims was collected in wooden spoons presented to the four cardinal points; and the offering that was made to the three gods of Ciguri: "Umarique" to the east, "Cocoyome" to the north, "Mulato" to the south; and the invocation to Taienari, the sun god. But the question of the authenticity of Artaud's experience has no meaning. For him, describing the peyote ritual was to be aware of an enchantment, a magic which completely transformed him, which turned him into another man.

"After an exhaustion so cruel, I repeat, that I can no longer believe that I was not in fact bewitched, or that these barriers of disintegration and cataclysms I had felt rising in me were not the result of an intelligent and organized premeditation, I had reached one of the last places in the world where the dance of healing by Peyote still exists, or at least the place where it was invented" (pp. 46–47).

For Artaud the Peyote dance was above all a way of no longer being "White:" that is, "one whom the spirits have abandoned"

(p. 48). The peyote ritual was the very expression of the "Red Race," of the most ancient possession by the gods. But for Artaud it was also the revelation of a poetry in its pure state; of creation outside of language: the creation of the gestures and rhythms of dance; pure creation, similar, he said, to a "boiling." Artaud thus thought he had found a pure art, free of all social conventions; a theater in an original state. This is what we sense especially in the strange text-poem Artaud entitled *Tutuguri*, after the name of the owl dance. It is about a dream of the dance of the Tarahumara, haunted by the image of the wooden crosses which six pure men are embracing, as if to marry them; the image of the initial fire which leaves the circle of crosses while the sun joined ranks. "It has formed in the middle of a celestial system. It has suddenly placed itself as if at the center of a tremendous explosion" (p. 103). The beating of the drums and the sound of the *sipirakas* accompanied the steps of the men and the dancer, whose body was carved with a bloody gash, seemed in ecstasy.

The text of that dream, written twelve years later, when Artaud was in the Ivry-sur-Seine clinic after his stay in the asylum in Rodez, in a certain way sealed the dream, closed the poet up inside himself. Artaud's experience in Mexico was the extreme experience of the modern man who discovers a primitive and instinctive people; the recognition of the absolute superiority of ritual and magic over art and science. Artaud, having returned from the Tarahumara Sierra, could no longer tolerate Mexican society. At the end of the month of October, he returned to Europe, heavy with that secret and the knowledge which was inadmissible for Westerners. From then on neither theater, poetry, nor even religion interested Artaud; only the idea of magic and his own intoxication concerned him. His experience in the Tarahumara Sierra marked a complete rupture with the Western world, and Antonin Artaud was unable to resume his previous occupations. He went to Ireland but was expulsed for his scandalous attitude and his use of drugs. His life was henceforth broken, his mind the prisoner of his dream in which the wooden cross of the Tarahumara priests of Ciguri became one with the holy staff of Saint

Patrick. But the modern world rejects dreamers and visionaries; and the poet Antonin Artaud died in isolation, burned up from the inside, after many years of poverty and suffering; from the hospital to the asylum; locked up in himself, carrying into his death the secret of his enchantment, and without the help of the Yumari, the funerary dance through which the Tarahumara help the soul to leave the body to travel to Rehuegachi, high, high up in the sky.[2]

7   The Interrupted Thought of Amerindian Civilizations

S URELY ONE OF THE STRANGEST THINGS about the beliefs of the ancient Mexicans is that in themselves they seemed to contain the means to their own end. We know the role played by omens and prophecies in the fall of the Amerindian civilizations upon the arrival of the first Europeans. Their destruction was foreseen, announced, one might even say expected in many of the Indian cultures, from the most advanced such as those of the Mexica or the Purepecha to the most "barbarian" seminomads from the north and northwest. When the dignitaries of the final cazonci Tangaxoan Zincicha learned that the soldiers of the Conqueror Cristobal de Olid were advancing onto the land of Michoacán, their terror was at its height: "Here they are, they are already arriving. Are we to disappear forever?"[1] All the auguries had already responded to that anguished question. The gods of the Tarascan pantheon had gathered at the top of Mount Xanoato Huacío, not far from the capital Tzintzuntzan, to hear the message of death: "Everything shall become a desert because other men are coming to the earth. They will spare no end of the earth, to the Left Hand and to the Right, and everywhere all the way to the edge of the sea and beyond. The sing-

ing will be all one for there will not be as many songs as we had b
only one throughout the land."[2]

The Maya of Yucatán and the Mexica of Tenochtitlán had r
ceived the same message. All the Amerindian peoples knew that time
had not been given to them. It was apportioned, and they would one
day be destroyed. Through myths, through religious beliefs, through
the laws of astronomy, the Indian world was impregnated with the
idea of a cycle; it lived while awaiting the return of time. The Indian
was not the master of the world. He was born of divine will, then he
was destroyed several times by successive cataclysms. The present
time was not a limitless time; in some ways it was a reprieve before
the coming destruction.

The most important festivals in ancient Mexico were those of the
new year, especially when they coincided with the coming of a new
astronomical cycle: there were the Tup Kaak of the Maya (the extinction of the fires), the Toxiuhmolpilia of the Aztecs (the binding of
our years), and the Hantsinansquaro of the Purepecha (that which
turns). There were also the Wikita of the Papagos, the festivals of the
new fire among the Coras and the Huichols, the ritual of the new
year among the Totonacs and the Otomis. The passage from one time
to another was not an abstraction. It was a dramatic reality, and in
the darkness the anguished people awaited the passage of the Pleiades
at the zenith which announced that the world was going to continue.

It was indeed that belief in an inevitable coming destruction
which caused the loss of the indigenous nations, in Mexico as in most
of the civilizations of the New World. The Conquerors immediately
understood the advantage they could derive from the Indians' anguished wait for the return of time. That belief was troubling for the
Conquerors themselves, for it was to convince them—men like Motolinia or Father Acosta—of the divine mission of which they were,
beyond the violence and injustice, the true instruments.

The belief in an inevitable destruction and the doubt the Indians
of Mexico felt—the myth of the return of the shaman warrior Quetzalcóatl, the waiting for the Uutz Katun, the century of change for

the Maya—were confirmed in the millenarian ideas of the first European voyagers, and in their confidence in the accomplishment of a divine project. Even Father Sahagun, so prudent when dealing with the evocation of the supernatural, saw the "plague" epidemics that decimated the Indian population in 1545 and 1576 as expressions of celestial punishment.

If the New World Christopher Columbus and Pinzón discovered by chance was the final stage of the coming of Christ the King, it was indeed because those lost peoples were also persuaded of the divine nature of the bearded strangers who had come from the other side of the seas, and because they were waiting for the change which was to occur. The Conquerors very quickly understood the benefits they could derive from that ambiguity. They were very careful to propagate and sustain that error beyond all probability. Without hesitation Cortés struck at the Indians' weak points; organizing terror and playing the role of a god: distributing green stones, symbols of prayer among the Maya, or cutting down the ceiba tree in the center of the villages, the only link between the terrestrial world and the empire of the gods. Alvarado had the bodies of the Spanish who died in combat hidden so that the Indians would continue to believe they were immortal. To appear supernatural the Conquerors quickly learned to use their horses (which the Indians confused with the fabulous deer of their legends), blunderbusses, and even alphabetic writing. Those Indians—notables, priests—who, once the moment of surprise had passed, sought to enlighten their compatriots and denounce the fraud were executed as traitors, after being accused of sorcery. In fact there were few contemporaries of the Mexican Conquest who denounced the abuse of the Indian myth of the gods returning to their ancient domain. Sahagun, Mendieta, and even Las Casas suffered the consequences of their moralistic attitude, and their works were held in disgrace until modern times. As for the great Indian texts condemning the lies and injustices of the Spanish Conquerors, they for the most part remained unpublished until the end of the nineteenth century. The taking of the New World could have only been based upon that silence, which erased all indigenous thought.

The silence was immense, terrifying. It engulfed the Indian world from 1492 to 1550, and reduced it to a void. Those indigenous cultures, living, diverse, heirs to knowledge and myths as ancient as the history of man, in the span of one generation were sentenced and reduced to dust, to ashes. How can we comprehend this? To carry out such destruction it took the power of all of Europe, of which the Conquerors were only the instruments: a power in which religion and morality were as important as military and economic strength. The European Conquest of the American continent is surely the only example of one culture totally submerging the conquered peoples, to the point of completely replacing their thought, their beliefs, and their soul. The Conquest was not just a handful of men taking over—a strange mixture of barbarism and daring—seizing the lands, the food reserves, the roads, the political organizations, the work force of the men and the genetic reserve of the women. It was the implementation of a project, conceived at the very beginning of the Renaissance, which aimed to dominate the entire world. Nothing that reflected the past and the glory of the indigenous nations was to survive: the religion, legends, customs, familial or tribal organizations, the arts, the language, and even the history—all was to disappear in order to leave room for the new mold Europe planned to impose upon them.

Such a monstrous project would seem impossible today. At the moment of their encounter with the New World—although the voyagers still had no idea of the origin and number of the populations they were to fight—the Conquerors had already formed the idea of total victory, the domination of bodies and souls. To realize that project, everything was permitted: the most terrible massacres—at Tlaxcala, in Mexico City in the courtyard of the temple of Huitzilopochtli, then during the final assault on the Aztec capital, and in the conquest of the distant lands of northern and western Mexico—

the war *a fuego y a sangre*, slavery, the disorganization of the Indian peoples. Idols were thrown down; priests, diviners, and rulers were killed. Ancient laws were abolished, customs were forbidden. To better achieve their ends the Spanish Conquerors took children from their parents and raised them in hatred of their own past. Denunciation and treason were encouraged, and an attachment to indigenous values was punished as a crime. Social organization was dashed to the ground: the Conquerors knew how to use ancient disputes, rivalries, and even alcoholism. Crossbreeding, aimed at creating a new race detached from its roots, was encouraged in spite of official prohibition. It created a multiplicity of rival castes fighting for individual profit and all showing scorn for the indigenous race. The dispossession of lands and the creation of new chieftaincies favorable to the Spanish Conquerors instituted abuses and legalized injustice. During the two decades of the first audiencia of Mexico, all means, especially violence, were used to carry out the program of the destruction of the indigenous societies: these means formed the set of rules which were to govern the American colonies until Independence.

In carrying out that destruction natural scourges played a primary role, and Indians and Spanish alike saw in them the manifestation of a destiny. Famine, epidemics, like fabulous signs which appeared in the sky, were proof of a divine will, of which the Conquerors had become sacred representatives. The frightful demographic shrinking which immediately followed the Conquest of the great empires of central Mexico—the Aztecs, Purepecha, Zapotecs, Nayars—reducing a population of several million to a few hundred thousand in less than a generation, that holocaust was not seen by the Spanish as a human tagedy (with the exception of a few, such as Mendieta or Las Casas), but rather as the clear manifestation of a divine project. Later, during the seventeenth century, the heirs of the Conquerors began to reflect upon the human catastrophe, yet the death of millions of Indians and the destruction of their culture continued to appear to them as a divine punishment. As Father Acosta expressed it, the punishment was directed against the Spaniards, since, to punish them for their impiety, God had deprived them of the benefits of indigenous manpower.

The Conquest of the New World was not the exchange that the disciples of Erasmus or of Thomas More might have imagined. If in a certain sense the Conquest brought a new *pax* Romana to those territories which were constantly torn apart by tribal wars, it was only able to do so on ruins and ashes. Empires destroyed, princes assassinated, priests stripped of their authority, the indigenous culture, religion, and social order reduced to silence, it was over that annihilated world that the *pax* Hispanica was finally able to reign. The Conquerors' seizing of all social structures rendered the survival of the indigenous values and ideas impossible. With ferocious blindness most of the Spanish chroniclers denied any spirituality to those peoples they had ruined. Having been reduced to a zero degree of culture, the Indians were ready to receive a new soul. Even in the works of the religious figures most favorable to the indigenous world, such as Bartolomé de Las Casas or Mendieta, we perceive the misunderstanding of the Conquest: the Indian, if he was no longer that demon thirsting for blood, given to all vices, closer to beasts than to man, was at the opposite extreme, the *parvulo*, miserable and abandoned by all, the *obejo manzo*, the sweet lamb offered up to the greed of the Spanish colonists. As a criminal or as an irresponsible victim, the Indian was therefore in any case deprived of his dignity as a human being. An irrational being, he could have no thoughts of his own, and his beliefs and customs could not have found a place in the harmony of cultures. The post-Conquest age inherited the destructive violence of the war *a fuego y a sangre*. The destruction wore another face: dispossessed of his lands, his forests, of his right to circulate freely, the Indian was also dispossessed of the most secret part of his being. He became a man without thought, without reason, without morality, a sort of brainless being whom his new master would fashion as he saw fit, in order to inculcate in him the principles of Christian morality and respect for the new political laws. It was that recasting of a being that motivated the mission, and which justified the system of the *encomienda*. Then, following Las Casas's denunciation of the abuses and the promulgation of the New Laws of the Indies, the Indians recovered a right over their own body, but did not for all that recover the right to think. It is significant that the Indians had to wait two centuries to obtain the right to enter the priesthood, and for Independence to have the right to participate in political life.

The silencing of the Indian world is without any doubt one of the greatest tragedies of humanity. At the very moment when the West was rediscovering the values of humanism and inventing the foundations of a new republic based on justice and respect for life, through the perversity of the Conquerors of the New World it initiated the era of a new barbarism, founded upon injustice, despoilment, and murder. It seems that man would never again be both so free and so cruel, discovering at the same time the universality of laws and the universality of violence; discovering the generous ideas of humanism and the dangerous conviction of the inequality of races, the relativity of civilizations and cultural tyranny; discovering, through that tragedy of the Conquest of Mexico, all that was to establish the colonial empires, in America, in India, in Africa, and in Indochina: forced labor, systematic slavery, the expropriation and profitable exploitation of lands, and above all that deliberate disorganization of peoples in order not only to hold on to them, but also to convince them of their own inferiority.

The silence of the Indian world is a tragedy whose consequences we have still not fully measured. It is a double tragedy, for in destroying the Amerindian cultures, the Conqueror also destroyed a part of himself, a part he will undoubtedly never find again.

Men or Gods?

What shocked the Spanish Conquerors upon their arrival in the New World was the strength of the pagan religions, a physical, carnal strength, a real connection between man and the supernatural. For the European of the Renaissance, a skeptic and a realist, that carnal relationship between men and their gods had something profoundly shocking about it, something disquieting which seemed closer to sorcery than to religion (and didn't he immediately think of Egyptian and Babylonian themes, of bloody Baal, and undoubtedly also of the pre-Christian superstitions which were still so much alive in Europe?)—this is why the indigenous religions were battled and condemned as true expressions of the demoniacal.

Inspired by their first contacts, the writings of the chroniclers were unanimous in their condemnation, although in them one can also perceive a sort of fascination. The religious faith of the Indians (Aztecs, Purepecha) was total, impassioned, stamped with a mystical fervor that the rituals of the ancient world did not have. When Father Pané undertook to write the first account of the inhabitants of that unknown world (*Relación acerca de las antigüedades de los Indios*) he could not help but closely tie the history of men into that of the divinities. Fra Andrés de Olmos, surely the first true historian of New Spain, whose work has today disappeared, primarily stressed that carnal relationship which connected men to their gods. When men were created, they were made with the blood and bones of the gods, and for that reason they were devoted to serving them forever and without restriction.[3] In another essential text regarding the culture of the ancient Purepecha, the *Relación sobre la Residencia de Michoacán* by Father Francisco Ramirez, it is the same consanguinity that is proclaimed: men were born of eight little balls made of ashes mixed with the blood of the god Curitacaheri. As in most of the Amerindian philosophies, the boundary between the divine and the human is indistinct: "They had," writes Father Ramirez, "many gods who, according to what we may believe, had been great men among them, who had once distinguished themselves through their actions."[4]

This indistinctness between human and divine nature is found in many of the myths of ancient Mexico. "That Quetzalcóatl," writes Father Sahagun, "even though he was a man, was considered to be a god."[5] This was the case with Kulkulcán, the Feathered Serpent of the Itzás, and with the god-hero Itzamná, whom the Maya venerated as the inventor of their calendar and of hieroglyphs. This was also the case with the founding father-gods of the cultures of the northwest; alongside Taoyappa, the sun, there ruled the *Mexe*, or the mummy of the giant Nayar, whom the Spanish burned after the conquest of Huaynamota.

Pre-Hispanic religions were basically characterized by a form of completeness. There was no break between the divine and the human, and the creation of the world of men occurred without a rupture between the natural and the supernatural. It was indeed that which most shocked and worried those strangers who disembarked onto the New World, bearers of the concepts and prejudices of Renaissance Europe. For the Conquerors, what was created could have no direct contact with its creator. To believe in the identity of man with the divine, and especially to believe in the reality of the supernatural, was both contrary to the laws of the Christian church and to the principles of reason. It was to enter into a magical world completely contrary to the concepts of the new man of the sixteenth century who was sure of his intelligence and his capacity to master reality.

That was indeed one of the aspects of Indian thought which the Spanish religious figures did all they could to strongly fight against. Worship services, pagan rituals, dancing festivals (the *mitotes*), sacrifices, and trances were abolished beginning with the first encounters, because they were the manifestation of that blending of the real and the divine which appeared so diabolical to the Europeans. The profanation of temples, the cutting down of the sacred trees of the Maya, and the massacre in the courtyard of the temple of Huitzilopochtli by Alvarado's soldiers were the first actions directed against Amerindian thought. Through the terror they inspired, those acts were also political, but they were above all a proclamation of the new order, in which only the Christian church would reign over the sacred. In one fell swoop they abolished all ancient mystical expressions, trances, dreams, songs, omens. From the start they excluded natives from the new clergy, because, as Father Sahagun expresses it, "they are considered unworthy and incapable of being priests."[6] The con-

sequence of that suppression was the distrust felt by the Spanish
priests for all popular manifestations of Christian faith in the New
World, beginning with the cult of the Virgin of Guadalupe.

At the time of the Conquest the indigenous religions of Mexico
all showed that cohesion of the human and the divine. Ritual dances,
shamanic ceremonies, the use of hallucinogens (peyote, datura,
mushrooms, but also tobacco and maguey or balche alcohol) were
the means through which any man, regardless of his past or his social
origins, could change his nature and become the incarnation of the
divinity.

The extraordinary spectacle of the pagan ceremonies, the beauty
of the costumes, the splendor of the feathered headdresses, the
dances, sometimes depicting battles, and the sacrificing of captives
dressed in the image of the gods, all of that spoke of the transfiguration which was at the heart of Indian thought. The second book of
Sahagun's *History* is a detailed inventory of these magical festivals,
some of which lasted without pause for several days, ending in the
transfiguration of the participants, victims and dancers joining in a
supernatural communion.

For the festival of the stellar god Tezcatlipoca, in the month of
toxcatl, a young man was prepped throughout an entire year, at the
end of which he became the god's representative on earth. He "went
through the whole town very well dressed, with flowers in his
hand, and accompanied by certain personalities (probably prominent
people). He would bow graciously to all whom he met, and they all
knew he was the image of Tezcatlipoca and prostrated themselves
before him, worshipping him wherever they met him." Twenty days
before the festival the young god was given four wives with the names
of goddesses: Xochiquetzal, Xilonen, Atlatonan, and Vixtocioatl. The
festival itself lasted five days, after which the young man went to the
temple of Tlacuchcalco, where, after breaking one of the flutes which
he had played during the previous year on each step of the temple,
he offered himself up to the knife of the sacrificers. In the seventh
month, one of his wives, Vixtocioatl, the eldest sister of the Tlaloc

gods of rain, in turn died, then in the eighth month Xilonen, the virgin mother, was sacrificed. In the eleventh month Teteo Inman, she whom the Indians affectionately called "Our Ancestor," began a silent dance which lasted eight days. Surrounded by women, "especially the women healers and midwives," she who represented the goddess participated in a battle of flowers, then she married a great dignitary and joined him at the top of the temple. Then, at the temple, the sacrificers cut off her head and flayed her, and the great priest danced around wearing her skin.

What was shocking, in the complicated rituals transcribed by Bernardino de Sahagun, and what without any doubt troubled him greatly, was the continual presence of divinities amidst men. On the eighteenth day of the festival of Teotleco ("the arrival of the gods") the priests made a pile of corn flour in front of the temples "in the shape of a bone. On this pile the gods imprinted the sole of one foot as a sign that they had returned." When the priest saw the sign of the foot he shouted "Our lord has arrived!"[7]

The extreme complexity of those rituals caused magic to surge forth, for the gestures, repeated year after year, century after century, affirmed transfiguration; slaves and priests, dignitaries and captives through the magic of that sacred theater identified fully with the forces they were representing.

The presence of gods among men was the very heart of the religious fervor of the ancient Mexicans, Aztecs, Maya, and Purepecha. Images, ornaments of feathers and precious stones, gold and silver had symbolic value. But the presence of the gods was above all an invisible, mysterious force that linked the actions of men, was blended with their breath and their words, haunted them, reassured them, and frightened them all at the same time. The gods were not those vain idols which the first European voyagers were content to see. Tezcatlipoca was the invisible, untouchable presence that directed every human life: "It is a fact that you are before him (in his presence), although you are not worthy to see him; and even if he doesn't speak to you, because he is invisible and not palpable," says the prayer reported by Sahagun.[8] And the hymn of Nezahualcóyotl uses the same words: "You are invisible and untouchable, as the wind and the night."[9]

For the Aztecs the wind was Quetzalcóatl Ehecatl, the breath that preceded the rain. Tezcatlipoca was like shadow, and Cihuacoatl, the goddess of origins, was like a groaning in the night. The Indian divinities all had that double appearance, one human and carnal, the other supernatural and fleeting. But the forces they incarnated were the very forces of existence: fire, water, clouds, wind, trees, stars. For the Europeans trained in the rationalism of the Renaissance, that plurality was the very sign of idolatry. They could not imagine the ambiguity that was the basis of Amerindian religions. No chronicler, at the time of the Conquest, seems to have perceived the unity of the indigenous world beyond the apparent contradiction between shamanic rituals and beliefs in a creator god, invisible, untouchable, "the master of the near and the far," as Nezahualcóyotl sang about him.

This is indeed because America, at the time when the foreign voyagers set foot on it, was living in religious reality, with the help of ceremonies and rituals of transfiguration.[10] The words "polytheism" and "monotheism" had no meaning for those cultures which represented the same natural force under various forms. One of the most surprising examples of their symbolism is in the religion of the Uacusecha, the faction that dominated the empire of the Purepecha in the fourteenth century. Curicaueri, the god of fire, also symbolized light, the heat of the sun, life. His earthly representation was in the form of the *padra*, the obsidian matrix from which were extracted the ritual knives used in sacrifices and the arrowheads used in war. This is the same abstraction one finds again among the peoples of Nayarit (the Coras and the Hueyquechales), who venerated the solar god in the form of the white Tayaoppa stone.

The term "idolatry," which all the Spanish chroniclers used to describe the Amerindian religions, clearly shows their incomprehension, their prejudice. It was easy for them to make caricatures of the rituals and symbols of those religions which, at the time they were writing their chronicles, had been reduced to clandestine ceremonies and superstitions. In an attempt to understand what the Indian religions truly were there remain only the testimonies written by the Indians themselves, the *Chronicles of Michoacán*, the codices (especially the *Codex Florentinus*), and the *Books of the Chilam Balam*. Thanks to these texts, miraculously saved from the burning stakes of the Inquisition, we can catch a glimpse of what their philosophy and religion might have been before the destruction of the Indian cultures, and imagine the direction of their evolution. Today, despite the gulf that separates us from those cultures, we can imagine what they might have created, using their original philosophical beliefs: the idea of transfiguration, trance, the corporality of faith, that universe where the earthly and the divine connected forming an indissociable whole. We might imagine the importance which that evolution could have had for the world, how it might have changed the European concepts of spirituality, the idea of man, morality, politics. In war and sacrifices as in the simplest acts of daily life, the Indian was connected to natural forces, to creation in its entirety. He was at the same time the food and substance of the gods. For him death was not a completion, nor the beginning of another life. It was a definitive union with the sacred universe.

Trance

It was perhaps the exaltation, the adventuring outside oneself that frightened the Europeans most when they landed for the first time on the American continent. Festivals of dancing, bloody sacrifices, hallucinations, dreams—for the Indians all of that tended toward immediate and irrational communication with the other world. Everything was done with a view to revealing the divine on earth. The Spanish chroniclers reported that mystical frenzy in tones of shock. Indian dancers were not symbols. With their tatoos, body and face painting, their clothes and feather headdresses, they truly were Xiuhtecuhtli, the lord of fire, "who appeared to throw flames," Yacatecuhtli, the black lord of merchants, Vixtocihuatl, the mistress of salt, or Xilonen, the goddess of young corn. They were even part of the body of the god Huitzilopochtli, who advanced by slithering like a snake into the courtyard of the chief temple.[11]

What struck the Spanish about Indian ritual was the cohesion between man and his myths. Those dances were not reserved for priests or princes alone. During the *macehualiztli*, the dance of the people, reports Sahagun, "many got together and paired off in twos and threes, in a large circle, according to their number. They carried flowers in their hands and with their finery they wore plumes. They all made the same motion with body, feet and hands at one time, which was worth seeing, for being very artistic. Their motions were executed to the beating of drums and rattles. They all sang together in chorus, with very sonorous voices, the praise of the god whose feast they celebrated. They have the same custom today, only dedicated to another personality. They govern their motions in posture and dress according to what they sing; they dispose of a great many different movements as well as a great variety of tunes for their singing, but it is all very graceful and even highly mystical. Idolatry is not uprooted as yet."[12] This emotional description by a witness indeed reveals the essential difference between the ancient Mexica or Michoaca and the Europeans: in those ardent, collective civilizations every man and woman could accede immediately to the supernatural order, and yet they did not exceed the limits permitted by society. Trance and revelation found their places in society. Thus each *macehual* [plebeian] could live the supreme gift of self-sacrifice, without the idea of redemption or martyrdom.

We understand today that there was very little difference between the Michoaca king Tariacuri demanding as an honor the sacrifice of his son and a Sioux Indian at the end of the last century convinced of the necessity of the bloody ritual of the Ghost Dance.

Trance and possession signified the entrance of the divine breath into the material body of men. The *Chronicles of Michoacán* give the most striking example of that belief: when the slave of Uiquixo, the lord of Ucareo, returns from an encounter with the gods, she is inhabited by the goddess-mother Cuerauaperi and demands to drink some blood. Those who were thus possessed by the goddess were in a state of trance and walked by themselves to the temple, where they offered themselves up to the sacrificers' knife.[13] Another example is that of the famous *nahual*, that animal form which a man could sometimes assume, and which turned him into a necromancer. In the diluted version Father Sahagun gives of it, the *nahualli* was a sorcerer who could change himself into various sorts of animals. The sorcerers' model was the stellar god Tezcatlipoca, he who was in fact also called Naualpilli, the prince-magician.[14] Indeed, the heritage of Amerindian shamanism is recalled under the lycanthropic theme common to most primitive cultures, and it was undoubtedly that which the Spanish Conquerors found most condemnable and incomprehensible about indigenous beliefs.

Shamanism

Little remains today of the shamanic rituals practiced in ancient Mexico. The *nahualli* of the Aztecs, the *hmen* of the Maya, the *sikuame* of the Purepecha have survived the destruction of Indian religious concepts, perhaps because their hidden role preserved them. A sorcerer, a doctor, an astrologist, the shaman was the symbol of man's direct contact with the other world. He was the diviner, he who healed or bewitched, he who conspired and revealed supernatural powers. Along with shamanism came a knowledge of plants, particularly poisons and hallucinogens: peyote, datura, mushrooms, and also *yauhtli* (the incense used to reduce suffering at the time of human sacrifices), tobacco, and alcohol.

But rather than black magic, there was a unique system of thought that inspired shamanism. Even the great theocratic civilizations of Mexico in the time that preceded the Spanish Conquest were under the influence of shamanism. Blood rituals, offerings, the use of tobacco and hallucinogens were proof of the importance of shamanic practices. Before any divination, or before healing ceremonies, re-ports Pedro Ponce de Leon, the doctor gave "a speech and prayed to the fire, then poured a little *pulque*,"[15] following a ritual which is still practiced today in some Indian cultures.

Shamanic themes also survive in myths. In the treatise by Jacobo de la Serna, the Aztec emergence myth is associated with healing formulas in which the female uterus is designated under the symbolic name of the "seven caves." The battle of Tezcatlipoca-Titlacaoan against the hero Quetzalcóatl is the mythical expression of shamanic rivalry, as was perhaps the feast of the god Huitzilopochtli, during which factions confronted each other in a simulated battle which ended in sacrifice. The festival dedicated to the Chichimeca god Mix-coatl was the occasion for propitiatory sacrifices which remind one of shamanic rituals, in which captives, feet and hands tied together, played the role of deer killed in the hunt.[16]

Among the ancient Mexicans and Purepecha, the shaman and the necromancer seem to have played an ambiguous role: both feared and hated, they were often denounced and put to death (as they later would be by the tribunal of the Inquisition). Yet it is the shamanic spirit that has remained alive in Indian thought. Shamanism expresses the individuality of religious faith, and above all, the necessary com-plementarity of the forces of good and evil which is the foundation of Amerindian beliefs. In addition, shamanism was the adequation of religious fervor to social structures, corresponding to divisions into factions and groups. This is why, despite the abolishment of the clergy and indigenous political authority, despite the banning of ceremonies and the destruction of temples, the ancient shamanic healing rituals were able to survive, and even, in some cases, adapt to the new laws and beliefs. In most of the indigenous societies of Mexico, nagualism, divination, and hallucinatory rituals have been maintained, not as archaisms, but because they have expressed the continuity of the indigenous way of thinking, symbolic and incanta-tory, another way of perceiving reality.

It is in the north and northwest of Mexico that shamanism has been best preserved, probably because the seminomadic societies had not developed a static structure or a true clergy. These societies, based on the family, the clan, or the tribe, valued above all the freedom to worship and divinatory practices. In those societies the shaman was almost always associated with war chiefs, and it was he whom the Christian missionaries would battle under the name of *hechicero* (the caster of spells). It was he who inspired and sometimes organized the indigenous resistance in the "barbarian" wars: among the Cazcanes, the Xiximes, the Acaxees, the Zuaques, the Tepehuanes, the Seris, the Yaquis. Messianic movements developed at the beginning of the seventeenth century throughout desert America under the impulse of those visionary, exalted shamans who preached "holy war" against the Christian invader.

The Diviners

One of the primary activities of the shaman was divination. The feature which most differentiated the Indians of middle America from their European conquerors was surely the former's belief in the truth of auguries and omens. Most of the Amerindian civilizations were troubled by those prophecies which announced the changes to come. For the Maya it was the return of the Itzá masters and their chief Kukulcán. Among the Aztecs there was a similar prophecy—which perhaps came from the Toltecs—which the prince-poet Nezahualcóyotl (if we are to believe his nephew Ixtlilxóchitl) contributed in spreading. Curiously, the terms of that prophecy were the same as those of their rivals, the Purepecha of Michoacán: "Even the little trees began to bear fruit, so much so that the branches were overloaded and bent downward, the magueys, even the little ones, began to shoot up long blades that looked like timbers, the little girls became pregnant while still children and had breasts as large as the women because of the pregnancy, and the children, small as they were, carried children on their backs. The older women began to produce knives made of black, white, red, and yellow stone."[17]

Omens and auguries signified the proximity of the real and the sacred. For the ancient Mexicans the fate of man was tightly linked to supernatural forces, and the greatest activity of the spirit consisted of seeking to pierce the mystery of their relationship. Dreams and omens were a means of discovering those laws, as if the divinities, through negligence or through a whim, sometimes allowed their creatures to approach their reign. Dreams were the privileged moment of that encounter. The great Indian texts are filled with the magic of dreams. In the *Chronicles of Michoacán*, when Tariacuri's nephews Hiripan and Tangaxoan finally receive royal investiture at the end of their wandering, it is through a dream that they obtain it. Through those dreams the future princes saw the god Curicaueri and the goddess Xaratanga, who showed them the location of future temples, steam baths, and ball courts where their cult was to be celebrated. Later, it was Tariacuri who evoked the quest for power of Caracomoco, a former slave. In order to be consecrated Lord by the god Querenda Angapeti, Caracomoco slept every night on the steps of the temple until the god, moved by so much stubbornness, sent him the dream which would make him a king.

As the art of divination, astrology had a privileged place in Aztec society. Rituals and legends emphasized the ties that joined men to the will of the gods. Forecasts were at the heart of the lunar calendar. The famous *Tonalamatl* (the *Book of Signs*), perhaps of Toltec origin (the legend has it that it was given to men by Quetzalcóatl), divided the twenty days of the lunar month into lucky or unlucky days. The signs predestined those who belonged to them: Ehecatl, the sign of the wind, made men avid and brutal. Mazatl, the sign of the deer, relegated men to fear. Tochtli, the sign of the rabbit, sentenced them to drunkenness and death by drowning. Ce Acatl, One Reed, the sign of Quetzalcóatl, the sign of misfortune, found its confirmation in the arrival of the Spaniards. Ce Miquiztli, the sign of Tezcatlipoca, asked that slaves be freed. Ce Malinalli, destined he who was born under it

to be fearful like a wild beast. Ce Ozomatli, the sign of the Cihuate-
teo harpies, caused sickness and death in children. Ce Cozcaquahtli
was the sign of happiness. Ce Atl, the sign of water, was the sign of
the evil Chalchiuhtlicue. Every day of one's life was ruled by a sign,
and none was indifferent. Only the magi ruled over time, capable of
foreseeing and changing the invisible forces that surrounded men.

Amerindian societies were troubled by the dreams and auguries,
and it was their anxiety which caused their destruction. But it was
also in their beliefs that they found a reason to live. Those societies,
guided by dreams, were naturally the opposite of the pragmatic and
materialistic West. But they represented above all another way of
thinking, another consciousness. The coherence between the diurnal
and the nocturnal expressed a necessary equilibrium between con-
traries, a harmony of life and death, of good and evil.

The theme of the fragility of terrestrial life, of the precariousness
of beauty and love is at the very heart of Amerindian thought, and,
in reading the songs and the hymns of the ancient Mexicans one can't
help thinking of the great themes of baroque poetry: thus, in Xayacamach's response to Tecayehuatzin:

> Let there be joy!
> Be truly joyful
> here in the place of flowers,
> O lord Tecayehautzin, you
> that are adorned with collars
> Is it true that we return to life again?
> Your heart knows the answer:
> We come here to live only once.[18]

Or the anonymous voice of Tenochtitlán:

> We have come only to sleep
> We have come only to dream.
> No, this is not true,
> We have not come to earth to live!

But none has surpassed the beauty of the song of Nezahualcóyotl:

> With flowers You write,
> O giver of Life;
> With songs You give color,
> with songs You shade
> those who must live on the earth.
>
> Later You will destroy eagles and ocelots;
> we live only in Your book of paintings,
> here, on the earth.[19]

The Cycle of Time

Among most Amerindian peoples the belief in dreams and auguries expressed a profound philosophical idea, that of the recurrence of time. The linear concept of time, born out of nothingness and returning to nothingness, was as foreign to Amerindian cultures as was the idea of a purely material world devoid of finality. Those men who intensely experienced the encounter of the real and the supernatural, who knew that their life was a parcel of divine existence, and who saw in the world which surrounded them, in the animals, plants, and natural phenomena that many expressions of the divinity, could not conceive of a universe without end, where time would flee into nothingness. The extraordinary success in the classic Mayan era was the calendar and Long Count [datation on steles with hieroglyphic numbers giving the full length of time from the mythical date of the creation of the world], which was based on the belief in a cyclical, spherical universe in which time endlessly began again. For the European of the Renaissance, in love with knowledge and skeptical, the Amerindian world, through its religious and symbolic system, was completely incomprehensible. The philosophy of recurrence, the idea of a finite and predestined universe, for the Conquerors became the very symbol of pagan darkness—"ridiculous fables provided by Satan," said Father Sahagun, in the prologue to book 7, which is devoted to astrology.

However, long before astronomy appeared in Europe, as early as the sixth century Mayan observers had developed that science and had perfected a remarkable calendar based on the course of Venus and those of the moon and the sun, which, using corrections, reduced error to a few hours per century. What essentially differentiated the Mayan astronomers from the scholars of the Renaissance was their philosophical conception. For the Maya (as for the Aztecs) the goal was not to master the laws of the universe, but to perceive its destiny. One might nevertheless imagine that the Mayan observers, when they carefully noted the course of the stars or established the plan of lunar eclipses, showed the same curiosity and the same excitement which later inspired Galileo, Tycho Brahe, or Copernicus. But unlike the Europeans, whose science was outside religion, the Amerindian astronomers conceived of a system that was entirely dedicated to the cults of the gods.

The civilizations of ancient Mexico were instilled with the idea of the return of time, of the wheel of destinies. Among the Maya the cycles of the *tun* years [360 days] were called *cuceb*, which evoked the wheel of the squirrel. Time was a prodigious set of gears turning at different speeds, from the movement of *uinal* days [a month of twenty days] to the *katun* centuries [twenty years] and to the great *Ahau katun* centuries, which had a duration of 23,040,000,000 days. But for the Maya, as for the Aztecs, those days, months, and years were not abstract. They were divine forces of which the stars and the designs in the sky were visible marks. The sacralization of numbers, their corporal representation gave time a supernatural and living value. The present—that passage of which the Mexican poets Xayacamach and Nezahualcóyotl speak—was linked to the past and the future by that wheel of time, a movement of numbers and stars. By numbering the days, by painting them on *amate* paper or engraving them on *tun* stones in the form of masked gods, the astronomer participated in the harmony of the universe. He was able to make the invisible seen.

The calendar was useful for harvests, for foreseeing epidemics, droughts, wars. But the finality of that representation of time was elsewhere; both prayer and knowledge, it was the very symbol of Indian thought.

There have been many questions about how astronomical calendars were circulated throughout America. How could the same calendar have been known simultaneously by peoples as different as the Toltecs, the Aztecs, and the barbarian nations of the northwest—the Apaches, the Sioux, the Arapahos—going as far as the limits of the continent to the Iroquois, the Algonquins, and the Kwakiutl? Whereas other knowledge and other technology remained localized—gold, the discovery of bronze, pewter, the use of poisons, and the rules of architecture—the invention of the calendar spread over the North American continent as easily as did agricultural techniques. This is because the calendar undoubtedly expressed a philosophical thought tied to the Amerindian cultures' genesis myths, which were dominated by a belief in a square world divided into directions and colors, and by a spherical conception of a universe in which everything endlessly begins again. One of the chiefs in the last Indian resistance in North America, the Oglala Sioux Yahaka Sapa (Black Elk) expressed this thought clearly:

You have noticed that everything an Indian does is inscribed in a circle. This is so because the power of the universe acts according to circles and because all things tend to become round. In ancient times, when we were a strong and happy people, all our power came from the sacred circle of the nation, and as long as it wasn't broken, our people remained prosperous. The flourishing tree was the living center of the circle, and the circle of the four quarters nourished it. The east gave peace and light, the south gave heat, the west gave rain, and the north, through its cold and powerful winds, gave strength and endurance. This knowledge came to us from the other world with our religion. All that the power of the universe does is done in a circle.[20]

We are aware of the importance of the wheel, the symbol of time (and of the calendar) in most pre-Hispanic cultures, particularly among the Aztecs. Among the ancient Purepecha one of the most important festivals was that of Hantsinansquaro (from the verb *Uantsikuarhini*, to turn), during which man was confronted with the movement of the stars. The idea of cyclical time saturates the mythology of the Maya and the Aztecs: the events of everyday life, like the great mythical facts, had universal value, because they would be reproduced. This is why magic was so important. Believing in a return of time, and in the rhythm of creation, the ancient Mexicans could not adhere to the scheme of Christianity, in which only the will of an omnipotent God-Father acted. Nor could they accept the pragmatic determinism which inspired the European Renaissance.

Before the Conquest all the efforts of Indian thought tended to divine and to write the recurrent design of the universe. It is not enough to say that magic was at the heart of those cultures; there was something more profound and more durable than a network of superstitions, as the first Western explorers wanted to interpret it: their's was a coherent system of thought, that is, a true philosophy.

In that system the experienced and the imaginary were in harmony, and ideas and social laws formed an indissociable whole. Because they believed in the rhythm of time, the ancient Mexicans knew the value of the world which carried them, and submitted to its natural laws. They also knew their own limitations, and the relativity of the human kingdom—that is, the doubting of oneself without which there could be no culture. At the same time they discovered the fundamental laws of science, numbers (the position of numerals and zero), geometry, the astronomical calendar. Above all else, they had conceived a society based on equilibrium, where each person, from the most humble to the highest up, was accountable before the gods.

The cyclical conception of time was clearly the starting point of a more complex philosophy tending toward the same perfection found in the great philosophies of India or China. The idea of metempsychosis is expressed in many myths and rituals of ancient Mexico, such as in the festival of Inextiua ("to search for good luck," as reported by Father Sahagun[21]), during which men and gods danced together, or in legends of nagualism created around the shamanic couple Quetzalcóatl-Tezcatlipoca. The wheel theme is also linked to that of the directions of the world, that is, from the axis of destiny around which figure the four beginnings of cycles: among the Maya, the years called Muluc (north), Cauac (south), Hix (east), and Kan (east); among the Aztecs, Tecpatl (the silex, to the north), Tochtli (the rabbit, to the south), Acatl (the reed, to the east) and Calli (the house, to the west). Among those peoples, life was linked to the movement of the wheel of time to such a degree that at the end of a cycle (when the year One Muluc of the Mayan Buc Xoc, or the year One Reed of the Aztec calendar returned), the fear of destruction took hold of them, and they waited in darkness for the sign that the world would continue to exist.

Catastrophe

Certainly no civilization has lived in such expectation of its final destruction. The Mayan astronomers anxiously watched for the coming of the time of the Utz Katun, the *katun* of the fold (the Katun 8 Ahau, whose sign coincided with the fold of the paper on which the passages of time were inscribed). All the prophecies evoked the *katun* of change in the same terms. First, Napuctun: "It will burn the earth, there will be circles of fire in the sky . . . It will burn the earth, the hooves of the deer during the katun of the new time."

That of Ah Xupan Nauat: "Then Kinich Kakmo will come, the Ara of Fire with the face of the Sun, during the Katun 8 Ahau. When he arrives, the sky will be turned over, the earth will move. When the sky moves, it will be the time of sin."

Napuctun again: "This shall happen in the sky and on the earth, in the time of the Twelfth year Tun. The sky will burn, the earth will burn, greed will reign. This will be caused by drought. Then Hunab Ku, the Unique God, will be implored, and the eyes of the governor will cry, during seven years of drought. Slabs of stone will shatter, the nests of birds will burn, the plains of grass will burn, in the valleys and between the mountains."[22]

The myth of destruction was also one of genesis, as among the Aztecs: *nahui ollin*, "4-Movement," the last sun which would bring the final destruction of the world:

The fifth Sun, its sign 4-Movement,
Is called the Sun of Movement because it moves and follows its path.
And as the elders continue to say, under this sun there will be earthquakes and hunger, and then our end shall come."[23]

There was also the ancient Purepecha myth of successive destructions: the gods, having at first made incomplete men who lacked joints, had to destroy the world three times.[24] What differentiates the myths of destruction from the myth of the flood is that, in Mexican thought, the destruction was connected to the creation of the world in an explicit way. All that the gods had made, they destined to destruction. Life on earth was but a brief instant between initial chaos and final chaos. The meaning of this myth is above all religious: to avoid destruction, men had to pray, offer blood sacrifices. But the myth of destruction also inspired Amerindian philosophy. Unlike the idea of a universe based on harmony and the golden age, as the idealists of the European Renaissance conceived it, the Indian world (and particularly that of the Aztecs, the Purepecha, and the Maya) saw creation as a succession of catastrophes, that is, as discontinuity, chaos. That conception was the complete opposite of the Christian one. In Europe, it was necessary to wait until the beginning of the scientific era with, for example, the theory of Max Planck, before the same concept of chaotic creation would be discovered. For the ancient Mexicans, as the world had not been ordered according to man's understanding, it could not be in his image. There was something quite profound in the Amerindian religions' refusal of anthropomorphism, a refusal the Western system could not accept, because it was above all an ethnocentric system. Stripped of their symbolic significance, Indian beliefs and myths were reduced by the Conquerors to the role of pagan figurations, that is, to absurdities or superstitions.

Blood sacrifices, a ritual identification with death, masks of divine representatives ceased to remind the faithful of the inevitability of destruction which presided over the creation of the world. The proximity of chaos and death which had been at the heart of Indian thought was erased in the presence of the new masters' rationalism and linear conception of time. How could the Indians have resisted such annihilation when those strangers brought the destruction of Indian values and beliefs precisely according to the terms of their destiny? The wheel of time, the knowledge of divine numbers, the laws of the stars, everything that had built Mexican thought, through the actions of the Conquest was then destroyed. The new religion could then be built upon that silence.

Thus, the plurality of the Indian kingdoms—a tripartite power among the Aztecs or the Purepecha, representation of professional bodies, public justice—that coherent and fragile whole had to concede before the political conception of the Conquerors, who were establishing in New Spain the foundations for a colonial administration.

By abolishing the element of doubt and the philosophy of a world devoted to catastrophe, the Europeans definitively prepared to establish their new empires all over the world. To instill their materialistic politics—that is, fundamentally to facilitate the rational application of the lessons of the *Prince*—western Europe halted the development of any original indigenous thought, beliefs which were the millenary heritage of the cultures of middle America. That thought, expressed entirely in rituals and mythical representations, had reached the moment in history when it could be refined, built upon. The destructive Conquest, through a cruel irony, occurred at a time when those rituals and myths might have given shape to a true philosophy, whose influence on the world might have had the same impact as that of Taoism or Buddhism. The silence that ensued, in the despair of repression, is the only measure we have left in our attempt to understand.

"Omeyocan," or the Gender of the Gods

"They also knew, asserted and said that there were twelve heavens, and in the highest were a great lord and his wife. They called the great lord Ometecuhtli, which means twice a lord, and his consort was called Omecíhuatl, which means two times a Lady. And they were both called such so that one would know they ruled over the twelve heavens and the earth. And it was said that upon that great lord depended the existence of all things, and through his rule came the influence or the heat that would engender the boys and girls in the wombs of their mothers."[25]

One of the most ancient myths of Mexico divided the universe into two distinct forces, a male principle and a female principle. We can imagine, along with Angel Maria Garibay and Miguel Leon-Portilla, a single and same deity, both male and female in the form of a couple reigning over Omeyocan, the place of duality. That couple was at the origin of all terrestrial life, for the ancient Mexicans did not separate existence from sexuality. The principle of sexual duality is constant in pre-Hispanic mythology, and most of the gods were evoked in their male or female form: Xiuhtecuhtli, the old god of fire, was one of the names of Ometecuhtli, as seen in the *Codex Florentinus*:

Mother of the gods, father of the gods, the old god
    Spread out on the navel of the earth,
    Within the circle of turquoise.[26]

The gods' double nature (male and female) is asserted in the Aztec religion: Xiuhtecuhtli, but also Mictlantecuhtli, the god of hell, was "our father and our mother of hells."[27] During difficult births, the midwife prepared the parturient for death by invoking the goddess Cihuacoatl (whom Sahagun compares to Eve): "Prepare to depart to that place of happiness which is the house of your father and your mother the sun."[28]

One might venture, as Miguel Leon-Portilla did (see *Aztec Thought and Culture*), to compare the idea of this double divine nature to the yin/yang philosophy of Chinese Taoism. Among the Purepecha of Michoacán, as among the Aztecs, the world was divided into two sexual tendencies which had to be balanced. If the Aztec pantheon included many goddesses in charge of rituals of love, fertility, and the uses of medicine, among the ancient Purepecha, heirs of the nomadic Chichimeca culture, creation seemed to be symbolized by those two complementary divinities Curicaueri, the god of fire and war, portrayed by the golden disk of the sun, and Xaratanga, his sister (and his consort), goddess of fertility and death, represented by the silver half-moon. This ancient symbolism is still alive among the Tarascan Indians of Michoacán: civil affairs and power are still under the protection of the patron saint, whereas female issues and traditional medicine are the responsibility of Nana Cutzi, the moon. As for the creator god, he is Kuerahpiri, the holy spirit, who evokes the goddess Cuerauaperi, mother of the world. Once again we find the bisexuality of the genitor principle, ruling over Omeyocan, the Aztec's place of duality.

The same fundamental sexuality existed among the Maya. The *Popul-Vuh* of the Quiché Maya of Guatemala relates the creation of the world in the form of a sexual act: on a mat the hero-god Ah Pu impregnates the virgin Ixquic, and from that union creation is born, the issue of the water of the sky.[29] This brings to mind the ancient myths of India, or the supernatural couple Isis and Osiris. For the ancient Mexicans, the world as it was was not the result of chance. It was the real image of a celestial existence, and carried within it, like a living secret, the creative force of the gods. A violent and beautiful explosion like desire, like love, creation necessarily had to carry out that revolution which, at the end of time, would lead it to destruction and chaos.

Earth Mother

All Amerindian civilizations expressed a sacralization of the earth. From the north to the south of the immense continent the earth mother was the beginning of life. Among the Quiché Maya it was the goddess Ixquic, among the Aztecs, Coatlicue, or Toci, Our Mother, she whom the Nahuas of Tamazula called Ehuacueye, She of the Leather Skirt. Among the Purepecha, it was Cuerauaperi, also called Pevame, She Who Gives Birth. The cult of the earth mother was not limited to the agricultural societies alone. For most of the nomads of the Mexican north and northwest creation was symbolized by the couple Sun Father and Earth Mother. The ritual of the *salva*—the offering of the first hunt—was practiced by the Chichimeca barbarians and by their heirs the Mexica and Purepecha, as it continued to be until modern time by the warrior Indians of the frontier, the Apaches, Comanches, and Lipans. For the chronicler Ixtlilxóchitl, that ritual was characteristic of the barbarians: "The head of the first prey they captured during the hunt was cut off and shown to the sun as during a sacrifice. They then worked the earth where the blood had been spilled." He adds: "They had no idols, but they called the sun their father and the earth their mother."[30]

Among the Na-u-ni, Comanches of Texas, offerings of blood and tobacco smoke were made to the Sun and Earth,[31] whereas among the ancient Purepecha, elaborate rituals during war festivals were directed toward the four parts of the world and to the goddess Cuerauaperi. During the preparations for those war festivals (Hicuandiro, Uazcuata Conscuaro, Unisperanscuaro) the challenge issued to the enemies had a ritual form, as related in the *Chronicles of Michoacán:* "Bring an offering of wood for the gods against us and let the priest cast the scents on the fire; let the sacrificer bring fragrances for the prayer to the gods against us. We, too, shall bring wood and the priest and the sacrificer will cast the incense on the fire. The third day, we shall meet and we shall all play behind the mountain and we shall learn how we are looked upon from on high by the celestial gods, the Sun, and the gods of the Four Quarters of the world."[32]

The earth mother's role as creator of men and mistress of death, both beneficial and evil, appears clearly in the Pure myth: the goddess takes her share of blood and places her victims in a sort of trance during which they go by themselves to the sacrificer's knife.

Among the Aztecs she appeared as the "Mother of the gods, heart of the earth, our ancestor."[33] She was *Temazcalteci*, the ancestor of the steam bath, *Yoalticitl*, "our mother the oven of the bath." Women gave birth in those symbols of the uterus, the Amerindian steam baths, which were undoubtedly also connected to the most ancient emergence myths. The earth goddess was also Coatlicue, She of the Skirt of Snakes, wearing the mask of death, whose colossal statue, several times unearthed and covered up after the Conquest, so profoundly affected the imaginary of Mexican artists at the beginning of the century.[34]

The symbol of an earth mother both nourishing and deadly was at the center of Amerindian philosophy. It is that symbol which explains the attitude of love and respect which the pre-Hispanic cultures had for nature. The world that surrounded them was much more than decor; it was the very expression of the divinity. If ownership of land was such a difficult notion for most Amerindian civilizations to conceive of, it is because the earth was without limits, like the sky, the sea, and the waters of the rivers.

Paradoxically, it was the nomadic civilizations of the north and northwest of Mexico, considered the most depredatory, which best expressed a feeling of great respect toward nature. The paradox was only superficial: for the hunting-gathering peoples agriculture was an infraction of the laws of nature, particularly when it was practiced as a means for enrichment and erected barriers preventing the free movement of men and game. There can be no doubt that the idea of land ownership was what most differentiated the Amerindians from the Europeans. Tecumseh, the chief of the Shawnee nation at the time of the Indian wars against the North American colonists, asserted for all Indians, regardless of their origins, "an equal right to this land, as in the past, as it should be today. For never was this earth divided in the past, and it belongs to all for the use of everyone."[35]

The love and respect the Indian peoples had for the earth was much more than an idea, it was a carnal connection. Through agrarian or funereal rituals, through war ceremonies or dances, this carnal attachment took on a cosmic significance. Tilling the soil to cultivate it, digging mines to extract minerals, and even taking earth to make pottery were serious acts, which could have consequences.

The carnal relationship with the earth was expressed most particularly through dancing, as is still done today among the Pueblos of New Mexico, who strike the ground with their bare feet following rhythms which are a language. It is that relationship which appeared in all its glowing beauty through the rituals and sacrifices described by the first chroniclers upon their arrival on the American continent. For the Aztecs, each moment of life, from birth until death, occurred in contact with this earth, on the unfolded mat which was the very symbol of human life. The solemn oath the Aztecs took at the time of public confession in front of the priest of Yaolli-Ehecatl was symbolic: "He took the oath to tell the truth—in their own way of taking an oath, which is touching the earth with the hand and licking off whatever had stuck to it."[36] It was with that mark of respect— Ontlaqualque, "they ate the earth," the hand touching the earth and bringing it to the lips—that Montezuma's delegates received the Spanish Conquerors when they alighted from their ship.[37]

Toci, Our Mother, and the goddess Cuerauaperi were in every respect similar to the divinity that inspired the armed struggle of the Winnebago Indians against the European invaders, she who was called "Our Holy Mother the Earth." The last nations to resist the destruction brought on by the Western world expressed the same indignation before the seizure and despoilment of the earth. We can hear the voice of Standing Bear, the chief of the Lakota Sioux: "The Lakota was filled with compassion and love for nature. He loved the earth and all things of the earth, and his attachment grew with age. The old people were literally in love with the ground and neither sat down nor lay down directly on the earth without having the feeling of coming close to maternal forces."[38]

Despite some exaggerations, the philosophers of the eighteenth and nineteenth centuries were not mistaken in describing the "savages" of the New World as the greatest defenders of nature. For the Amerindian peoples equilibrium was the very expression of divine creation. All activities—agriculture, hunting, or war—were carried out with a view to preserving that equilibrium. According to what Diego de Landa writes (*Historia de las cosas de Yucatán*), the Maya were horrified by any shedding of blood caused by an act other than sacrifices: "For they considered abominable any shedding of blood outside of their sacrifices, and for that reason every time they went hunting they invoked the devil and offered incense to him, and if they could they anointed their faces with the blood of the game they had killed."[39]

For the Aztecs, even cutting down a tree was a serious act, and, as Pedro Ponce relates, to do that they had people who "at the moment a tree was cut down to make beams they went into the mountains or the forest, and before entering offered a prayer to Quetzalcóatl to ask his permission so that he would not see as disrespectful the fact that they wanted to take wood from his forest, and so he would permit them to take that wood from his side."[40]

The Interrupted Thought of Amerindian Civilizations

The great question we are asked by the indigenous cultures of Mexico—and in a general way, by the entire Amerindian continent—is indeed this: How might those civilizations, those religions have evolved? What philosophy might have developed in the New World if the destruction of the Conquest had not taken place? In destroying those cultures, by abolishing so completely the identity of those peoples, what richness did the European Conquerors deprive us of? For it is indeed a deprivation, an exile, of which we must speak. The Spanish, Portuguese, then French and Anglo-Saxon conquerors who subjugated the vast territory of the Amerindian continent were not responsible for just the destruction of beliefs, art, and the moral virtues of the peoples they captured. Through a sort of backfiring which they themselves could not have imagined, they were at the beginning of a profound change in our own civilization, they were the first adventurers of this materialistic and opportunistic culture which has spread over the entire world, and which has gradually taken the place of all other philosophies.

People carped at length about the inequality of cultures at the time when on the soil of the New World "primitive" peoples from the neolithic age and Renaissance uniformed soldiers armed with cannons suddenly confronted each other. Although it is true that the shock of cultures was above all a shock of technology, we need however to remember all the realms in which the Amerindian civilizations, and particularly those of Mexico, were ahead of Europe: medicine, astronomy, irrigation, drainage, and urbanism. But we must especially remember the chapter in the history, ignored at the time by Europeans, which is today of vital importance to us: the harmony between man and the world, that balance between the body and the spirit, the union of the individual and the collectivity which were the foundations of most Amerindian societies, from the strongly hierarchical society of Anáhuac or Michoacán to the seminomadic societies of desert America of the north and northwest—those of the Seris, the Yaquis, the Tarahumara, the Pimas, and the Apaches.

Specifically, the inequality of armed strength succeeded in obscuring all other values. Because the Indian peoples were persuaded of the communality of the earth and of the impossibility of dividing up the body of the goddess-mother, they abandoned their rights to inhabit their own continent, and found themselves excluded from

progress. The *macehuales*, the *purepecha*, those men of the common ex-
traction, servants of the gods, became, through the movement of the
colony, and through the abuses of the *encomenderos*, the mass of forced
laborers, dispossessed of their land. Because in a certain sense beyond
the Conquest they continued to respect the equilibrium of natural
forces, the Indians could not enter into the system of the exploitation
of goods, and condemned themselves to exile in the poorest and most
inaccessible regions of the continent: stark mountains, deserts, or sti-
fling forests. In these refuges of Indian societies, nature itself imposed
its limits, and what was once spiritual value and reflection became a
fatality. Through the force of events the Indian was sentenced to
poverty and unproductiveness.

Similarly, after the Conquest the traditional values of the indigenous cultures were sometimes transformed into an insurmountable
weight. The unity between the mythical and the real, that sort of
harmony between dreams and the body which once made the great
strength of the ancient Mexica, Purepecha, Maya, and Toltecs, was
then shattered. Traditional values served as a refuge, a shield. On
the one side were the Conquerors, representing all the values of civilization—right, morality, religious truth. On the other, "barbarism,"
ignorance, vice, superstition. The isolation of the Indians, their mar-
ginalization, was not accidental. It was in truth the ultimate stage of
colonization, following a plan about which one might say that it was
the only coherent force of the colonial empire in America. Excluded
from temporal power, from progress, deprived of a voice in the exercise of justice, and subject to a clergy of another race, the Indians
became strangers on their own land.

The last representatives of the Aztec kingdom expressed it a final
time, before dying: "For we believe that the said Spaniards are acting
thus so that we will all be finished and will fade away, and so there
will no longer be any memory of us on earth."[41]

Today, after so much destruction and injustice, we can dream of
what the great Amerindian civilizations might have been, the Mexica,
Maya, Purepecha, Mixteca, Zapotec, Cora, Seri, Yaqui, Otomi civi-

lizations, and all those peoples who now no longer exist. Each group had its importance in the concert of Amerindian cultures, each one might have played its role in the development of a Mesoamerican classicism, which would undoubtedly have been the most complex and the most coherent ensemble in the New World.

Upon the arrival of the Spanish explorers in Mexico, the great empires of Anáhuac, Michoacán, and Nayar were still recent. Most of the great discoveries in irrigation, agriculture, and architecture were only a few centuries old.

In Tzintzuntzan, in Mexico/Tenochtitlán, unity had just begun to be accomplished. In Yucatán the renewal of the Tutul Xiu in Mani was underway. The armed peace which had just been made between the two greatest ethnic groups, the Mexica and the Purepecha, was finally enabling a cultural exchange, the exchange of ideas, beliefs, and technology. The art of writing and the science of the stars were in full development. In the region of Zacapu, metallurgists were inventing that mixture of pewter and copper which enabled the manufacture of bronze.

The spread of the cult of Quetzalcóatl, the civilizing hero, was undoubtedly the sign of that search for a unity, as was the tendency toward monotheism, affirmed by Nezahualcóyotl and by the cult of Hunab Ku, the Unique God of the Maya. The great lords of Anáhuac and the cazonci of Michoacán were not just war chiefs. They were also philosophers and poets, urbanists. They ruled, like the monarch of Michoacán, at the center of a system of representation of corporations which was as yet unknown in Europe in the sixteenth century. In most of those kingdoms moral harmony and the respect for laws would win the admiration of the first voyagers. It was all that which collapsed at the time of the Conquest, leaving room for destruction and silence.

It was perhaps in art and religion that Amerindian civilizations contributed the greatest innovations. The Mexicans were on the verge of developing a philosophical system which might have resolved the contradictions of the ancient world. Through trance and revelation, it was the harmony between reality and the supernatural which was achieved. The conception of cyclical time, the idea of a creation based upon catastrophe might have been the points of departure for a new scientific and humanist way of thinking. Finally, the respect for natural forces, the search for an equilibrium between man and the world might have been the necessary braking of technological progress in the Western world. Only today we are measuring what that equilibrium might have brought to medicine and psychology. The Indian heritage of shamanism, if it had not been fought by the purgers of sorcery, might have integrated dream and ecstasy into daily life, and enabled that equilibrium to be achieved.

Therefore it is not by chance that our Western civilization today rediscovers the philosophical and religious themes of the Indians of America. Because he has put himself in a position of disequilibrium, because he has let himself be carried away by his own violence, Western man must reinvent all that once made up the beauty and harmony of the civilizations he has destroyed.

The last survivors of the greatest disaster in human history, the Indian peoples refuged in the mountains, the deserts, or hidden in the depths of the forests continue to give us the image of an absolute fidelity to the principles of freedom, solidarity, and the dreams of the ancient pre-Hispanic civilizations. They continue to be the guardians of "Our Mother the Earth," the observers of the laws of nature and the cycle of time.

It is impossible for us today not to perceive their life, their way of seeing, as being fundamentally ours, as if all could, now, begin again. In the *Codex Florentinus*, the admirable summa left as a testimony by the Mexican people, is it not that impossible hope which reaches out to us?

"Another time, it shall be thus, another time things shall be thus, in another time, in another place. What happened long ago and which now is no longer done, another time it shall be done, another time it shall be thus, as it was in very distant times. Those who live today shall live another time, they shall live once again."[42]

Notes

Chapter 1

1. The page references in parentheses are from Bernal Díaz del Castillo, *Historia verdadera de la conquista de la Nueva España* (Madrid: Espasa-Calpe, 1968). Where possible I have quoted from the following English language editions: *The Bernal Diaz Chronicles: The True Story of the Conquest of Mexico*, translated and edited by Albert Idell (New York: Doubleday & Co., 1957); *The True History of the Conquest of Mexico By Captain Bernal Díaz del Castillo, One of the Conquerors*, translated by Maurice Keatinge, Esq. (London: J. Wright, 1800). The appropriate editions are noted with the page references.—Trans.

2. Bartolomé de Las Casas, *The Devastation of the Indies: A Brief Account*, translated from the Spanish by Herma Briffault (New York: The Seabury Press, 1974), pp. 54–55.

3. *The Chronicles of Michoacán*, translated and edited by Eugene R. Craine and Reginald C. Reindorp (Norman: University of Oklahoma Press, 1970), p. 57.

4. Beaumont, *Chronique du Michoacán*, 1932, II, pp. 64–65.

5. Cited by José Miranda, *Le tribut indigène dans la Nouvelle-Espagne*, 1952, p. 51.

6. *An Account of the Conquest by an Anonymous Author from Tlatelolco*, printed in 1528, translated from the Nahuatl by Angel Maria Garibay in Bernardino de Sahagun, *Historia general de las cosas de Nueva España* (Mexico: Porrua, 1975), pp. 813–14.

Chapter 2

1. Fernando de Alva Ixtlilxóchitl, *Obras históricas* (Mexico: Porrua, 1977), I, p. 479.

2. The page references in parentheses are from Bernardino de Sahagun, *Historia general de las cosas de Nueva España* (Mexico: Porrua, 1975). Where possible I have quoted from the following English language edition: *A History of Ancient Mexico*, by Fray Bernardino de Sahagun, vol. I, translated by Fanny R. Bandelier (Nashville: Fisk University Press, 1932). The appropriate editions are noted with the page references.—Trans.

3. Fernando de Alva Ixtlilxóchitl, *Obras históricas*, II, p. 7.

4. Francisco Ramirez, in *Monumenta Mexicana* (Rome, 1959), II, pp. 492–95.

5. Undoubtedly the three stars forming Orion's belt.

6. Fernando de Alva Ixtlilxóchitl, *Obras históricas*, I, p. 264.

7. From the Nahuatl *caltzontzin* (The Lord of many houses). This was one of the titles of the Irecha, kings of the ancient Tarascans (or Purepecha) of Michoacán.

8. *Relation de Michoacán* (Paris, 1984), pl. VI.

Chapter 3

1. Cited in *Native Mesoamerican Spirituality: Ancient Myths, Discourses, Stories, Doctrines, Hymns, Poems from the Aztec, Yucatec, Quiché-Maya and other Sacred Traditions*, edited with a foreword, introduction and notes by Miguel Leon-Portilla (New York: Paulist Press, 1980), p. 237.

2. Peter Furst, *Mitos y arte huicholes* (Mexico: S.E.P., 1972), p. 80.

3. In Del Paso y Troncoso, *Biblioteca Nahuatl*, vol. V (Mexico, 1903).

4. In Ramirez, *Monumenta Mexicana* (Rome, 1959), II, p. 495.

5. *Histoire du Méchique*, ed. Lehmann, *Journal de la Société des Américanistes* II (Paris, 1905), p. 8.

6. Ramirez in *Monumenta Mexicana*, p. 492.

7. Peter Furst, *Mitos y arte huicholes*, p. 59.

8. *Les prophéties du Chilam Balam* (Paris: Gallimard, 1976), p. 63.

9. Sahagun, *Historia general de las cosas de Nueva España* (Mexico: Porrua, 1975), p. 700.

10. In Doris Heyden, *Mitologia y simbolismo de la flora en el Mexico prehispánico* (Mexico, 1983). In the Embera myth of Panama, man, guided by the ant, discovers water enclosed in a tree. Helped by the green woodpecker, he knocks down the tree, which then turns into a river.

11. Miledred Kiemele Muro, *Cuentos Mazahuas* (Mexico, 1979).

12. Cruz Refugio Acevedo Barba, *Mitos de la meseta tarasca* (Thesis for the University of Aguascalientes, 1981).

13. Peter Furst, *Mitos y arte huicholes*, p. 80.

14. In Doris Heyden, *Mitologia y simbolismo*.

15. *Popul Vuh: The Sacred Book of the Ancient Quiché Maya*. English version by Delia Goetz and Sylvanus G. Morley (Norman: University of Oklahoma Press), 1950.

16. Cruz Refugio Acevedo Barba, *Mitos de la meseta tarasca*, p. 71.

17. Cited by Americo Paredes, *Folktales of Mexico* (Chicago: University of Chicago Press), 1970.

18. Peter Furst, *Mitos y arte huicholes*, p. 8.

19. Jacinto de la Serna, *Tratado de las idolatrías, supersticiones, dioses, ritos, hechicerias*, in *El alma encantada* (Mexico, 1987). Doris Heyden ("Un Chicomostoc en Teotihuacan," *Bulletin de l'INAH*, 2d series, no. 6) has written interesting material on the cave hidden under the pyramid of the sun in Teotihuacán, perhaps the first site to offer proof of emergence rituals among the ancient Toltecs.

20. Sahagun, *Historia general de las cosas de Nueva España* (Mexico: Porrua, 1975), p. 555.

21. Ibid., pp. 157, 277: "And they said that Tezcatlipoca often turned himself into an animal that they called *coyotl*, which was like a wolf . . ." For sorcery practices in colonial Mexico see Luis Gonzales, "El siglo mágico," in *Historia Mexicana*, vol. V (Mexico, 1954).

22. *The Chronicles of Michoacán*, translated and edited by Eugene R. Craine and Reginald C. Reindorp (Norman: University of Oklahoma Press, 1970), p. 112.

23. Cruz Refugio Acevedo Barba, *Mitos de la meseta tarasca*, p. 12.

24. Roberto Williams Garcia, *Mitos tepehuas* (Mexico, 1972), p. 112.

25. Roberto Weitlaner, *Cuentos chinantecos* (Mexico, 1977), p. 179.

26. Miledred Kiemele Muro, *Mitos y cuentos mazahuas* (Mexico, 1979), p. 39.

27. *The Chronicles of Michoacán*, p. 58.

28. Walter Miller, *Cuentos Mixes* (Mexico, 1956), p. 110.

29. R. H. Barlow, "Kwawxochipixkeh y otros temas del cuento indigena," *Anuario de la Sociedad folklorica de México* V (1950).

30. Miledred Kiemele Muro, *Mitos y cuentas mazahuas*, p. 50.

31. Cruz Refugio Acevedo Barba, *Mitos de la meseta tarasca*, p. 80.

32. Americo Paredes, *Folktales of Mexico*.

33. R. W. Garcia, *Mitos tepehuas*, p. 112.

34. R. H. Barlow, "Kwawxochipixkeh y otros temas del cuento indigena," *Anuario de la Sociedad folklorica de México* VI.

35. *The Chronicles of Michoacán*, pp. 207–11.

36. See Riva Palacio and Juan de Dios Peza, *Tradiciones y leyendas mexicanas* (Mexico, 1957).

37. Sahagun, *Historia general*, p. 889.

38. Stanley L. Robe, *Mexican Tales and Legends from Los Altos de Jalisco* (Los Angeles: University of California Press, 1970).

39. The prevalence of *A Thousand and One Nights* is a curious aspect of Mexican folklore. Pedro Carrasco (*El catolicismo popular de los Taroscos* [Mexico: S.E.P., 1976]) notes the presence of two copies of *A Thousand and One Nights* in Jaracuaro, a village of eight hundred inhabitants.

40. Ruth Giddings, *Yaqui Myths and Legends* (New York, 1959).

41. Sahagun, *A History of Ancient Mexico*, translated by Fanny R. Bandelier (Nashville: Fisk University Press, 1932), p. 146.

Chapter 4

1. The exact translation of the Nahuatl formula would be "Master of the near and of the ring of the confines of the world" (see Baudot, *Récits aztèques de la Conquête* [Paris, 1983], p. 400).

2. Fernando de Alva Ixtlilxóchitl, *Obras históricas* (Mexico, 1975), II, p. 132.

3. In Leon-Portilla, ed., *Native Mesoamerican Spirituality* (New York: Paulist Press, 1980), p. 241.

Chapter 5

1. Juan Bautista Pomar, *Relación de Tezcoco* (Mexico: Ed. Chavez Hayhoe, 1941).

2. *Crónica Mexicayotl* (Mexico, 1949), p. 18.

3. Ibid., p. 19.

4. Fernando de Alva Ixtlilxóchitl, *Obras históricas* (Mexico, 1977), I, p. 16.

5. *The Chronicles of Michoacán*, translated and edited by Eugene R. Craine and Reginald C. Reindorp (Norman: University of Oklahoma Press, 1970), p. 105.

6. Thus in Sahagun, the ritual hunt and the ritual of the man/deer. *Historia general de las cosas de Nueva España* (Mexico: Porrua, 1975), pp. 90, 139.

7. See Peter Furst, *Mitos y arte huicholes* (Mexico: S.E.P., 1972).

8. "The God Cupanzieri played ball with another God, Achurihirepe, won over him and sacrificed him in a village called Xacona. He also left the latter's wife pregnant with his son Siratatapeci. When the son was born, he was taken to another village to be raised, as if he were a foundling. As a youth he went bird hunting with a bow and on one of those hunts he came upon an iguana which said to him, 'Don't shoot me and I'll tell you something. The one you now think is your father is not because your real father went to the house of the God Achurihirepe to conquer, and he was sacrificed there.' When Siratatapeci heard this he went to the village of Xacona to get vengeance on his father's murderer. He excavated the place where his father was buried, exhumed him, and carried him on his back. Along the way there was a weed patch full of quail which took to flight. In order to shoot the quail he dropped his father, who turned into a deer with a mane on his neck and a long tail like those that come with the strange people. He went east for he had come with those newcomers to this land." *The Chronicles of Michoacán*, pp. 63–64.

9. Andrés Perez de Ribas, *Historia de los triunfos de Nuestra Santa Fe* (Mexico, 1944), II, pp. 247–48.

10. *The Chronicles of Michoacán*, p. 15.

11. Ibid., p. 224.

12. Sahagun, *Historia general*, p. 599.

13. *The Chronicles of Michoacán*, p. 224.

14. *Cartas Anuas*, in Ernesto Burrus, *Misiones Norteñas Mexicanas de la Compañía de Jesús* (Mexico, 1963), p. 30.

15. José Ortega, *Historia del Nayarit* (Mexico, 1887), p. 471.

16. *Cartas Anuas*, p. 35.

17. Perez de Ribas, *Historia de los triunfos*, I, pp. 126sq.

18. Sahagun, *Historia general*, p. 599.

19. James Ohio Pattie, a prisoner of the Apaches in 1825, gives the same description of the Indians' arrows: The "arrows of the Apaches are three feet long, and are made of reed cane, into which they sink a piece of hardwood, with a point made of iron, bone, or stone. They shoot this weapon with such force, that at the distance of 300 paces they can pierce a man. When the arrow is attempted to be drawn out of the wound, the

wood detaches itself, and the point remains in the body." Cited in John Upton Terrell, *Apache Chronicle* (New York: World Publishing, 1972), p. 157.

20. Antonio de Ciudad Real, *Tratado curioso y docto* (Mexico, 1975), II, pp. 160–61.

21. José Ortega, *Historia del Nayarit*, p. 149.

22. Sahagun, *Historia general*, 1938, II, p. 116.

23. *The Chronicles of Michoacán*, pp. 106–7.

24. Ibid., p. 157.

25. Perez de Ribas, *Historia de los triunfos*, p. 174.

26. The only time the calendar is mentioned in the *Chronicles* it is in a negative sense. When Hiuacha boasts to Hiripan about knowing the Mexican calendar, Tangaxoan, indignant, answered: "Who told you to count the days?" P. 212.

27. See Kirchhoff, "Gatherers and Farmers of the Greater Southwest." *The American Anthropologist* 54, no. 4, part I (August 1954), p. 529.

28. Fernando de Alva Ixtlilxóchitl, *Obras históricas*, I, p. 76.

29. Ibid., p. 30: "They cut the head off the first catch killed during the hunt, showed it to the sun as a sacrifice, and worked the land in the place where the blood had been spilled."

30. Sahagun, *Historia general*, pp. 399, 328, 431, 433.

31. Juan de Torquemada, *Monarquía Indiana* (Mexico: Porrua, 1969), I, p. 580.

32. José Ortega, *Historia del Nayarit*, p. 16.

33. Juan de Torquemada, *Monarquía Indiana*, I, p. 580.

34. *Anales de Cuauhtitlan*, translated by Primo Feliciano Velasquez (Mexico, 1975), p. 5.

35. *Relation de Michoacán* (Paris, 1984), pp. 163–64.

36. Perez de Ribas, *Historia de los triunfos*, I, p. 20.

37. Sahagun, *Historia general*, p. 439.

38. *The Chronicles of Michoacán*, p. 109.

39. *Relation de Michoacán* (Paris, 1984), p. 149.

40. José Ortega, *Historia del Nayarit*, p. 24.

41. Perez de Ribas, *Historia de los triunfos*, I, p. 54.

42. Francisco de Saliedo in *Archives du Fondo Franciscano* (Guadalajara, 1755).

43. José Ortega, *Historia del Nayarit*, p. 40.

44. *The Chronicles of Michoacán*, pp. 20–21.

45. Sahagun, *A History of Ancient Mexico*, translated by Fanny R. Bandelier (Nashville: Fisk University Press, 1932), p. 33.

46. Ocaranza, *Crónica de las Provincias Internas* (Mexico, 1939), p. 268.

47. Perez de Ribas, *Historia de los triunfos*, p. 300.

48. *The Chronicles of Michoacán*, p. 20.

49. The name of this planet is perhaps related to the Quangariecha, the Uacusecha order of warriors whose god, Urendecuauecara, was considered to be the founding hero.

50. *Anales de Cuauhtitlan*, p. 11.

51. *The Chronicles of Michoacán*, p. 25.

52. Antonio de Ciudad Real, *Tratado curioso y docto*, II, pp. 160–61.

53. Ocaranza, *Crónica de las Provincias Internas*, p. 50.

54. Perez de Ribas, *Historia de los triunfos*, I, p. 86.

55. Ocaranza, *Crónica de las Provincias Internas*, p. 60.

56. Perez de Ribas, *Historia de los triunfos*, I, p. 126.

57. See Philip Wayne Powell, *La guerra Chichimeca* (Mexico, 1971), and Tello, *Crónica miscelanea* (1891), II, p. 219. Bartolomé de las Casas even accused the Conquerors Pedro de Alvarado and Nuño de Guzmán of having encouraged anthropophagy to feed their troops of native mercenaries.

58. *The Chronicles of Michoacán*, p. 140.

59. When Tariacuri learns of the death of his son, sacrificed by the people of Yzipamucu, he cries out: "I have given food to the Sun and to the Gods of the Heavens. I begot that head which satisfied them and that heart which they cut out of him. My son was as delicate pigweed bread. Now I have given food to all the Gods in the Four Quarters of the world." *The Chronicles of Michoacán*, pp. 225–26.

60. Saliedo, in *Archives du Fondo Franciscano* (Guadalajara, 1755), vol. 41.

61. Fernando de Alva Ixtlilxóchitl, *Obras históricas* (Mexico, 1977), II, p. 37.

62. *The Chronicles of Michoacán*, p. 55.

63. *Relation de Michoacán*, p. 218.

64. Paul H. Nesbitt, *The Ancient Mimbreños: Based on Investigations at the Mattocks Ruin, Mimbres Valley, New Mexico*, Logan Museum Bulletin no. 4 (The Logan Museum, Beloit College, Beloit, Wisconsin, 1931).

65. Rupert N. Richardson, *The Comanche Barrier to South Plains Settlement* (Glendale: The Arthur H. Clark Co., 1933), p. 30.

66. Russell, *The Pima Indians*, B.A.E., vol. 26.

67. Perez de Ribas, *Historia de los triunfos*, I, p. 134.
68. Ibid., II, p. 32.
69. Ibid., II, p. 32.
70. Although the use of the tobacco pipe has disappeared today, gathering and offering incense (*thiuxunganda*) is practiced in most of the villages of the Tarascan meseta.
71. Sahagun/Bandelier, *A History of Ancient Mexico*, p. 146.
72. *The Chronicles of Michoacán*, pp. 185–86.
73. Ibid., p. 55.
74. Perez de Ribas, *Historia de los triunfos*, III, p. 166.
75. Tello, *Crónica miscelanea* (1891), II, p. 34.
76. In the same town of Tzenticpac, two hundred years later, there appeared the same strange figure of the "Indian king," Mariano, who came to reclaim his kingdom wearing as insignia the crown of thorns of Christ and the golden mask of the idols. The "king" Mariano is the central character of the beautiful novel by Jean Meyer, *Al Nombre del rey* (Mexico, 1990).
77. John Clum, letter of April 14, 1854, Archives B.I.A., Santa Fe, 1849–60.
78. Sahagun, *Historia general*, III, p. 118.
79. Although there is no mention of it in the *Chronicles of Michoacán*, we cannot exclude the use of hallucinogens in the religious rituals of the ancient Purepecha. The turquoise-studded gourds worn by the Petamuti priests are not unlike the ritual peyote containers worn by the Huichols and the Coras of Nayarit. Diego Muñoz, in his *Descripción de la Provincia de San Pedro, San Pablo de Michoacán*, mentions a use among the Chichimeca barbarians, who "using fruit soaked in water make a bad-tasting wine, with bad color and odor, with which they are accustomed to getting drunk, and which, mixed with certain roots, gives them very great vigor and fortifies them" (1965, p. 30).
80. Perez de Ribas, *Historia de los triunfos*, III, p. 23.
81. José Ortega, *Historia del Nayarit*, p. 22.
82. Perez de Ribas, *Historia de los triunfos*, III, p. 248. It is possible to associate the magical cults of most of the barbarian peoples of the north with peyote. Among the Yaquis, for example, the only reference made by Vildosola in the eighteenth century to *bolsas de peyote* worn by the rebel sorcerer Muni enables us to assume the existence of other cults not men-

tioned by the chroniclers. Cf. Evelyn Hu Dehart, *Missionaries, Miners, and Indians* (Tuscon: University of Arizona Press, 1981), p. 122, n. 20.

83. Fray Diego Muñoz, *Descripción* (Mexico, 1965), p. 28.

84. *Crónica mexicayotl* (Mexico, 1949), p. 12.

85. The name of the priest Hiripati (Swadesh: from the stem *hiri*—to hide) evokes the secret of the shaman. We are reminded here of the Chilam Balam of the Mayas (from the Mayan *chi*, mouth, and *bal*, to hide in the night). Cf. Ralph Roys, *The Book of Chilam Balam of Chumayel* (Carnegie Institution of Washington, 1933).

86. *The Chronicles of Michoacán*, p. 103.

87. Perez de Ribas, *Historia de los triunfos*, I, p. 134.

88. Father Pedro Mendez wrote in 1621 regarding the Opatas of Sonora: "Those whom they called sorcerers (*isaribe* in their language) are valiant men in combat." Cited by Maria Elena Galaviz de Capdevielle, *Rebeliones Indigenas* (Mexico, 1967), p. 45.

89. Perez de Ribas, *Historia de los triunfos*, II, p. 32.

90. E. Burrus, *Misiones norteñas de la Compañía de Jesús, 1751–1757* (1963), p. 27.

91. Tello, *Crónica miscelanea*, I, p. 175.

92. In this augury one can see a manifestation of the eddy god *Cachinipa* of the Parras Indians.

93. Philip Wayne Powell, *La guerra Chichimeca*, p. 57.

94. *Cartas de Franciscanos de la Provincia de Santiago de Jalisco* (1585), in Diego Muñoz, *Descripción*, p. 100.

95. Tello, *Crónica miscelanea*, I, p. 143.

96. Despite the cedula of 1531 through which Charles V forbade the selling of Indians as slaves, Nuño de Guzmán, after Cortés's disgrace, became so "arrogant," says Father Tello (*Crónica miscelanea*, I, p. 81) "and absolute, full of himself and a judge, with so much power, that he frightened all of New Spain . . . and granted every license to brand the Indians as slaves, for he, himself, while he was at Panuco, cruelly caused many Indians to die, and those who were still living, he sold and in such large numbers that that Province was practically emptied of its population."

97. Isidro Felix de Espinosa, *Crónica de la Provincia Franciscana* (Mexico, 1945).

98. José de Arlegui, *Crónica de la Provincia de N.S.P.S. Francisco de Zacatecas* (Mexico, 1851), p. 282.

99. Tello, *Crónica miscelanea*, II, p. 146.

100. *Relation de Michoacán*, p. 238.

101. See Mircea Eliade, *Shamanism: Archaic Techniques of Ecstasy*, translated from the French by Willard R. Trask (Princeton: Princeton University Press, 1964).

102. *Relation de Michoacán*, p. 285.

103. Cited by Maria Elena Capdevielle in *Rebeliones indigenas in el norte del reino de la Nueva España* (Mexico, 1967), p. 130.

104. Antonio de Remasal, *Historia de la Provincia de San Vicente de Chyapa y Guatimala* (Madrid, 1619), I, p. 595.

105. Perez de Ribas, *Historia de los triunfos*, III, p. 166.

106. José de Arlegui, *Crónica de la provincia de N.S.P.S. Francisco de Zacatecas* (1851), p. 287.

107. José Antonio Gay, cited by Casarrubias, *Rebeliónes indigenas en la Nueva España* (Mexico, 1945), p. 78.

108. Diego López de Cogulludo, *Historia de Yucatan* (Campeche, 1955), p. 123.

109. Cogolludo, ibid., p. 123.

110. For the history of the Tzendal uprising of Cancuc see Herbert S. Klein, "Peasant Communities in Revolt: The Tzendal Republic of 1712," *Pacific Historical Review* (August 1966), p. 247.

111. Francisco Ximenez, *Historia de la Provincia de San Vicente de Chiapa y Guatemala* (quoted in Klein's article cited in previous footnote, p. 257).

112. Casarrubias, *Rebeliónes indigenas en la Nueva España* (Mexico, 1945), p. 179.

113. Luis Navarro Garcia, *Sonora y Sinaloa en el siglo XVI y XVII* (Seville, 1967).

114. Maria Isaura Pereira de Queiroz, *Historia y etnologia de los movimientos mesianicos* (Mexico, 1978), p. 177 n. 2.

115. Antonio de Ciudad Real, *Tratado curioso y docto*, II, p. 160: "All the Chichimeca, men, women and children, are warriors, for they all help each other in making bows and ammunition."

116. Tello, *Crónica miscelanea*, II, p. 219.

117. Ibid., II, p. 226.

118. Ibid., II, p. 303.

119. Ibid., II, p. 294. Father Tello adds that at the time when he wrote that "in the year 1652, there were not six Indians left in Cuina."

120. *The Chronicles of Michoacán*, p. 74.

121. Tello, *Crónica miscelanea*, II, p. 26.

122. We might also think of the messianic religions of the Indians of North America, such as the Handsome Lake ritual of the Seneca Indians (in 1799), or of the role of visionaries and dreamers, such as the shaman Noch-ay-del-klinne of the Indians of Fort Apache. See Vittorio Lanternari, *Movimentos religiosos y de libertad y salvación de los pueblos oprimidos* (Barcelona, 1965), p. 135; and John Upton Terrell, *Apache Chronicle*, p. 157.

123. See Philip Wayne Powell, *La guerra Chichimeca* (Mexico, 1977), pp. 57sq.

124. See Niño Cochise, *The First 100 Years of Niño Cochise* (London: Abelard-Schuman Ltd., 1971).

125. Ralph Hedrick Ogle, *Federal Control of the Western Apache, 1848–1886* (The University of New Mexico Press, 1970), p. 127.

126. C. L. Sonnichsen, *The Mescalero Apaches* (Norman: University of Oklahoma Press, 1958), p. 98.

127. Ralph Hedrick Ogle, *Federal Control of the Western Apache*, p. 130.

128. See Dan L. Thrapp, *Juh: An Incredible Indian* (Oklahoma, 1973).

129. Morford, regarding the Indians of Camp Apache, wrote that they are so attached to White River that they say they love it as they do their own parents (*Archives of the U.SB.I.A.*, 1875–80).

130. John Upton Terrell, *Apache Chronicle*, p. 150.

Chapter 6

1. This is part of *Les Tarahumaras*, tome 9, *Oeuvres complètes d'Antonin Artaud* (Paris: Gallimard, 1971). Translated by Helen Weaver as *The Peyote Dance* (New York: Farrar, Straus and Giroux, 1976). Page numbers given with quotations from Artaud's text refer to Helen Weaver's translation.—Trans.

2. Le Clézio originally wrote this chapter in Spanish, and it was translated into French by Anne-Marie Meunier. The author has kindly authorized the English translation from the French version.—Trans.

Chapter 7

1. *Relation de Michoacán* (Paris, 1984), p. 261.

2. *The Chronicles of Michoacán*, translated and edited by Eugene R. Craine

and Reginald C. Reindorp (Norman: University of Oklahoma Press, 1970), p. 57.

3. Juan de Torquemada, *Monarquía Indiana* (Mexico, 1969), I, p. 577.

4. *Monumenta Mexicana* (Rome, 1959), II, p. 495.

5. Sahagun, *Historia general de las cosas de Nueva España* (Mexico: Porrua, 1975), p. 579.

6. Ibid., I, p. 32.

7. Sahagun, *A History of Ancient Mexico*, translated by Fanny R. Bandelier (Nashville: Fisk University Press, 1932), pp. 60–61.

8. Ibid., p. 31.

9. Sahagun, *Historia general*, p. 299.

10. The transfiguration ritual is described by Sahagun in the festival of *teonenemi:* "they walk like the gods." Sahagun, *Historia general*, p. 439.

11. Sahagun, *Historia general*, p. 90.

12. Sahagun/Bandelier, *A History of Ancient Mexico*, p. 38.

13. *The Chronicles of Michoacán*, p. 55.

14. Under the name of Titlacaoan, Tezcatlipoca is one of the three necromancers who, with Huitzilopochtli and Tlacauepan, triumphed over Quetzalcóatl during a magical duel. See Sahagun/Bandelier, *A History of Ancient Mexico*, pp. 180sq.

15. Angel Maria Garibay, *Teogonia e historia de los Mexicanos* (Mexico: Porrua, 1979), p. 124.

16. The hunting ritual, which can be associated with the Mayan ceremonies dedicated to the god Zuhuy Sip, is described in Sahagun, *Historia general*, pp. 90, 139.

17. *The Chronicles of Michoacán*, p. 183.

18. Cited in Leon-Portilla, ed., *Native Mesoamerican Spirituality* (New York: Paulist Press, 1980), p. 275.

19. Ibid., p. 244. See also *Romances de los Señores de la Nueva España* (Mexico: Ed. Garibay. UNAM, 1963); and *Les Chants de Nezahualcóyotl*, translated by Pascal Coumes and Jean-Claude Caer (Obsidiane-Unesco, 1985), pp. 62–63.

20. Cited by Philippe Jacquin, *La Terre des Peaux-Rouges* (Paris, 1987), p. 142. More about Black Elk's concepts can be found in John G. Neihardt, *Black Elk Speaks* (New York: William Morrow, 1932) and *When the Tree Flowered* (New York: MacMillan, 1951).

21. Sahagun/Bandelier, *A History of Ancient Mexico*, p. 146.

22. Napuctun and Xupan Nauat were Ah Kinob (Priests of the Sun); they both lived in Uxmal in the eleventh century. Their words form part of the *Prophéties du Chilam Balam* (Paris, 1976), p. 119.

23. Cited in Leon-Portilla, *Native Mesoamerican Spirituality*, p. 137.

24. See Ramirez, *Relación, Monumenta Mexicana* (Rome, 1959), II, p. 495.

25. Sahagun, *Historia general*, p. 197.

26. Cited in Leon-Portilla, *Native Mesoamerican Spirituality*, pp. 201–2.

27. Sahagun, *Historia general*, p. 322.

28. Ibid., p. 382.

29. *Pop Wuj*, translated by Adrian Chavez (Mexico, 1979).

30. Fernando de Alva Ixtlilxóchitl, *Obras históricas* (Mexico, 1977), I., p. 176.

31. Rupert Narval Richardson, *The Comanche Barrier to South Plains Settlement* (Glendale: The Arthur H. Clark Co., 1933), pp. 38–39.

32. *The Chronicles of Michoacán*, pp. 121–22.

33. Sahagun, *Historia general*, p. 33.

34. Justino Fernandez (*Coatlicue, estetica del arte indigena antiquo*, Mexico, 1954) defines the goddess as "the dynamic and cosmic form which gives life and is sustained in death."

35. T. C. MacLuhan, *Pieds nus sur la terre sacrée* (Paris, 1974).

36. Sahagun/Bandelier, *A History of Ancient Mexico*, p. 31.

37. Sahagun, *Historia general*, p. 760.

38. Cited by Philippe Jacquin, *La Terre des Peaux-Rouges*, p. 146.

39. Diego de Landa, *Relation des choses du Yucatan*, edited by Brasseur de Bourbourg (Paris, 1864).

40. *El Alma encantada* (INI and FCE, Mexico, 1986), p. 10.

41. "Carta de los Señores y Principales de las Provincias y Ciudades de la Nueva España," *Codice Mendieta* (Guadalajara, 1971 [facsimile of Mexico, 1892]), I, p. 130.

42. *Codex Florentinus*, facsimile edition (Mexico: AGN, 1969), book VI, p. 196 (translated by Alfredo Lopez Austin).